Praise from the Experts

"Michael Raithel has written an excellent learning and reference manual about SAS indexes. This book is well thought out, and the information is presented aptly so it can be used by a SAS beginner as well as the most advanced SAS developer to learn more about SAS indexes. Michael covers indexes so that you will understand when, why, and where to use indexes. He includes plenty of easy-to-follow code examples to help you fully comprehend the strengths and weaknesses of indexes. He also explains when and where NOT to use indexes. You need this manual in your SAS library when building SAS applications involving the need for performance and speed to deliver your data to your end users or clients.

"I strongly encourage ALL SAS users (beginners to advanced levels) to purchase this manual as an effective learning and reference tool. Your money will be well spent on this book. I am pleased to add this to my 'must have' SAS manuals. Now that I have read Michael's new book, I will be looking for more books by this author knowing how well he presents his materials to an audience of varied experiences and skill levels."

Charles Patridge
Sr. Data Engineer
Full Capture Solutions, Inc

"I thought I knew indexes inside out, but I certainly learned more about how SAS processes, and how I can exert more control over index usage. This book begins with excellent background on 'what's in it for me' and then provides a solid explanation of what SAS is actually doing. Michael Raithel effectively demonstrates HOW to create and use indexes; but more importantly, he explains WHEN to use (and NOT use) indexes.

"The beginner will be able to make smart choices about index creation and usage and will be able to easily implement indexes. The experienced user will learn excellent tuning tips.

"This book is a 'must read' for any SAS programmer who works with large SAS data sets!"

Marje Fecht
Partner
Prowerk consulting

SAS Publishing

The Complete Guide to SAS® Indexes

Michael A. Raithel

The correct bibliographic citation for this manual is as follows: Raithel, Michael A. 2006. *The Complete Guide to SAS® Indexes.* Cary, NC: SAS Institute Inc.

The Complete Guide to SAS® Indexes

Contents

x

Acknowledgments

The reason authors pen acknowledgments is that they are so richly deserved by the many other people who help to bring a book from inception to production. Working on my third publication for SAS Press, I was once again impressed by the solid professional support that I got from my publisher. SAS Press provided me with a stellar team of publishing professionals, lined up a great group of in-house technical reviewers, and allowed me to pick an assemblage of top technical reviewers from the wide world of SAS programming professionals. All of this resulted in a book that I am very proud of and that I know you are really going to like.

Professional

Once again, my first thank you goes to Judy Whatley, my editor. This is the second book that I have been lucky enough to work on with Judy. Her easy-going working style, patience, and professionalism are beyond compare. I hope that I will have the opportunity to work with Judy again on my next book for SAS Press!

I had an amazing amount of intellectual firepower in the lineup of technical reviewers for this book! I would like to thank the following well-known SAS superstars for their painstakingly accurate technical reviews: Richard DeVenezia, Paul Dorfman, Toby Dunn, and Jack Hamilton. I would also like to thank these very sharp, very talented, technical reviewers from SAS: Billy Clifford, Charley Mullin, Matt Starbuck, Jane Stroupe, Jack Wallace, and Kim Wilson. All of the reviewers caught my errors, made great suggestions, and helped me to craft a book that is light years better than the original draft.

If you like the look and feel of this book as much as I do, then you should join me in thanking Patrice Cherry, the designer. Kathy Underwood's copyediting helped to keep me from tripping over my own words. Candy Farrell did a great job as the technical publishing specialist. Jennifer Dilley deserves praise for creating the spiffy figures in Chapter 1. Finally, the very fact that you have this book in your hand, dear reader, means that Liz Villani and Shelly Goodin, who are in charge of marketing, did a very good job.

Personal

I am dedicating this book to the memory of my mother, Emma Raithel, who taught me love, honesty, thriftiness, compassion, and devotion to family. It is also dedicated to my father, Hal Raithel, who taught me that hard work and perseverance pay off and who wrote this sound advice in the front of a math book that he and my mother gave me when I was nine years old: "Numbers are your very good friends. They will help you if you use them right." His words couldn't have been more correct!

Chapter 1

Introduction to Indexes

The Index Concept

The concept of an index is hardly new to us. We use indexes in everyday life without giving them a second thought. For example, if I were to ask you to find every page in this book that contains the word "centiles," what would you do? You would not read through every page of this book, searching for the word "centiles." Instead, you would go directly to the index in the back of the book, search the index pages for the word "centiles," determine on which non-index pages it could be found from the index entry, and then go directly to those pages. Using the index would have saved you a lot of time and effort.

A similar example would be if I were to ask you to find the pages in this book that contain the name of the first president of the United States. You would go to the index, search through it, and find that no such index entry exists. You would tell me that there is no entry for the name of the first president of the United States, and you would not bother searching through all of the non-index pages of the book. Using the index would have saved you the time and effort of searching through every page in the entire book for an entry that does not exist.

Both examples illustrate how an index improves the efficiency of a search for data. If we find an entry in the index of a book, we can streamline our search effort and go directly to the pages that contain information about that entry. If we do not find an entry for a particular topic, we can conclude that it is not in the book and move on to looking for other entries, or to searching the indexes of other books. Thus, indexes save us time and effort when we are searching for information on a particular topic in a particular venue.

The Index as a SAS Performance Tool

A SAS index is functionally similar to an index in a book. It is used to look up whether a particular value of a key variable exists in the data pages of a SAS data set. If so, then only those pages are accessed; if not, then no data set pages are accessed. In this way, an index is a SAS data set performance tool, because it limits the amount of processing that is done to a given SAS data set. But, it is a performance tool that you must specifically build and overtly use.

When SAS reads a SAS data set without using an index, it reads the entire data set sequentially. SAS data sets are actually segmented (behind-the-scenes) into *pages* on which observations are stored. SAS moves each data set page from disk to computer memory, starting with the first data set page and ending with the very last data set page. Once a page is in memory, SAS can read the observations stored on that particular page. This process happens with every SAS program you execute that does not use an index.

The movement of SAS data set pages between disk and computer memory is done via Input/Output (I/O) events. I/Os take time to execute and are the slowest events in the life of your SAS program. The more I/Os your SAS program consumes, the longer it takes for your program to run. Conversely, the fewer I/Os your SAS program consumes, the quicker it runs. So you can see that it is advantageous to limit the number of I/Os your SAS program uses, whenever possible.

The main goal of using a SAS index is to read only a small portion of a large SAS data set, instead of reading the entire SAS data set. As with the book index example, above, you want to use the SAS data set index to reduce the time and effort consumed reading observations with a specific value. With SAS, it is a specific index key variable value that you are looking for. When using an index, SAS first consumes I/Os by reading the index pages, searching for the specified value of the key variable. Then, if the value is found in the index, SAS consumes additional I/Os by directly reading *only* those pages that contain the specified value of the index key variable. If a large SAS data set is being accessed and only a few pages contain the specified key variable value, then you have saved many I/Os by having avoided reading the entire SAS data set.

Using a SAS index to access observations in a SAS data set with a specific key variable value can drastically reduce the I/Os and wall clock time of your SAS program. It can also lower CPU time, because less processing is necessary on the fewer pages that are returned to your SAS program. A decline in wall clock time can be good for SAS programmers in all environments. Cutting I/Os and CPU time can be especially beneficial for SAS programmers who work in organizations that have instituted computer resource chargeback programs. Such organizations often charge for CPU time and for I/Os. Using SAS indexes to decrease both of these resources helps you by lowering the amount that you are charged for running your SAS application programs.

Besides reducing computer processing resources, using a SAS index returns the observations in sorted order. They are sorted into ascending key variable(s) value order in your output SAS data set. This eliminates the need to execute subsequent SORT procedures and enhances BY statement processing.

Types of SAS Applications That May Benefit from Indexes

Just about any type of SAS application can benefit from the use of SAS indexes because of the decreased run time that they facilitate. SAS batch applications generally run faster when indexes are used within them to extract small subsets of observations from large SAS data sets. Using SAS indexes can be advantageous when you have a series of long-running batch applications that must be run sequentially. Shrinking a batch window—the time it takes for your SAS batch programs to run each day or night—would definitely be a visible benefit of using SAS indexes.

SAS/IntrNet applications that access small subsets of large SAS data sets certainly profit from the use of SAS indexes. Users of Web applications are sensitive to response time issues. They do not expect to have to wait very long after pressing ENTER to receive their results back in their Internet browsers. Using an index behind-the-scenes to subset a SAS data set that is being queried by a SAS/IntrNet program results in better response time for your users. This gives them greater confidence in the reliability of the SAS/IntrNet Web applications and greater productivity in their use of those applications.

SAS stored procedures used by groups of programmers and non-programmers via SAS Enterprise Guide benefit from the use of indexes. Like the SAS/IntrNet application users, Enterprise Guide users expect good response times from the stored procedures that have been written for them. When the stored procedures that they are invoking access small subsets of observations stored in large SAS data sets, users get their result sets far faster when SAS indexes are judiciously employed behind-the-scenes.

How SAS Indexes Are Structured

Indexes are separate SAS files with a member type of INDEX. Internally, they are divided into pages the same way that SAS data sets are. Indexes are stored in the same SAS data library that contains the data set they are associated with. SAS maintains the relationship between the index and its data set. When observations are added, updated or deleted from the data set, the index file is updated to reflect the changes. All indexes for a given SAS data set are stored in the same index file.

The logical organization of an index is based on the data storage structure known as a B-tree. This means that index entries are grouped into one of three node types: the root node, branch nodes, and leaf nodes. Each node contains a number of individual index entries and is stored on an index page. A particular index page may contain only entries of a single node type. The various nodes are logically connected through a series of node pointers and through pointers within the entries. The function and structure of an entry varies according to node type.

The following sections explain how the entries in each node are organized.

Root Node

The root node is the highest level node in an index. All accesses of the index begin with the root node and then follow the pointers down to other nodes. There is one root node entry for each child (or subordinate) branch node. Each root node entry contains the highest key variable value stored in a child branch node and a pointer to the beginning of that branch node. The root node is stored on a single index page.

Root node entries contain only two fields: a value field, and a node identifier (NID) field. The value field is equal in length to the key variable (for a *simple* index), or key variables (for a *composite* index), of the indexed SAS data set. The value field contains the highest key variable value stored in the branch node the entry points to. The NID contains a pointer to the subordinate branch node.

Branch Nodes

Branch nodes are the intermediate level nodes in an index. Accesses of the index proceed from the root node to the branch nodes—via a binary search—and then follow pointers down to the leaf nodes. Each branch node is stored on an index page that is filled with only branch node entries. There is one branch node entry per leaf node. Branch node entries contain the highest key variable value stored in a subordinate branch node or leaf node and a pointer to the beginning of that subordinate branch node or leaf node.

The structure of branch node entries is identical to that of root node entries. The value field entry in a branch node contains the highest key variable value stored in the leaf node pointed to by the entry. The NID contains a pointer to the subordinate leaf node.

Leaf Nodes

Leaf nodes are the lowest level nodes in an index. An index search culminates when the entries in a leaf node are examined for the requested key variable value. If the key variable value is found, SAS follows leaf node pointers to specific observations in the SAS data set. Like branch nodes, leaf nodes are stored on index pages that are populated exclusively by leaf node entries. There is one leaf node entry per unique key variable value in the SAS data set that the index is associated with.

Leaf node entries contain a value field and one or more record identifier (RID) fields. The value field is equal in length to the index key variable (for a *simple* index), or to the combined length of the index key variables (for a *composite* index), of the indexed SAS data set. The value field contains a unique key variable value that can be found in one or more observations within the SAS data set. The RID contains a pointer to an observation in the SAS data set that has the value field value in it. SAS uses the RID to directly access the SAS data set and return the observation with the requested key variable value. If key variable values are unique in a SAS data set and the UNIQUE option is specified, then there is only one pair of value field and RID per leaf node entry. See Chapter 5, "Index-Related Options," for a complete explanation of the UNIQUE option. If the key variable values are not unique, a value field can have any number of RIDs associated with it. Thus, the size of leaf node entries can vary in indexes where the key variable values are not unique.

When an index search finally arrives at a leaf node, the entries are examined in a binary search. The value fields in leaf node entries are compared against the key variable value the program is looking for. If SAS reaches the end of the leaf node binary search without finding the specific key variable value, the value does not exist in the SAS data set.

Figure 1.1 depicts the composition of root node, branch node, and leaf node entries. For any index, the size of the root and branch node entries is always the same. However, indexes with non-unique key variable values can have leaf node entries of varying sizes. Each entry contains one RID for every observation with a specific key value. For example, if three observations have the same key variable value, the leaf node entry will have three RIDs associated with the value field. Node identifiers are 4 bytes on a 32-bit host and 8 bytes on a 64-bit host. Record identifiers are 8 bytes on a 32-bit host and 12 bytes on a 64-bit host.

Figure 1.1 The Structure of Root, Branch, and Leaf Nodes

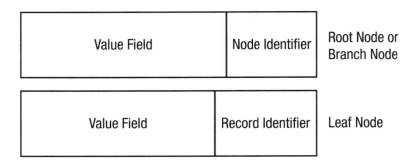

Figure 1.2 illustrates the tree structure of a SAS data set index. In the figure, the root node (RN) has pointers down to the branch nodes (BN). Each branch node has a pointer to the next branch node and pointers down to the leaf nodes (LN). Index searches begin with the root node and follow NIDs down to the lower levels of the index.

Figure 1.2 The Index Tree Structure

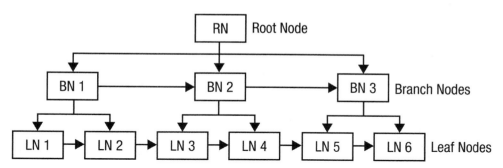

SAS keeps the structure of an index symmetric by balancing the index. It balances the index by keeping each leaf node exactly the same number of levels in distance from the root node. This means that accessing any particular leaf node consumes exactly the same amount of computer resources as accessing any other. If observations are added or deleted from the data set, index node entries are created or deleted at all appropriate levels of the index, depending on the key variable values. If a preponderance of new key variable values falls into a specific range, index nodes are added to expand the index "horizontally," to avoid adding new levels to the index. If a large number of observations are deleted, the index may contract "horizontally." This ensures that changes in the population of a SAS data set do not have a negative impact on the performance of its indexes. SAS performs index balancing tasks at the end of the DATA step in which the index was updated.

Large SAS indexes, especially those with small index page sizes, tend to have more index levels. The greater the number of levels an index has, the more I/Os are consumed during an index search and the longer it takes to complete the search. Conversely, indexes with fewer levels require fewer I/Os to traverse the index during an index search. So it is advantageous to increase the index page size to try to keep the number of levels that an index occupies as low as possible. This may be done with the IBUFSIZE option, discussed in Chapter 5, "Index-Related Options." Because SAS does not report the number of levels an index occupies, you must specify a large index page size value on the IBUFSIZE option and hope that it minimizes the number of index levels, thereby promoting good index performance.

Figure 1.3 presents an example of an index search. In this example, the program is using the index to return all observations with the key variable value of *Barre*.

Figure 1.3 Example of an Index Search

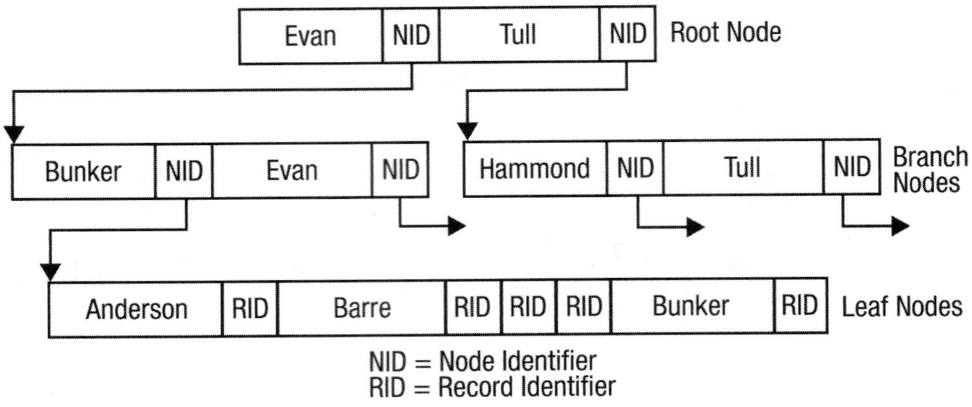

```
                    ┌──────────┬─────┬──────────┬─────┐
                    │   Evan   │ NID │   Tull   │ NID │ Root Node
                    └──────────┴─────┴──────────┴─────┘
```

```
┌──────────┬─────┬──────────┬─────┐   ┌───────────┬─────┬──────────┬─────┐ Branch
│  Bunker  │ NID │   Evan   │ NID │   │  Hammond  │ NID │   Tull   │ NID │ Nodes
└──────────┴─────┴──────────┴─────┘   └───────────┴─────┴──────────┴─────┘
```

```
┌──────────┬─────┬──────────┬─────┬─────┬─────┬──────────┬─────┐
│ Anderson │ RID │  Barre   │ RID │ RID │ RID │  Bunker  │ RID │ Leaf Nodes
└──────────┴─────┴──────────┴─────┴─────┴─────┴──────────┴─────┘
```

NID = Node Identifier
RID = Record Identifier

Here is the sequence of events that transpire during the index search:

1. The index search begins with a binary search of the entries in the root node. Each root node entry value field contains the highest key variable value stored in the branch node it points to. The first root node entry, *Evan*, is of a higher key variable value than *Barre*. If *Barre* does exist in the index, it is in one of the subordinate nodes pointed to by this root node entry. SAS follows the NID pointer down to the branch node.

2. SAS starts a binary search of the branch node. The first branch node entry, *Bunker*, is of a higher key variable value than *Barre*. So the index search continues by following the NID pointer from the branch node entry to the beginning of its associated leaf node.

3. When the index search arrives at the leaf node, another binary search is initiated. The first entry in the binary search, *Barre,* is a direct match to the key variable value being sought. There are three RIDs associated with the value field containing *Barre*. Thus, there are three observations in the SAS data set containing the key variable value of *Barre*. SAS follows each RID, one by one, to the SAS data set and returns each of the three observations to the program. When the last observation has been obtained, the SAS program is finished with the index search for *Barre*.

Types of SAS Indexes

SAS gives you the ability to construct two different types of indexes. The difference between the two index types is simply a matter of whether the index is built from a single variable or from multiple variables. Because there are different considerations to keep in mind when constructing either type, both are described separately.

Simple Indexes

A SAS index created from a single variable is known as a *simple index*. The variable that is used to create the index is known as the *index key variable*. You can create a simple index for any variable that exists in a SAS data set. Index key variables may be numeric or they may be character. When you create a simple index, SAS gives the index the same name as the index key variable. Consequently, you can find an index with the same name as the index key variable in the "Alphabetic List of Index and Attributes" section of a CONTENTS procedure listing for the indexed SAS data set.

Here is an example of a DATA step that creates a simple index:

```
data  indexlib.prodindx(index=(state));
set   indexlib.prodsale;
run;
```

In the example, above, a new SAS data set named INDEXLIB.PRODINDX contains a simple index named STATE after the DATA step executes. The STATE simple index contains one entry for every value of the index key variable STATE found in the INDEXLIB.PRODINDX SAS data set, along with pointers (RIDs) to each observation that contains that value.

If you know that you are going to use a particular variable to obtain small subsets of a large SAS data set on a frequent basis, then you should consider creating a simple index from that variable. If there are other variables that are also often used to subset the SAS data set, then you can make simple indexes for them, too. A SAS data set may have multiple simple indexes associated with it. Chapter 3, "Index Variable Selection Considerations," provides a discussion on how you may determine which variables make good index variable candidates.

Composite Indexes

A SAS index created from two or more variables is known as a *composite index*. Composite index key variables may be numeric, character, or any combination of the two. You may choose to construct a composite index key from variables that occur in any order within an observation—composite index key variables do not need to be adjacent fields. (SAS actually concatenates the variable values together in the value fields of the index entries that are created for the index.)

Because a composite index is created from two or more variables, SAS cannot pick a name for a composite index. You are responsible for providing a name. You may choose any valid SAS variable name for the name of a composite index. After a composite index is created, you can find the composite index name in the "Alphabetic List of Index and Attributes" section of a CONTENTS procedure listing for the indexed SAS data set. (To see other places that you may get index information, refer to Chapter 6, "Identifying Index Characteristics.")

This is an example of a DATA step that creates a composite index:

```
data  indexlib.prodcomp(index=(country_state=(country state)));
set   indexlib.prodsale;
run;
```

In this example, the newly created SAS data set INDEXLIB.PRODCOMP contains a composite index named COUNTRY_STATE after execution of the DATA step. That composite index contains every distinct combination of the values of COUNTRY and STATE found in the INDEXLIB.PRODCOMP SAS data set and pointers to each observation containing that distinct value.

SAS often uses composite indexes to surface observations when only the first variable in a composite index is used in a WHERE expression or BY statement. You should keep this in mind when determining the order of variables to specify in a composite index.

SAS compares the WHERE or BY variables, one by one, from left to right, with the variables in an existing composite index. SAS stops when it reaches the end of the shortest list of matching variables. If one or more of the WHERE or BY variables match one or more of the variables in the composite index, then that composite index may be used.

For example, if you are creating a composite index based on variables COUNTRY and STATE, your first instinct might be to list COUNTRY first in the composite index so that it is COUNTRY/STATE. However, if many of your SAS programs subset the SAS data set with WHERE expressions based on STATE, you would consider creating a STATE/COUNTRY composite index. This increases the likelihood that the composite index will be used in the aforementioned types of queries and can save you the trouble of building a simple index based on STATE.

When Indexes Are Used

SAS does not automatically use an index to access data in a SAS data set just because you have created one. There are four specific constructs that allow SAS to use an existing index:

- a WHERE expression in a DATA or PROC step (see Chapter 10, "Using Indexes with a WHERE Expression")

- a BY statement in a DATA or PROC step (see Chapter 11, "Using Indexes with a BY Statement")

- the KEY option on a MODIFY statement (see Chapter 12, "Using Indexes with the KEY Option on a MODIFY Statement")

- the KEY option on a SET statement (see Chapter 13, "Using Indexes with the KEY Option on a SET Statement")

SAS does *not necessarily* use an existing index even when you do use a WHERE expression or a BY statement. SAS first calculates if using an index would be more efficient than reading the entire data set sequentially. The internal algorithms take a lot of factors into consideration, including data set size, the index or indexes that are available, and *centile* information. (For more information on centiles, see Chapter 4, "Index Centiles.") Here is the three-step algorithm that SAS uses (Clifford 2005):

1. **Compute estimated number of observations qualified by the index.** SAS uses the index's centiles to estimate the total number of observations that would be qualified to be returned by the index. This estimate is accurate to within 5% as long as the centiles are up-to-date.

2. **Calculate the I/O cost per RID.** SAS examines the RIDs (record identifiers) on the first qualifying leaf node index page and calculates the number of different data pages that those RIDs point to. SAS computes an I/O cost per RID by dividing this number into the number of RIDs on an index page. This results in a decimal number that is less than or equal to one.

3. **Calculate the number of data pages that would be read by the index.** SAS multiplies the estimated number of qualified observations (#1 above) by the I/O cost per RID (#2 above) to get the number of SAS data set pages that would be read if the index was used. This number should be much smaller than the total number of pages in the entire SAS data set.

If SAS predicts that it would be more efficient to use a specific index to return observations than to read the entire data set, then it uses that index. If not, then it reads the entire data set sequentially to return the observations. However, SAS does not consider using an index if you do not use a WHERE expression or a BY statement.

SAS automatically uses an index when you specify the KEY option on either a MODIFY statement or a SET statement. It does so because the KEY option specifies exactly which index should be used. You do not have to be concerned with whether or not an existing index is used with the KEY option in a MODIFY or SET statement.

Most of the time, SAS makes good decisions regarding whether or not to use an index. But its internal calculations are not infallible, and sometimes the resources consumed when reading a large subset of data via an index *are* greater than reading the entire SAS data set. You can use the IDXNAME and IDXWHERE options to override SAS default index usage. Both of these options are discussed in Chapter 5, "Index-Related Options."

Estimating the Size of an Index

SAS stores index entries in a separate index file. These index entries take up space, so it is natural to ask just how much space a prospective index will occupy. SAS Technical Support has created a program that enables you to get a fair estimate of the size of your SAS index. You can find a copy of that program in Appendix D, "Estimating the Number of Pages for a SAS 9 Index." It is also included in the example code for this book, found on its companion Web site at support.sas.com/companionsites.

The index estimation program requires that you provide five values for the computation:

- **PSIZE** This refers to the page size of the index file. Set PSIZE equal to the current value of IBUFSIZE. See the section titled "The IBUFSIZE System Option" in Chapter 5, "Index-Related Options," for a thorough discussion of this index option.

- **VSIZE** This is the total length, in bytes of the variable that you intend to use to create a simple index. If you are going to create a composite index, add the lengths of all variables that will make up the composite key. You can find variable lengths in a CONTENTS procedure listing of the data set you are going to index.

- **UVAL** This parameter is the number of unique values that you expect in your SAS data set for the particular index key. If all values are unique for a simple index, then UVAL should be equal the total number of observations in the SAS data set. If not, or if you are going to create a composite index, you need to run the FREQ procedure to get an idea of the number of unique values. Because this program is computing an estimate, do not worry if you are in the position of estimating the number of unique values.

- **NREC** This value is the total number of observations in the SAS data set. If you are building an index for an existing SAS data set, find this value from a PROC CONTENTS listing. Otherwise, you can estimate this value from how many observations you expect to have in a SAS data set that you are creating.

- **Host** This identifies the operating system hosting the SAS data set and where the index is built. There are ten possible host values:

MVS	OS/390 and z/OS
WIN	Windows NT, 2000, and XP
LNX	RedHat Linux on Intel servers
ALP	OpenVMS Alpha
ALX	Compaq Digital UNIX
HP64	HP 64 UNIX
S64	Solaris 64 UNIX
R64	AIX 64
H6I	HP/UX for Itanium Platform Family, 64-bit
W64	Windows for IPF, 64-bit

Once you supply the five main values and execute the program, it computes the index size and creates a formatted report in the SAS log.

Here is an example of the output from the index size estimation program. In this example, the size of an index created from variable SEQNUM for INDEXLIB.PRODINDX was computed.

```
Index characteristics:
   Host Platform          = WIN
   Page Size (bytes)      = 32256
   Index Value Size (bytes) = 8
   Unique Values          = 2304000
   Total Number of Values = 2304000
   Number of Index Levels = 2

Estimated storage requirements for a V9 index:
   Number of Upper Level Pages =        1
   Number of Leaf Pages        =     1145
   Total Number of Index Pages =     1146 or      36,965,376 bytes

Note: the above estimate does not include storage for the index
      directory (usually one page) or the host header page.

Estimation of index size complete.
```

The program first reiterates the five values that were supplied in a section labeled "Index characteristics." Then it displays the number of "Upper Level Pages" (which are used to store the root node and branch nodes), the number of "Leaf Pages," and the "Total Number of Index Pages." In this example, you can see that one index page would be enough to contain the root node and the branch nodes. It would take 1,145 pages to store all of the leaf nodes for the SEQNUM simple index. The total number of index pages would be 1,146. SAS multiplies this by the page size (you entered this value in as PSIZE=) to get the total number of bytes, which is 36,965,376—or about 35 megabytes.

If you are going to create multiple indexes for a SAS data set, then you need to calculate each index separately. When you're done, add the number of pages for each index together to get the total index pages used by *all* indexes for the SAS data set. You can stop there, or multiply *total index pages* by the index page size to get the total number of bytes for the entire index file.

The index size estimate program is a great tool for getting a reasonable estimate of the amount of space needed for your SAS indexes. It is probably most useful for people in organizations where disk space is at a premium, or where people are charged for the disk space that their data sets occupy.

Summary

This chapter introduced the concept of SAS indexes, discussed how SAS indexes are actually performance tools, and described how indexes can benefit various types of SAS applications. Next, the structure of an index was described, including the root, branch, and leaf nodes and the entries that reside within them. An example was provided to illustrate how SAS traverses an index during an index search.

The chapter presented the two types of SAS indexes: a *simple* index made from a single variable and a *composite* index made from two or more variables. It discussed the four SAS programming structures that use SAS indexes: the WHERE expression, the BY statement, the KEY option in a MODIFY statement, and the KEY option in a DATA statement. Then, the three-step algorithm that SAS uses to determine whether or not to use an index for WHERE or BY statement processing was discussed. The chapter concluded by presenting how to estimate the size of an index.

Chapter 2

Index Considerations for SAS Data Sets

Introduction

Perhaps the most common question associated with SAS indexes is this: *When is it appropriate to create an index for a SAS data set*? The basic goal of having a SAS index is to be able to efficiently extract a *small* subset of observations from a *large* SAS data set. When the goal is achieved, the amount of computer resources—measured in CPU time, I/Os, and elapsed time—expended by your program should be less than if SAS reads the entire data set sequentially. If your applications are extracting small subsets from large SAS data sets, then it is usually appropriate to create SAS indexes to improve the performance of those applications. However, though it is a very important consideration, the size of the subset is not the only criteria for determining whether or not to create and use an index for a specific SAS data set.

Before attempting to build a SAS index or to use one, you should determine whether an index will truly improve the efficiency of your application. There are three main issues that influence the effectiveness of indexes:

- the size of the subset and the size of the SAS data set
- the frequency of use of the index
- the variability of the data

All three of these issues must be examined to ensure the success of any indexes that are built. Each of these issues is discussed in this chapter.

Size of the Subset and Size of the SAS Data Set

An index is most effective when it is used to access a *small* subset of observations from a *large* SAS data set. When this happens, the overhead of processing index pages and data set pages is lower than the overhead of reading the entire data set. As the size of the subset increases, the efficiency of using the index to read the data decreases. There is a finite point at which the size of the subset becomes too large, relative to the size of the data set. At this point, the overhead of using the index becomes greater than the overhead of a sequential read of the entire data set. (This is due to the additional CPU time and I/Os consumed moving index pages from disk into the buffers in memory and then following the pointers to read the data set pages.) When the size of the subset reaches this point, the index is not an efficient means of accessing the data and should not be used.

The break-even size of the largest subset of observations that should be accessed through an index is not always obvious. Specific characteristics of a particular data set, such as its size, how discriminant and uniformly distributed its key variables are, and whether the key variables are sorted, affect the upper limits for efficient subset size. Programmers have reported maximum efficient subset sizes ranging up to 50% of the data set. Though this is often data- and application-dependent, some good basic guidelines have emerged. Table 2.1 contains some basic indexing guidelines.

Table 2.1 Indexing Guidelines[1]

Subset Size	Indexing Action
1% to 15%	An index will definitely improve processing. There should be dramatic resource savings in the lower end of this range.
16% to 30%	An index will improve processing. However, the resource savings will not be as dramatic as in the lower range.
31% to 60%	An index may improve processing, or it might worsen processing. Be very careful in this subset range.
61% to 100%	Do not use an index. A sequential read of the entire data set is very likely to be more efficient.

[1] These guidelines provide rules of thumb that you can generally count on. However, they have not been subjected to rigorous testing with many different sized SAS data sets across all of the computer platforms that SAS currently runs on. Therefore, your own experience may differ slightly, especially along the boundaries of the percentage categories in the Subset Size column.

While the indexing guidelines in Table 2.1 are general rules for you to use when considering the relationship between subset size and data set size, as evidenced by the table, the smaller the subset, the more efficient is the use of the index. Do not be overly concerned if you have a subset size that is on the upper boundaries of one of the first two percentage categories in the table when making an index usage decision. These are basic guidelines, and the composition and nature of the SAS data sets that you are processing may slightly blur the results you actually get for percentage categories stated in the guidelines. However, following the guidelines should keep you in the right ballpark in terms of index resource usage.

It is much harder to characterize what is meant by *a large SAS data set* than it is to characterize *a small subset*, because *large* is a relative term when it comes to SAS data sets. In some organizations a *large* SAS data set is one that contains several thousand observations, while in others a *large* SAS data set is one that holds several million observations. People normally consider a SAS data set to be large when it contains tens of thousands, hundreds of thousands, millions, or tens of millions of observations. Because SAS normally reads SAS data sets sequentially, an appreciable amount of computer resources are consumed when larger SAS data sets are read. The larger the SAS data set the more computer resources are needed to perform a sequential read of the entire SAS data set. It takes more resources to read a SAS data set that is ten million observations *large* than to read one that is fifty-thousand observations *large*.

You can still achieve significant computer resource savings whether your SAS data set has a few thousand observations or several million observations when you access a small subset of observations via an index. However, the winning combination for SAS indexes is accessing a *small subset* from a *large SAS data set*. The smaller the subset and the larger the SAS data set the more resource savings you get from using an index. Keep this in mind when determining whether an index might help the performance of your SAS applications.

Frequency of Use

An index must be used often enough to make the computer resources expended for its creation and upkeep worthwhile. This fact is frequently overlooked when programmers evaluate the performance of an index. Some programmers only consider how many I/Os and how much CPU time were saved through the use of an index. What is less obvious is that it took I/Os and CPU time to initially build the index. These computer resources were pure overhead because no data or result set was actually returned to a user. Additionally, when the indexed SAS data set is updated, still more overhead is required to maintain the index. A particularly costly scenario, in terms of overhead, occurs when large numbers of observations are appended to an indexed data set.

For an index to really be resource and cost-effective, the resources saved through using it must surpass those spent to create it. The break-even point comes when the CPU time and I/Os avoided by using the index are finally greater than those used to create it. This can be expressed by the following algorithm:

A = resources consumed building the index

B = resources necessary to read the entire data set

C = resources expended by any program using the index

D = (B – C) resources saved by any program that used the index

When the accumulated value of D (for all programs that use the index) becomes greater than A, the index becomes cost-effective.

This algorithm can be better understood with an example that illustrates the break-even point of a hypothetical index. For this example, let's assume that applications always access the same subset size of the data each time they use the index. The CPU times are in seconds.

A = CPU time = 30; I/O count = 400   building the SAS index

B = CPU time = 10; I/O count = 150   reading the entire SAS data set

C = CPU time = 2.0; I/O count = 15   using the index to read the SAS data set

D = CPU time = (10 - 2) = 8   CPU time difference
      I/O   count = (150 - 15) = 135   I/O difference

It would take four (4 $*$ 8 = 32, which is greater than 30) accesses to pass the CPU time break-even point. It would take three (3 $*$ 135 = 405, which is greater than 400) accesses of the data set through the index to pass the break-even point for I/O count.

From this example it should be clear that frequently used indexes have the greatest potential to be the most resource and cost-effective. After the break-even point has been reached, all future accesses of the SAS data set through the index reap great computer resource savings. So the frequency of index use is an important item to establish. If using the index does not exceed its initial cost, it may not be worth the effort to build it at all.

Occasionally, there may be other factors that override *frequency of use* as being an important consideration for creating an index. Sometimes the speed of data retrieval gained through using an index is more important. For example, consider a mission-critical SAS/IntrNet application that requires fast end-user response time. Building indexes for the SAS data sets involved in the application might require more overhead resources than are recouped from subsequent aggregated indexed data retrievals. However, the fast retrieval of data by end-users may be more important to the organization than the resources used to build and maintain the index. When this is the case, the only appropriate action to take is to ignore the index *frequency of use* rule and build the index to speed up the productivity of the end-users.

As discussed, the use of indexes must be frequent enough to overcome the cost of building, storing, and maintaining them. So, it is usually not cost-effective to build an index for use in an ad hoc SAS program that is run only once or twice. Rather, it is far more cost-effective to build an index that is used in SAS programs that are executed tens, scores, hundreds, or thousands of times. That is where you get your greatest payback from the computer resources spent in creating the index.

Variability of the Data

Static SAS data sets make better index candidates because no index maintenance is required. When indexes are built for a SAS data set that remains static, all of the index overhead is spent up front when the indexes are first created. As the indexes are used more and more, the up-front index-creation resource overhead is recouped and then surpassed as the index provides greater efficiency than reading the entire SAS data set. The longer the data set remains static, the greater the overall savings.

SAS data sets that change often are not the strongest index candidates. We know that when observations are added to an indexed SAS data set, the index is updated to account for the key variable values of the new observations. When observations are deleted, the index is again updated to reflect the changes. Such changes to the index consume computer resources that are pure overhead. That is, the computer resources consumed are for index housekeeping only and do not provide any type of result set that can be given to your users. Consequently, the more often the data set is updated, the more computer overhead is expended to keep the index updated.

This discussion is not intended to imply that you should not add and delete observations from an indexed SAS data set. Rather, it points out that frequent additions and deletions of observations to an indexed SAS data set require an index update overhead "penalty." That penalty increases as the percentage of updated observations rises in the original SAS data set. As mentioned earlier in this chapter, it can be particularly costly when large numbers of observations are appended to an indexed data set.

A different slant to this overall issue involves SAS data sets that are re-created on a cyclic interval. Some applications require that a SAS data set be completely re-created from new data every day, week, month, or quarter. If that data set is indexed, then the indexes must be rebuilt when the SAS data set is re-created. This may consume a significant amount of computer resources depending on the size of the data set and the number of indexes that are created. In order to make the resources spent building them worthwhile, the SAS indexes must be used often enough between the time they are created and the next time that the data set is refreshed and they are re-created.

It is difficult to formulate a rule of thumb for determining the break-even point when considering how the variability of the data should influence your decision to create indexes. This is so because the speed of retrieving observations through an index might be more important to your application than the resources exhausted by index creation and housekeeping. It can be especially true if your indexed SAS data sets are the back-end for SAS/IntrNet applications, SAS Enterprise Guide applications, or SAS BI applications where you want to provide the best possible response time to users. Or you may have critical batch applications running against indexed SAS data sets that must complete in a tight, nightly batch window. If these types of considerations outweigh the cost of re-creating or maintaining SAS indexes, then the variability of the data is probably not an issue for you to be overly concerned about.

The following issues that mitigate the variability of a SAS data set should be considered:

- how often the data set is re-created
- how often and how many observations are added to the data set
- how often and how many observations are deleted from the data set
- how often and how many observations are updated
- how often large amounts of data are appended to the data set
- what are the interactive application response time demands for data in the data set
- what are the batch application program run time demands for data in the data set

If you consider the issues above and determine that your SAS data set is relatively static, then building SAS indexes for that data set is probably worthwhile. Similarly, if interactive response time demands—or batch job turnaround time demands—outweigh the issue of having a constantly changing data set, then creating SAS indexes should be a viable option for you.

Summary

This chapter provides guidelines to help answer this question: *When is it appropriate to create an index for a SAS data set*? There are three main factors that you should consider when determining whether or not to create an index for a particular SAS data set. First, you should consider the size of the subsets you will obtain and the size of the SAS data set. Indexes are more efficient when they are used to access small subsets of large SAS data sets. Second, you should consider the frequency of use of an index. Because it takes a specific amount of computer overhead to create and to maintain an index, you should use the index often enough to make spending those resources worthwhile. Finally, the variability of the data is a consideration. Indexed SAS data sets that change a lot require index maintenance, which is pure overhead that costs additional computer resources. From time to time the last two considerations may be mitigated by the need to quickly access data in an interactive or critical batch application. When that is the case, using an index is appropriate if you are willing to make the trade-off between consuming more computer resources for index creation and maintenance and faster access to the data.

C h a p t e r **3**

Index Variable Selection Considerations

Introduction

If SAS indexes are such powerful performance tools, then why doesn't SAS
automatically build an index for every variable in a new SAS data set? The most obvious
reasons are that indexes consume computer resources when being built and maintained
and that they take up disk space. Less obvious is the fact that not every variable in a SAS
data set makes a good index key variable. Many data set variables contain pure data that
may be used in computations but that would not normally be used to subset or to order

the data. Other variables contain values that recur in large numbers of data set observations so that attempting to select a particular value via an index would return a very large subset of the original SAS data set. Another reason is that data sets often contain various variables that are informational and *do* have distinct values but are never used to subset or order the data in the normal processing done within an application. These are some of the reasons that SAS leaves it up to you to determine which variables should become index key variables.

This chapter discusses the three factors that you should consider when determining whether a particular variable, or variables, make good index key variable candidates. You need to answer the following questions, which will determine how you should proceed:

- Which variables are used most often to subset the data?
- Are the proposed index key variables discriminant?
- Is the data sorted into ascending order of the proposed index key variables?

For you to adequately consider the factors above, you need to know something about the variables in the data set that you are examining. The first thing you should do is to run the FREQ procedure against the variables that you think might possibly make good index key variables. This will give you a good idea of the range of values for these particular variables.

Here is an example of the SAS code needed to run the FREQ procedure for selected variables found in the INDEXLIB.PRODSALE SAS data set:

```
proc freq data=indexlib.prodsale;
    table country state county product year quarter month
    daymonyr / missing;
run;
```

PROC FREQ above creates a long output listing of frequencies for the specified variables. Because the MISSING option was used, missing values appear as entries in the frequency tables. The entire PROC FREQ output listing can be found in Figure 3.1, "FREQ Procedure List of Selected Variables in INDEXLIB.PRODSALE," at the end of this chapter. It is used in the following discussions about index key variable viability.

After reviewing the output of the FREQ procedure, you should analyze the applications that access the data set(s) in question. Keep your answers to the questions, discussed above, in mind while analyzing your applications so that you can look for good indexing opportunities. When you find a variable, or variables, that make good index key variable(s), act immediately to create the requisite indexes and to modify your application's programs so that they exploit the new SAS indexes.

Variables Used Most Often to Subset the Data

If you always find yourself using a particular variable to subset a large SAS data set, then that variable is a good candidate for becoming an index key variable for a simple index. For example, consider an application that continually subsets the INDEXLIB.PRODSALE SAS data set by variable MONTH to obtain a small subset of observations. The obvious action would be for you to create a simple index from MONTH. On the other hand, if you are always extracting subsets of a large SAS data set using two or more variables, then you should consider making a composite index out of them. For instance, if you are always looking for observations in INDEXLIB.PRODSALE based on STATE, YEAR, and MONTH, it makes sense to create a composite index built from the three variables.

You should ask yourself which variables are used to subset your large SAS data sets and which are to be used for computation and reporting purposes. Variables that are used to subset data sets are prime candidates for indexing. Examine your SAS application programs and decide which of the candidate variables are used the most frequently within the various SAS programs for subsetting purposes. Such variables are most often found in subsetting IF statements and WHERE expressions.

If a cohesive application does not yet exist, try to envision which variables are the most likely candidates. It usually does not take too much imagination to see which variables are the most likely contenders. They are often the variables that are used in CLASS and BY statements in the SUMMARY and MEANS procedures, the TABLE statement in the FREQ procedure, the ORDER or GROUP statements in the REPORT procedure, or they are the category variables in reports. Armed with a CONTENTS procedure listing and an idea of the probable reporting needs, you should be able to pick out the variables that should be indexed.

You do not want to build indexes for variables that are seldom used. Doing so is a waste of the computer processing power used to create and to maintain those indexes. So you should be judicious about which variables you pick to be index variables. It might be wise to start with the ones that you know will be used and then examine your application on a periodic basis. As the application changes and other variables frequently emerge as subsets, you can build indexes for them as well.

Proposed Index Key Variable Discriminant

Index key variables should be discriminant. A *discriminant* variable is one with values very specific to a small set of observations within a data set. The ideal discriminant variable has a one-to-one correspondence between specific values and observations. This means that each observation has a unique value stored in the variable. Variables with a one-to-many correspondence between specific values and observations can also be discriminant. If very small subsets of the observations in a data set share a particular set of values, then the variable is discriminant. In summary, discriminant variables have a large number of distinct values so that subsets based on any particular value are typically a small percentage of the entire SAS data set.

Some types of variables tend to be more discriminant than others. For instance, Social Security number, zip code, part number, and last name are fairly discriminant. However, gender, age, first name, region, and country are not. Variables that have binary values, such as gender, are not discriminant and make poor key variables. In general, the variables within a data set with values that are shared by the smallest subsets of observations make the best discriminant variables.

To better understand the nature of discriminant variables, consider the FREQ procedure listing for INDEXLIB.PRODSALE in Figure 3.1, located at the end of this chapter. The variable COUNTRY does not make a good discriminant variable because 60% of the observations have the value "U.S.A.," 20% have "Canada," and 20% have "Mexico." Because hundreds of thousands of observations exist for each value of COUNTRY, the variable is not discriminant. Similarly, the variable QUARTER is not very discriminant because 25% of the total observations in the entire data set contain each distinct value. If you were to subset INDEXLIB.PRODINDX for QUARTER=2, you would end up with one-fourth of the observations in the data set, that is, 576,000 observations.

The variable MONTH is more discriminant than COUNTRY or QUARTER because fewer observations in the data set share the same values. Only about 8% of the variables in INDEXLIB.PRODINDX share the same value of MONTH. Still, MONTH is not overly discriminant because 192,000 observations have the same value for any month that you may select. DAYMONYR is a far more discriminant variable than any of the variables previously discussed. Specifying a particular value for DAYMONYR would net you about 1% or fewer observations from INDEXLIB.PRODINDX. Because relatively small subsets of the data set share the same values in DAYMONYR, it is a *very* discriminant variable. Consequently, COUNTRY and QUARTER are not discriminant, MONTH is somewhat discriminant, and DAYMONYR is very discriminant.

Using an index built from a discriminant variable enables SAS to read the fewest possible observations from the data set. This is important because it reduces the I/O count and CPU time that the program expends obtaining data. These computer resources are reduced because fewer data set pages are transferred between disk and computer memory. Thus, using discriminant variables for index key variables promotes good program performance.

Discriminant index key variables enable your applications to read in only the observations that you need. It is far more efficient for SAS to *not* read in unwanted observations than it is to read them in, decide that they are not needed, and skip them. This can be illustrated by considering an application that requires observations with specific zip codes within certain states. If the application uses an index built on variable STATE, it reads in all of the observations from the states it needs to process. Unfortunately, it reads in many observations that are not needed because they do not have the required zip code values. Additional program logic must be written to identify and omit the unwanted observations. If an index were built on variable ZIP_CODE, which is more discriminant, then the application could use that index so that only the observations containing the specific zip code values that are wanted are actually read. Consequently, fewer overall observations would be read, and no additional program selection logic would be required.

Composite indexes may also be discriminant even if their component variables are not. They can be discriminant by offering unique combinations of the values of their component variables. For example, we already know that in the INDEXLIB.PRODSALE SAS data set, COUNTRY, QUARTER, and MONTH are not particularly discriminant variables. However, a composite index key variable built from COUNTRY/QUARTER/MONTH is actually pretty discriminant. In this composite index, each of the index keys where COUNTRY = "U.S.A." represents 5% of the observations in the data set no matter what the values of QUARTER and MONTH are. Similarly, index keys where COUNTRY = "Mexico" or "Canada" represent about 2% for every combination of COUNTRY/QUARTER/MONTH. If you were often going to access the INDEXLIB.PRODSALE SAS data set by COUNTRY, QUARTER, and MONTH, you could feel confident that a composite index built from those variables would give you a discriminant index that would be able to return small subsets of data.

When building a composite index, the first variable specified in the key should be the most discriminant of the key variables. However, you must base your decision on whether or not the most discriminant variable is also one of the variables most often used to subset the data. When there is a choice, the variable most often used to subset the data should be selected over that which is most discriminant.

If the most discriminant variable is first in the composite index key, the original subset will be smaller. For example, a composite index of MONTH/QUARTER/COUNTRY would be better than one of COUNTRY/QUARTER/MONTH. This is true because MONTH is the most discriminant variable, QUARTER is the next most discriminant, while COUNTRY is the least discriminant variable.

A SAS Data Set Sorted into Ascending Order of the Proposed Index Variable

If a SAS data set is sorted into ascending order by a proposed index key variable, the resulting index will be more efficient. You can determine whether a SAS data set is sorted by a particular variable by looking at a CONTENTS procedure listing of the data set. The first section of the listing would list YES for the Sorted field, indicating that the data is sorted. When Sorted equals YES, the listing contains a subsection titled Sort Information. This section reports the variable or variables used to sort the data set. If you see that a particular SAS data set is sorted into ascending order by a variable you are considering for an index key variable, that is very good news.

Here is an excerpt from the CONTENTS procedure listing found in Appendix A:

```
                         The CONTENTS Procedure

Data Set Name:  INDEXLIB.PRODSALE              Observations:          2304000
Member Type:    DATA                           Variables:             12
Engine:         V9                             Indexes:               0
Created:        16:37 Saturday, January 15, 2005   Observation Length:    128
Last Modified:  16:37 Saturday, January 15, 2005   Deleted Observations:  0
Protection:                                    Compressed:            NO
Data Set Type:                                 Sorted:                YES
Label:
```

Notice that the YES in the Sorted field indicates that the data set is sorted. Noting this, you would look at the Sort Information section of the listing to determine which variable or variables were used to sort the data.

```
            -----Sort Information-----

            Sortedby:        DAYMONYR
            Validated:       YES
            Character Set:   ANSI
```

The Sort Information section states that the data is sorted by variable DAYMONYR. So, a SAS index built from variable DAYMONYR would be more efficient than one built from any other variable in the INDEXLIB.PRODSALE data set.

Sorting a SAS data set by a key variable *before* creating the index results in an index that will more efficiently subset data. The reason for this is that observations with like values are grouped together on the same—or on adjacent—data set pages. When the index is used to read a range of values, fewer pages have to be moved from disk to computer memory because observations with similar values are concentrated together. When a data set page is read into memory, most of the observations that are needed to satisfy the program's value-range selection criteria are likely to be found on the same page. SAS will not have to read a new data set page from disk until it has processed all of the observations on the page currently in memory.

In a SAS data set that is not sorted by key variable value, the next required observation may be on any page anywhere in the data set. The likelihood that the next required observation is on a page that is currently in computer memory is very low. Therefore, the probability that another I/O is needed to read in a new data set page is very high. Some data set pages may be read in again and again as SAS follows index pointers to them, then to other pages, and back again. All of this results in more I/Os and CPU time being expended to process the data set through the index. It is a direct result of the data not being sorted into ascending index key variable value.

To determine whether the data should be sorted by ascending key variable value before building the index, consider how the index will normally be used. If disparate, or truly random, key variable values are usually processed and sorting probably does not improve performance. This could be the case if you had a SAS/IntrNet application that accessed data by a very discriminant variable such as client-ID or Social Security number, in an ad hoc, random pattern. Because users would be accessing very targeted single observations at a time, there is no particular advantage to having the data set sorted. However, if homogeneous ranges of key variable values are often accessed, then sorting the data *will* improve performance. This could be the case for the INDEXLIB.PRODINDX SAS data set, which has multiple records for each DAYMONYR and is updated by a transaction data set in a nightly batch job. Because the data is sorted by DAYMONYR, there is a high likelihood that all observations for a given DAYMONYR will be on the same data set page. This would reduce the total number of data set pages read from the master data set—if the transaction data set is also sorted by DAYMONYR.

This same discussion pertains to composite indexes as well. If you know that you are always going to access subsets of the INDEXLIB.PRODINDX SAS data set by DAYMONYR and STATE, then you are probably considering creating a composite index built from DAYMONYR/STATE. You should presort the data by DAYMONYR/STATE to get it into an advantageous sort order before the index is built. Doing so allows observations with the same values of STATE to be together on data set pages for any given value of DAYMONYR. Thus, an index search for a particular value combination of DAYMONYR and STATE will return all qualifying observations as efficiently as possible.

Another consideration of whether or not to presort a SAS data set by the proposed index key variable is how often the data will be accessed through the index. The data must be accessed often enough through the index to make the sort processing overhead worthwhile. If, on balance, most accesses of the data set do not come through the index, and the key variable sort order is not often used, then sorting the data set is not worthwhile. This is so because the CPU time and I/Os spent sorting the data set will never be recouped by the CPU time and I/Os avoided through the use of the index.

There may be some circumstances under which having the data sorted by proposed index key variable value is impractical. One circumstance is when you want to create multiple simple indexes for a particular SAS data set. Because the SAS data set may only be sorted into order for a single variable at a time, you cannot have it sorted into primary order for multiple distinct variables. That is, if you were to sort INDEXLIB.PRODSALE by PRODUCT, it would not be in the proper sort order for STATE and vice versa. The same holds true for composite indexes. If INDEX.PRODSALE is sorted by YEAR/QUARTER, it is definitely not sorted by COUNTRY/STATE. Thus, you may have to settle for having the data set sorted into order of the proposed index key variable, or variables, *most often* used to subset the data when you are considering creating multiple simple or composite indexes. This issue should not influence you to abandon creating a SAS index for a particular variable when the data is already sorted by another variable in order to optimize that variable's index. You should create the index anyway if you believe that the new index will help with your application's overall performance.

Summary

This chapter discussed the three major considerations for determining whether or not to create an index for a given variable or variables. The first consideration is that you should create indexes for variables that are used most often to subset your SAS data sets. The second consideration is that index variables must be discriminant—they must have values that are very specific to a small set of observations within a data set. The final consideration is that indexes are more efficient if they are sorted in ascending order by the proposed key variable. You should use these considerations when determining whether or not a particular variable makes a good index variable. Doing so helps you to build effective indexes that promote good performance in your SAS applications.

Figure 3.1 FREQ Procedure List of Selected Variables in INDEXLIB.PRODSALE

```
                              The FREQ Procedure

                                   Country

                                          Cumulative    Cumulative
         COUNTRY       Frequency    Percent    Frequency      Percent

         Canada         460800      20.00       460800        20.00
         Mexico         460800      20.00       921600        40.00
         U.S.A.        1382400      60.00      2304000       100.00

                                State/Province

                                          Cumulative    Cumulative
   STATE                Frequency    Percent    Frequency      Percent

   Baja California Norte   115200     5.00        115200         5.00
   British Columbia        115200     5.00        230400        10.00
   California              115200     5.00        345600        15.00
   Campeche                115200     5.00        460800        20.00
   Colorado                115200     5.00        576000        25.00
   Florida                 115200     5.00        691200        30.00
   Illinois                576000    25.00       1267200        55.00
   Michoacan               115200     5.00       1382400        60.00
```

(continued on next page)

Figure 3.1 *(continued)*

New York	115200	5.00	1497600	65.00
North Carolina	115200	5.00	1612800	70.00
Nuevo Leon	115200	5.00	1728000	75.00
Ontario	115200	5.00	1843200	80.00
Quebec	115200	5.00	1958400	85.00
Saskatchewan	115200	5.00	2073600	90.00
Texas	115200	5.00	2188800	95.00
Washington	115200	5.00	2304000	100.00

County

COUNTY	Frequency	Percent	Cumulative Frequency	Cumulative Percent
	1728000	75.00	1728000	75.00
Adams	115200	5.00	1843200	80.00
Cook	115200	5.00	1958400	85.00
Fayette	115200	5.00	2073600	90.00
McLean	115200	5.00	2188800	95.00
Winnebago	115200	5.00	2304000	100.00

The FREQ Procedure

Product

PRODUCT	Frequency	Percent	Cumulative Frequency	Cumulative Percent
BED	576000	25.00	576000	25.00
CHAIR	576000	25.00	1152000	50.00
DESK	576000	25.00	1728000	75.00
SOFA	576000	25.00	2304000	100.00

(continued on next page)

Figure 3.1 *(continued)*

Year

YEAR	Frequency	Percent	Cumulative Frequency	Cumulative Percent
1995	115200	5.00	115200	5.00
1996	230400	10.00	345600	15.00
1997	230400	10.00	576000	25.00
1998	345600	15.00	921600	40.00
1999	230400	10.00	1152000	50.00
2000	115200	5.00	1267200	55.00
2001	230400	10.00	1497600	65.00
2002	115200	5.00	1612800	70.00
2003	115200	5.00	1728000	75.00
2004	115200	5.00	1843200	80.00
2005	115200	5.00	1958400	85.00
2006	115200	5.00	2073600	90.00
2007	115200	5.00	2188800	95.00
2008	115200	5.00	2304000	100.00

Quarter

QUARTER	Frequency	Percent	Cumulative Frequency	Cumulative Percent
1	576000	25.00	576000	25.00
2	576000	25.00	1152000	50.00
3	576000	25.00	1728000	75.00
4	576000	25.00	2304000	100.00

(continued on next page)

Figure 3.1 *(continued)*

```
                        The SAS System

                      The FREQ Procedure

                            Month

                              Cumulative    Cumulative
  MONTH    Frequency    Percent    Frequency     Percent
  _____

     1       192000       8.33       192000        8.33
     2       192000       8.33       384000       16.67
     3       192000       8.33       576000       25.00
     4       192000       8.33       768000       33.33
     5       192000       8.33       960000       41.67
     6       192000       8.33      1152000       50.00
     7       192000       8.33      1344000       58.33
     8       192000       8.33      1536000       66.67
     9       192000       8.33      1728000       75.00
    10       192000       8.33      1920000       83.33
    11       192000       8.33      2112000       91.67
    12       192000       8.33      2304000      100.00


                        The SAS System

                      The FREQ Procedure

                         Day/Month/Year

                               Cumulative    Cumulative
 DAYMONYR    Frequency    Percent    Frequency     Percent
  _____

  01JAN95      9600        0.42        9600        0.42
  01FEB95      9600        0.42       19200        0.83
  01MAR95      9600        0.42       28800        1.25
  01APR95      9600        0.42       38400        1.67
  01MAY95      9600        0.42       48000        2.08
  01JUN95      9600        0.42       57600        2.50
```

(continued on next page)

Figure 3.1 *(continued)*

01JUL95	9600	0.42	67200	2.92
01AUG95	9600	0.42	76800	3.33
01SEP95	9600	0.42	86400	3.75
01OCT95	9600	0.42	96000	4.17
01NOV95	9600	0.42	105600	4.58
01DEC95	9600	0.42	115200	5.00
01JAN96	19200	0.83	134400	5.83
01FEB96	19200	0.83	153600	6.67
01MAR96	19200	0.83	172800	7.50
01APR96	19200	0.83	192000	8.33
01MAY96	19200	0.83	211200	9.17
01JUN96	19200	0.83	230400	10.00
01JUL96	19200	0.83	249600	10.83
01AUG96	19200	0.83	268800	11.67
01SEP96	19200	0.83	288000	12.50
01OCT96	19200	0.83	307200	13.33
01NOV96	19200	0.83	326400	14.17
01DEC96	19200	0.83	345600	15.00
01JAN97	19200	0.83	364800	15.83
01FEB97	19200	0.83	384000	16.67
01MAR97	19200	0.83	403200	17.50
01APR97	19200	0.83	422400	18.33
01MAY97	19200	0.83	441600	19.17
01JUN97	19200	0.83	460800	20.00
01JUL97	19200	0.83	480000	20.83
01AUG97	19200	0.83	499200	21.67
01SEP97	19200	0.83	518400	22.50
01OCT97	19200	0.83	537600	23.33
01NOV97	19200	0.83	556800	24.17
01DEC97	19200	0.83	576000	25.00
01JAN98	28800	1.25	604800	26.25
01FEB98	28800	1.25	633600	27.50
01MAR98	28800	1.25	662400	28.75
01APR98	28800	1.25	691200	30.00
. . .	. . .	. . .	. . .	. . .

Chapter 4

Index Centiles

Introduction

Centiles are a very important but not very well understood feature of SAS data set indexes. Centiles are important because SAS uses them to determine if it is more efficient to use an index or more efficient to read the entire SAS data set sequentially.[1] Centiles are found in the header page of an index file and contain a mapping of the distribution of index key values throughout the index. SAS initializes each index's centiles when the index is created and keeps them updated when a certain percentage of the index key variable's values have changed within the data set. The default value for updating centiles is 5%. This means that when 5% of the variables in the SAS data set that are index key variables have their values changed, SAS will recompute the centiles for that index.

The word *centile* is a contraction of the term *cumulative percentile*. There are 21 centiles for each index, representing the 0, 5th, 10th, 15th, 20th, 25th, 30th, 35th, 40th, 45th, 50th, 55th, 60th, 65th, 70th, 75th, 80th, 85th, 90th, 95th, and 100th percentiles. The first centile, corresponding to the 0 percentile, has the minimum value of the entire index. The last percentile, corresponding to the 100th percentile, has the maximum value of the entire index. The other centiles, 5th, 10th, 15th, etc., are such that 5% of the data has index values less than the 5th percentile, 10% of the data has index values less than the 10th percentile, and so on. Centiles give you a very valuable peek into how the index key variable values are spread out throughout your indexes.

To better understand centiles, consider Table 4.1, below, which displays the centiles for three indexes that exist for SAS data set INDEXLIB.PRODINDX. The 0 centile shows that the minimum values for PRODUCT, YEAR, and DAYMONYR are *BED*, *1995*, and *12784*, respectively. The 100th centile indicates that the maximum values for PRODUCT, YEAR, and DAYMONYR are *SOFA*, *2008* and *17867*, respectively. Thus, the centiles disclose the minimum and maximum index key variable values at a glance.

The centiles reveal something very interesting about the PRODUCT index. They show that PRODUCT is a relatively poor index. This is true because for any given value of PRODUCT, the index would return about 25% of the observations in the SAS data set. It might be more efficient to have SAS read the entire SAS data set sequentially and have program statements subset the data rather than use this index to subset the data for a

---

[1] See the "When Indexes Are Used" section in Chapter 1, for an explanation of how SAS uses centiles in its three-step algorithm that determines whether or not it is more efficient to use an index or to read the entire SAS data set sequentially.

single value of PRODUCT. If more than one value of PRODUCT is to be used to subset the data, it would *definitely* be more efficient to read the entire SAS data set than to use the PRODUCT index.

The centiles show that YEAR is a much better variable for indexed processing of the INDEXLIB.PRODINDX data set than PRODUCT. This is true because for any given value of YEAR from 5% to 10% of the observations contain that value. Therefore, it would be more efficient to use YEAR to subset INDEXLIB.PRODINDX for a single value of YEAR than it would to read the entire SAS data set.

Finally, Table 4.1 shows that DAYMONYR is an excellent index variable. In this example, let's suppose that there are 168 distinct values of DAYMONYR in the INDEXLIB.PRODINDX SAS data set. The DAYMONYR index was created without the UNIQUE option. Using any specific value of DAYMONYR in an indexed search would return 5% or less of the observations in the SAS data set. This would be far more efficient than reading the entire SAS data set to find a subset match for a particular variable value, which is exactly what indexes were designed for.

Table 4.1 Centiles for SAS Data Set INDEXLIB.PRODINDX's Simple Indexes Based on the Values of the PRODUCT, YEAR, and DAYMONYR Variables

Centile	Index Variable PRODUCT	Index Variable YEAR	Index Variable DAYMONYR
0	BED	1995	12784
5	BED	1995	13118
10	BED	1996	13301
15	BED	1996	13484
20	BED	1997	13666
25	BED	1997	13849
30	CHAIR	1998	13970
35	CHAIR	1998	14092
40	CHAIR	1998	14214
45	CHAIR	1999	14396
50	CHAIR	1999	14579
55	DESK	2000	14945
60	DESK	2001	15127

(continued on next page)

Table 4.1 *(continued)*

Centile	Index Variable PRODUCT	Index Variable YEAR	Index Variable DAYMONYR
65	DESK	2001	15310
70	DESK	2002	15675
75	DESK	2003	16040
80	SOFA	2004	16406
85	SOFA	2005	16771
90	SOFA	2006	17136
95	SOFA	2007	17501
100	SOFA	2008	17867

The power of centiles should have emerged from this discussion. You can craft your SAS program to use a specific index when the centiles reveal that using it would improve performance. You can do this through the use of a WHERE expression or with the IDXNAME option. Conversely, you can override your SAS program to *not* use an index when the centiles indicate that using an index would probably degrade performance. You can do this through the IDXWHERE option. (The IDXNAME and IDXWHERE options are discussed in Chapter 14, "Overriding Default Index Usage.")

The previous discussion is not meant to imply that you are responsible for determining which index SAS is to use. SAS is designed to exploit centiles and use the index that returns the smallest possible subset. SAS internal algorithms usually choose the optimal index. The IDXNAME and IDXWHERE options are simply designed to give you the ability to specify preferences if and when you decide that it is desirable to override the SAS default behavior.

Specifying the UPDATECENTILES Option for a New Index

Because centiles are so important to SAS making a good choice as to whether or not it should use a particular index, it is necessary for you to make a good choice as to when they are updated. The choice of when centiles are updated is controlled by the UPDATECENTILES option. As mentioned in Chapter 8, "Creating Indexes with the DATASETS Procedure," the default value for UPDATECENTILES is 5, meaning that when 5% of an index changes, SAS recomputes the centiles for that index. Indexes created by DATA steps, PROC steps, and PROC SQL have their UPDATECENTILES value automatically set to 5. The DATASETS procedure is the only SAS PROC that allows you to specify a different value for UPDATECENTILES when an index is first created. It is also the only procedure that allows you to change the value of UPDATECENTILES after an index has been created.

Here is an example of specifying UPDATECENTILES in the DATASETS procedure as an index is being created:

```
proc datasets library=indexlib;
  modify prodindx;
    index create state /nomiss updatecentiles=15;
  run;
quit;
```

In this example, the UPDATECENTILES value for the new STATE index is 15%. When 15% of the values of STATE change in INDEXLIB.PRODINDX, the centiles for the STATE index are recomputed. If the UPDATECENTILES option had been omitted from this example, the STATE index would have had the default value of 5.

Here is the general format of the UPDATECENTILES option:

UPDATECENTILES = ALWAYS | 0 | NEVER | 101 | INTEGER

The acceptable values for UPDATECENTILES are as follows:

- **ALWAYS or 0** Specifies that centiles are to be updated when a SAS data set is closed after changes have been made to a data set that affects its index. If you want SAS to always have the best information for deciding whether or not to use an index, then use this value. However, you should be prepared for your program to consume extra I/Os and extra CPU time when the updated indexed SAS data set is closed, because SAS takes the time to recompute the centiles. Depending on the size of the index, this may or may not be noticeable.

- **NEVER or 101** Specifies that centiles are not to be updated when a SAS data set's index has been changed. This is a dangerous value to use. If your SAS data set is updated frequently, the centiles stored in the index may become very out-of-date. If so, the out-of-date centiles may cause SAS to make a poor, badly informed decision about whether or not to use an index. This can lead to unnecessarily high I/O counts and CPU time if SAS chooses to use an index when using it *is not* optimal or if SAS does not choose to use an index when using it *is* optimal.

- **INTEGER** Specifies the percent of values of the indexed variable that can be updated before the centiles are recomputed. This number can range from 0 to 100. If you feel comfortable with your centiles being somewhat out-of-date, you can choose a specific percentage. For example, 15 would mean that SAS does not recompute the centiles until 15% of the index key variable values have changed. Specifying an integer enables you to choose a centile recompute value that falls somewhere between the values of ALWAYS, 5% (the default), and NEVER.

Here is an example of creating a new index and using the 0 value for UPDATECENTILES:

```
proc datasets library=indexlib;
   modify prodindx;
      index create seqnum / unique nomiss updatecentiles=0;
   run;
quit;
```

In this example, the SEQNUM index has its centiles updated every time a value of SEQNUM changes in the INDEXLIB.PRODINDX SAS data set. Remember that the value of *0* is synonymous with *always* for UPDATECENTILES.

Here is an example of creating a new index and specifying that centiles are never to be recomputed when the index is updated:

```
proc datasets library=indexlib;
   modify prodindx;
      index create state /nomiss updatecentiles=never;
   run;
quit;
```

The centiles for the STATE index are never recomputed, no matter what changes are made to the data set. You could also have coded the value of 101 to achieve the same result.

The default value of 5% is a good all-around value of UPDATECENTILES to choose. It allows for small changes in the index without recomputing the centiles. In most situations, you would not want your centiles to get too outdated. That would defeat the purpose of having them in the first place.

Resetting the Value of UPDATECENTILES for an Existing Index

The DATASETS procedure is the only tool at your disposal for resetting the value of UPDATECENTILES for an existing index. To reset the value of UPDATECENTILES, you must use the MODIFY statement to name the SAS data set that has the index, or indexes, that you want to modify. You must also use the INDEX CENTILES statement to identify the index that you want changed and to specify the new value of UPDATECENTILES. The value that you specify represents the percentage of the key variable values that must change before SAS recomputes the centiles.

The general format of the INDEX CENTILES statement is as follows:

INDEX CENTILES *index-name* / <UPDATECENTILES = ALWAYS | 0 | NEVER | 101 | INTEGER >;

In the statement, you must specify the name of the index that is to have its centiles modified, as well as the new value of UPDATECENTILES.

Here is an example of resetting centiles:

```
proc datasets library=indexlib;
   modify prodindx;
      index centiles product / updatecentiles=20;
   run;
quit;
```

In the example above, UPDATECENTILES specifies that the centiles for the PRODUCT index are to be updated only when 20% of their values are changed since the last time the centiles were recomputed.

This is what the SAS log for the code above looks like:

```
77    proc datasets library=indexlib;
                                -----Directory-----

Libref:          INDEXLIB
Engine:          9.0101M3
Physical Name: C:\Data Files
File Name:       C:\Data Files


          #   Name      Memtype   File Size  Last Modified

          1   PRODCOMP  DATA      297255936   05FEB2005:18:20:28
              PRODCOMP  INDEX      57377792   05FEB2005:18:20:28
          2   PRODINDX  DATA      296332288   13FEB2005:12:37:09
              PRODINDX  INDEX     170344960   13FEB2005:12:37:09
          3   PRODSALE  DATA      298021888   15JAN2005:18:03:25
          4   TRANCAN   DATA       22475776   28MAR2004:13:41:42
78    modify prodindx;
79       index centiles product / updatecentiles=20;
NOTE: Index product centiles update percent changed to 20.
80       run;
81    quit;
```

The NOTE in the log lets you know that the centiles for the PRODUCT index have been successfully updated and will be recomputed when 20% of the values of PRODUCT change in the future.

Why might you want to reset the value of UPDATECENTILES? One scenario might be if you had an indexed SAS data set that was going to undergo heavy amounts of updating during several phases of a batch cycle. If the various updates did not use the index, then you would reset the value of UPDATECENTILES to a high value, say 50, at the beginning of the batch processing. This would keep SAS from taking the extra time and resources to recompute the centiles each time the SAS data set was updated during the batch cycle. At the end of the batch program, you could reset UPDATECENTILES back to a lower value, say 5. That would force SAS to recompute the centiles and make sure that they were staged to be recomputed when smaller amounts of updates took place within the SAS data set in the future.

How to Refresh Centiles

If you would like to manually force SAS to refresh the centiles for a particular index, you can do so with the DATASETS procedure. *Refreshing* the centiles means that you direct SAS to recompute the centiles for a specific index on the spot. SAS recomputes the centiles immediately, even if the current percentage of changes to the key variable values has not reached the specified UPDATECENTILES value currently in effect for the index.

You might want to refresh an index's centiles when a SAS data set is updated and the percent of index key variable values changed significantly but are too low to trigger SAS to recompute the centiles. If you had some important processing that relied heavily on the data set's indexes, you could consider refreshing the centiles before running your programs.

Here is an example of how to refresh centiles:

```
proc datasets library=indexlib;
   modify prodindx;
       index centiles product / refresh;
   run;
quit;
```

In this example, the centiles for the PRODUCT index are refreshed. SAS recomputes the index centiles to reflect the current values of PRODUCT in the SAS data set. This is a one-time refresh that does not affect the threshold at which the centiles are next recomputed. The current value of UPDATECENTILES is still in effect. If the current value of UPDATECENTILES is 5%, the next time that the centiles will be refreshed is when 5% of the values of PRODUCT change.

The code, above, results in the following note in the SAS log:

```
81    proc datasets library=indexlib;
                                 -----Directory-----

Libref:          INDEXLIB
Engine:          9.0101M3
Physical Name: C:\Data Files
File Name:       C:\Data Files

                 #   Name       Memtype   File Size   Last Modified

                 1   PRODCOMP   DATA      297255936   05FEB2005:18:20:28
                     PRODCOMP   INDEX      57377792   05FEB2005:18:20:28
                 2   PRODINDX   DATA      296332288   05MAR2005:12:35:33
                     PRODINDX   INDEX     170344960   05MAR2005:12:35:33
                 3   PRODSALE   DATA      298021888   15JAN2005:18:03:25
                 4   TRANCAN    DATA       22475776   28MAR2004:13:41:42
82       modify prodindx;
83          index centiles product / refresh;
NOTE: Index product centiles refreshed.
84       run;
85    quit;
```

The NOTE states that the centiles for PRODUCT have been refreshed. Therefore, a CONTENTS procedure listing of the centiles shows zero in the Current Percent Update column, which is discussed in the next section.

How to Review Centiles

You can display centiles for a specific index via the CONTENTS procedure. Then you can examine the centiles in the CONTENTS procedure listing to determine how effective a given index might be for processing a subset of the particular SAS data set it is associated with. By specifying the CENTILES option in the CONTENTS procedure, you can discover if the index key variable values are really spread throughout the entire SAS data set. If so, then the index yields efficient processing of the data set. If not, then you might want to reexamine why that particular variable, or variables, were used to create an index in the first place.

Here is an example of the CONTENTS procedure with the CENTILES option:

```
proc contents data= indexlib.prodindx centiles;
run;
```

Here is an annotated portion of the "Alphabetic List of Indexes and Attributes" for the execution of this CONTENTS procedure:

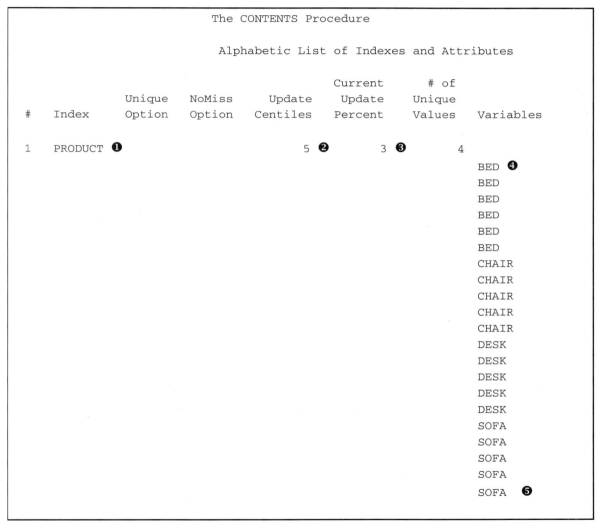

(continued on next page)

(continued)

```
 2 STATE_PRODUCT    ❻                        15 ❼    7 ❽  64 STATE PRODUCT ❾
                                                Baja California Norte ,BED  ❿
                                                Baja California Norte ,SOFA
                                                British Columbia       ,SOFA
                                                California             ,SOFA
                                                Campeche               ,SOFA
                                                Colorado               ,SOFA
                                                Florida                ,SOFA
                                                Illinois               ,BED
                                                Illinois               ,CHAIR
                                                Illinois               ,DESK
                                                Illinois               ,SOFA
                                                Illinois               ,SOFA
                                                Michoacan              ,SOFA
                                                New York               ,SOFA
                                                North Carolina         ,SOFA
                                                Nuevo Leon             ,SOFA
                                                Ontario                ,SOFA
                                                Quebec                 ,SOFA
                                                Saskatchewan           ,SOFA
                                                Texas                  ,SOFA
                                                Washington             ,SOFA ⓫
```

In the example, above:

❶ The first index is a simple one built from the PRODUCT variable.

❷ The UPDATECENTILES option has been set to 5%.

❸ 3% of the PRODUCT variables in the data set have had their values updated.

❹ The lowest value in the index is *BED*.

❺ The highest value in the index is *SOFA*.

There are four unique values of the PRODUCT index in the SAS data set. You can also see that the first 25% of the values of PRODUCT have a value equal to *BED*, that the next 25% have a value equal to *CHAIR*, that the next 25% have a value equal to *DESK*, and that the top 25% have a value equal to *SOFA*.

❻ The second index is the STATE_PRODUCT composite index.

❼ This index's centiles are recomputed when 15% of the values of STATE/PRODUCT have been changed.

❽ Currently 7% of the values of STATE/PRODUCT have been modified since centiles were last computed. Once another 8% change, SAS recomputes the centiles for the STATE_PRODUCT index. Then this value is reset to 0.

❾ This composite index is built from the STATE and PRODUCT variables.

❿ The lowest value for this index is *Baja California Norte , BED.*

⓫ The highest value for this index is *Washington   , SOFA.*

There are 64 unique values of the STATE_PRODUCT composite index. You can see that this is a relatively discriminant composite index. Five percent or fewer observations have the same combined values of STATE/PRODUCT for most observations in the SAS data set. The exception is that about 10% have the STATE/PRODUCT combined value of *Illinois, SOFA.* Therefore, most attempts to subset the data through the use of STATE_PRODUCT would extract about 5% of the data, while a single combination (*Illinois, SOFA*) would extract, at most, 10%.

Though executing the CONTENTS procedure with the centiles option produces a long listing, it is well worth the effort. The centiles list reveals a lot about how the values of index variables are actually distributed throughout the SAS data set. As previously discussed, SAS uses centiles to make index usage decisions. Now that you know how to produce a listing of the centiles, you can too.

Summary

Centiles are a built-in feature of SAS indexes and are essentially 21 separate values saved in the index descriptor. These values represent the 0, 5th, 10th, 15th, 20th, 25th, 30th, 35th, 40th, 45th, 50th, 55th, 60th, 65th, 70th, 75th, 80th, 85th, 90th, 95th, and 100th percentile values of key variables in an index. SAS uses centiles to determine if it is more efficient to use an index to read a SAS data set or whether it is more efficient to just read the entire SAS data set.

SAS initializes each index's centiles when the index is created and keeps them updated when a certain percentage of the index key variable's values have changed within the data set. The default value for updating centiles is 5%. This means that when 5% of the variables in the SAS data set that are index key variables have their values changed, SAS recomputes and updates the centiles for the index.

The DATASETS procedure is your tool for resetting the value at which SAS updates centiles and for having centiles refreshed on the spot. The UPDATECENTILES statement on PROC DATASETS enables you to specify that centiles always be updated, never be updated, or be updated after a specific percentage of index key variable values are changed. The REFRESH option on the INDEX CENTILES statement in the DATASETS procedure permits you to refresh centiles on the spot.

You can examine a SAS index's centiles to determine just how balanced the index is. By executing the CONTENTS procedure with the CENTILES option, you can discover if the index key variable values are really spread throughout the entire SAS data set. If so, then the index will yield efficient processing of the data set. If not, then you might want to reexamine why that particular variable, or variables, were used to create an index.

C h a p t e r 5

Index-Related Options

Introduction

It should probably come as no surprise to you that there are several SAS options that have a direct effect on SAS indexes. Three of the options, NOMISS, UNIQUE, and UPDATECENTILES, are pretty obvious because they are specified in either a DATA step or a PROC step. Three others, IBUFSIZE, IBUFNO, and MSGLEVEL=I, are less well known and must be specified in OPTIONS statements. You should become familiar with all six of these options so that you have better control over the structure and usability of your SAS indexes.

This chapter provides an overview and discussion of all six of the options that affect SAS indexes. These options are discussed in passing when used in other chapters of this book. However, this chapter provides an in-depth discussion of how and where they can be specified, what the values may be, and what you can expect from specifying them. You should refer back to this chapter if and when you are curious about how a specific option affects your SAS indexes.

DATA Step and Procedure Options

Three SAS index options can be specified in a DATA step or a PROC step. The first two, NOMISS and UNIQUE, must be specified when a SAS index is first created because they affect the structure of the index. The third, UPDATECENTILES, can be specified when an index is created, or some time afterward, because it affects the operation of the index, not its structure. Unlike the NOMISS and UNIQUE options, the UPDATECENTILES option may only be specified in the DATASETS procedure.

The NOMISS Option

The NOMISS option specifies that index entries *are not* to be built for observations with missing values in the key variable (simple index) or key variables (composite index). It is a good option to have in effect if you know that chances are very good that your key variable(s) have a large number of missing values in them. It helps keep the index smaller; without it the observations with missing key variable values would have a single leaf node entry. That entry would contain missing values in the value field, followed by hundreds, thousands, or tens of thousands of record identifiers pointing to each one of the many observations with missing values in the key variable field. This would most likely not be a discriminant value and would bog down your index with unnecessary entries. It could increase the size of your index and the number of index levels, leading to longer index processing times.

Using the NOMISS option does not block your ability to build an index for a data set that has missing values for some key variables. Nor does it block your ability to update the data set with observations containing key variables with missing values in them. Using this option simply means that the addition or deletion of observations with missing key variable values has no effect on the index in any way. No index entries are created for those observations.

Here is an example of the NOMISS option being specified in a DATA step:

```
data listeners(index=(studentid / nomiss));

input @1 name      $10.
      @12 studentid 4.;

datalines;
Lionel      3525
Edward
David       1892
Zachary     4444
Elvira
Patricia    2269
run;
```

Once the DATA step has run, data set STUDENTS contains six observations and has an index based on variable STUDENTID. The index only contains four entries because the second and fifth entries had missing values for STUDENTID (the index key variable) and the NOMISS option was in effect when the index was built.

Using the NOMISS option to create a slimmer index determines whether the index is used for BY statement or WHERE expression processing. You should be aware of the following limitations before deciding to use the NOMISS option:

- **BY statement limitations** SAS *does not* use an index that was created with the NOMISS option when executing a BY statement. If you intend to use your index to return observations in sorted order, that is, sorted into ascending index key variable order, do not use the NOMISS option when creating the index.

- **WHERE expression limitations** SAS does not use an index built with the NOMISS option when executing a WHERE expression if observations with missing values fulfill the WHERE expression condition. Put another way: if observations with missing values fulfill the WHERE expression, SAS does not use the index because it was built using the NOMISS option. An example of this would be *where age ne 21*. That WHERE expression would be fulfilled by all observations with missing values. An index built on variable AGE, using the

NOMISS option, would not be used by SAS to satisfy the WHERE expression. Instead, SAS would process the data set sequentially.

The NOMISS option can help to limit the size of your SAS indexes when you have a lot of missing values in index key variables within your SAS data sets. You need to be familiar with the limitation to BY statement and WHERE expression processing to know if the NOMISS option is right for a particular SAS index.

The UNIQUE Option

The UNIQUE option specifies that the index key variable values must be unique for each observation of your SAS data set. If you are creating a simple index, no two key variable values may be the same within the SAS data set. If you are creating a composite index, the combination of the various key variable values must be totally unique for every observation in the SAS data set. Let's consider the following simple DATA step to better visualize the distinction that is being made here:

```
data students;

input @1   name       $10.
      @12  studentid   4.
      @18  state       $2.;

datalines;
Lionel     3525   MA
Edward     8175   NC
David      1892   MA
Zachary    4444   MD
Elvira     4523   CA
Patricia   2269   AL
Paul       1129   AK
Edward     3456   AK
Lionel     8965   AK
Ivan       0234   NM
Nancy      7523   MD
;;;;
run;
```

After the STUDENTS data set is created, you can use the UNIQUE option to create simple indexes and composite indexes. The simple index contains STUDENTID. Because the value of STUDENTID is unique for every observation, this is the only variable in the data set that may be used to create a simple index using the UNIQUE option. You could create four unique composite indexes for the STUDENTS data set.

In this example, composite indexes contain the following:

- NAME/STUDENTID   Though there are duplicate values of NAME, adding STUDENTID makes the composite index values unique.

- NAME/STATE   Though there are duplicate values of NAME and duplicate values of STATE, the combination of the two variables' values is unique throughout the entire SAS data set.

- NAME/STUDENTID/STATE   The combination of NAME and STATE is unique as is the value of STUDENTID. The combination of all three creates unique composite key variable values.

- STUDENTID/STATE   Though there are duplicate values of STATE, STUDENTID makes the composite index value unique.

If you attempt to use the UNIQUE option and the values of your proposed index key variables are not unique, then SAS will not build the index. If you are using a DATA step or PROC SQL to create the index, it creates the new data set successfully, but the index is not created. The following error message is returned by the DATA step, PROC DATASETS, and PROC SQL:

```
ERROR: Duplicate values not allowed on index name for file
       STUDENTS.
```

A good reason for creating an index using the UNIQUE option is that SAS prevents the addition of new observations with duplicate index key variable values when the data set is updated. This is handy because you are essentially giving SAS the job of maintaining the integrity of your data set's unique key variable values. If an attempt is made to add an observation with a duplicate index variable key value via the APPEND procedure or the KEY option on a MODIFY statement, SAS rejects the offending observation and issues a warning.

To best illustrate the warnings that you can expect in your SAS log, consider the following transaction SAS data set named TRANSACT. The first observation has a STUDENTID value of 3525, which is a duplicate of the STUDENTID in the first observation of the STUDENTS SAS data set used in the previous example. The TRANSACT SAS data set is used in the two following subsections to precipitate duplicate index key variable warnings.

```
data transact;
input @1   name       $10.
      @12  studentid  4.
      @18  state      $2.;

datalines;
Jeffrey    3525  WY
Winston    1234  NC
;;;;
run;
```

APPEND procedure warning This occurs when attempting to append a SAS data set to an existing SAS data set that has an index. If there are duplicate index key variable values in the data set being appended, the observations containing them are not appended to the BASE SAS data set. Observations in the appending SAS data set that have index key variable values that are not found in the BASE SAS data set append in the normal manner. Therefore, it is possible to have a mixture of appended and rejected observations when attempting to append to a SAS data set with a UNIQUE index.

This SAS code produces the following SAS log:

```
proc append base=students data=transact;
run;
```

```
1007  proc append base=students data=transact;
1008  run;


NOTE: Appending WORK.TRANSACT to WORK.STUDENTS.
INFO: Engine's fast-append process in use.
WARNING: Duplicate values not allowed on index studentid for file
         STUDENTS, 1 observations rejected.
NOTE: There were 2 observations read from the data set WORK.TRANSACT.
NOTE: 1 observations added.
NOTE: The data set WORK.STUDENTS has 12 observations and 3 variables.
NOTE: PROCEDURE APPEND used:
      real time           0.01 seconds
      cpu time            0.01 seconds
```

Note that the WARNING message reports that one observation was rejected because it had a duplicate value. The other observation, the one with a STUDENTID value of 1234 was successfully appended to the STUDENTS SAS data set so that there are now 12 observations in that data set.

Using PROC APPEND to update a SAS data set is explained in detail in Chapter 15, "Preserving Indexes During Data Set Manipulations."

KEY option on a MODIFY statement warning   Attempting to add observations from a transaction SAS data set with duplicate values of index key variables in a master data set fails when using the KEY option on a MODIFY statement. Transaction data set observations with matching key variable values are rejected while observations with unique values are added to the master data set.

The following SAS code attempts to add the observations in TRANSACT to the STUDENTS data set when there is a match on the index key variable as illustrated by the IF statement:

```
data students;
set transact(rename=(name = tranname state = transtate));
modify students key=studentid;
if _iorc_ = %sysrc(_sok) then output;
else do;
  _error_ = 0;
  _iorc_  = 0;
  name = tranname;
  state = transtate;
  output;
end;
run;
```

The DATA step, above, produces the following SAS log:

```
1281   data students;
1282   set transact(rename=(name = tranname state = transtate));
1283   modify students key=studentid;
1284   if _iorc_ = %sysrc(_sok) then output;
1285   else do;
1286       _error_ = 0;
1287       _iorc_  = 0;
1288       name = tranname;
1289       state = transtate;
1290       output;
1291   end;
1292   run;
tranname=Jeffrey studentid=3525 transtate=WY name=Lionel state=MA
_ERROR_=1 _iorc_=630058 _N_=1
```

(continued on next page)

(continued)

```
NOTE: There were 2 observations read from the data set WORK.TRANSACT.
NOTE: The data set WORK.STUDENTS has been updated.  There were 0
      observations rewritten, 1 observations added and 0 observations
      deleted.
NOTE: There were 0 rejected updates, 1 rejected adds, and 0 rejected
      deletes.
NOTE: DATA statement used:
      real time           0.01 seconds
      cpu time            0.01 seconds
```

At the end of the programming statements, you can see a list of the values of the rejected observation from TRANSACT. The third NOTE states that there was "1 rejected adds." That would be the first observation in the TRANSACT data set, which had a duplicate value of STUDENTID.

Updating a SAS data set via the KEY option on the MODIFY statement is fully explained in Chapter 12, "Using Indexes with the Key Option on a Modify Statement."

If having unique index key variable values throughout a SAS data set is important to you, consider using the UNIQUE option. It puts the burden on SAS to identify observations with duplicate index key variable values when you attempt to update your SAS data set. But you must be careful to check the SAS log to see if observations were rejected after attempting to add new observations to a SAS data set that has a unique index.

The UPDATECENTILES Option

The UPDATECENTILES option specifies when centiles are to be recomputed after changes have been made to an index. The word *centiles* is a contraction of the term *cumulative percentiles*, which are the 21 centiles that characterize values in a SAS index. SAS uses centiles to determine if it is more efficient to use an index or more efficient to read the entire SAS data set sequentially. (Centiles are discussed more completely in Chapter 4, "Index Centiles.")

The default value of UPDATECENTILES is 5, meaning that when 5% of an index's key values are changed, SAS recomputes the centiles for that index when the data set is closed. Indexes created by DATA steps and PROC SQL have an UPDATECENTILES value of 5. Indexes created by the DATASETS procedure have a default value of 5. However, the DATASETS procedure enables you to override the default and specify a different value for UPDATECENTILES when an index is first created.

The DATASETS procedure is also the single means by which the value of UPDATECENTILES can be changed after an index is created. You must use the INDEX CENTILES statement within a MODIFY RUN group. Here is an example of an invocation of PROC DATASETS with a MODIFY RUN group that uses the INDEX CENTILES statement to execute the UPDATECENTILES option:

```
proc datasets library=indexlib;
  modify prodindx;
    index  centiles state updatecentiles = 15;
  run;
quit;
```

Here is the general format for the UPDATECENTILES option:

UPDATECENTILES = ALWAYS | 0 | NEVER | 101 | INTEGER

Here is what the values for the UPDATECENTILES option mean:

- **ALWAYS or 0**   Specifies that centiles are to be updated when a SAS data set is closed after changes have been made to the data set's index. This value ensures that SAS always has the best information for making decisions on whether or not to use an index. All programs that update the data set consume additional CPU time and I/Os as SAS recomputes and then updates the centiles. This may or may not be noticeable, depending on the size of the index.

- **NEVER or 101**   This is an index option setting that you do not want to use because it specifies that centiles are never to be updated when a SAS data set's index has been changed. The value freezes the current centile values in place. It is not a good idea to use this value, especially if your SAS data set is updated frequently. As your centiles get more and more out-of-date, SAS makes poorer and poorer decisions on whether or not to use the index. This could cause unnecessarily high CPU time and I/Os if SAS chooses to use an index when using it *is not* optimal. Alternatively, you could have a performance penalty if SAS does not choose to use the index when using it *would be* optimal.

- **INTEGER**   Specifies the percentage of the values of the indexed variable that can be updated before the centiles are recomputed. The value of INTEGER may range from 0 to 101. A value of 20 would mean that SAS would not recompute the centiles until 20% of the index key variable values have changed. If you are comfortable with your centiles being somewhat out-of-date, then you can choose a specific percentage. However, the default value of 5% is a good all-around value to stick with. It allows for small changes in the index before the centiles are recomputed. You would not normally want to let your centiles get too outdated because that would defeat the very purpose of having them in the first place.

Here is an example of executing the UPDATECENTILES option for an existing SAS data set using the DATASETS procedure:

```
proc datasets library=indexlib;
  modify prodindx;
    index  centiles state updatecentiles = 15;
  run;
quit;
```

This is the SAS log for the execution of the example above:

```
1414  proc datasets library=indexlib;
                                  -----Directory-----


Libref:         INDEXLIB
Engine:         V9
Physical Name: C:\Documents and Settings\Michael\My Documents\SUGI
               29\Indexes III - SUGI\Data\Data Files
File Name:     C:\Documents and Settings\Michael\My Documents\SUGI
               29\Indexes III - SUGI\Data\Data Files


      #  Name       Memtype   File Size  Last Modified
      _____

      1  PRODINDX   DATA      298034176    10JAN2007:17:51:45
         PRODINDX   INDEX      18678784   10JAN2007:17:51:45
      2  PRODSALE   DATA      298034176   08JAN2007:11:42:33
      3  TRANCAN    DATA       22475776   28MAR2004:13:41:42
1415     modify prodindx;
1416        index  centiles state / updatecentiles=15;
NOTE: Index state centiles update percent changed to 15.
1417     run;
1418  quit;


NOTE: PROCEDURE DATASETS used:
      real time           0.20 seconds
      cpu time            0.01 seconds
```

The NOTE in the SAS log clearly states that the centiles update percent for the STATE simple index was changed to 15%.

Executing PROC CONTENTS for INDEXLIB.PRODINDX with the CENTILES option enabled would produce the following report (partial view):

```
                         The CONTENTS Procedure

               -----Alphabetic List of Indexes and Attributes-----

                                  Current      # of
                         Update   Update      Unique
     #    Index         Centiles  Percent     Values    Variables
    ─────────────────────────────────────────────────────────────────────
     1    STATE            15        0          16
          ---                                             Baja California Norte
          ---                                             Baja California Norte
          ---                                             British Columbia
          ---                                             California
          ---                                             Campeche
          ---                                             Colorado
          ---                                             Florida
          ---                                             Illinois
          ...                                             ...
```

Notice that the Update Centiles value is now set to 15. This is further verification that the centile update value was successfully updated via the DATASETS procedure.

System Options

There are three SAS system options that affect indexes. The IBUFSIZE system option affects the structure of indexes and must be specified before an index is created. The IBUFNO system option affects the performance of SAS applications that use a particular index. Lastly, the MSGLEVEL=I system option affects what index usage information is written to the SAS log. All three of these options may be specified in a number of different places in your SAS programs. Here is the hierarchy in order of precedence of where they may be specified:

1. in a source program OPTIONS statement

2. in an autoexec file OPTIONS statement

3. in the OPTIONS parameter in a .bat file (Windows), batch script (UNIX and Linux), SAS EXEC JCL statement (z/OS), or SAS CLIST invocation command (z/OS)

4. in the user configuration file

5. in the system configuration file

6. the default options shipped with SAS

In the hierarchy above, the lower option numbers take precedence over the higher option numbers. That is, options specified in a source program OPTIONS statement (#1 above) take precedence over options specified in the system configuration file (#5 above). OPTIONS statements in the source program override the default values for SAS system options, the system configuration file options, the user configuration file options, options designated within the OPTIONS parameter in a batch invocation of the program, and options specified in an autoexec file OPTIONS statement. An OPTIONS statement in the SOURCE program is usually the best place to specify the IBUFSIZE, the IBUFNO, and the MSGLEVEL=I options.

The IBUFSIZE System Option

The IBUFSIZE option specifies the physical size that SAS uses for the index file page (block size) for all new SAS indexes. The option applies whether the new indexes are created for permanent SAS data sets or for temporary data sets in the WORK library. An index's page size is set at the time that it is first created and cannot be modified during the life of the index. If several indexes are created for the same SAS data set, the IBUFSIZE of the index created first will be the IBUFSIZE in effect for all other indexes. SAS does not maintain multiple indexes with varying page sizes for a SAS data set.

Because index pages are moved between memory and disk during I/O operations, the value of IBUFSIZE can have a profound effect on the I/O count of SAS programs using indexes. A smaller index page size means fewer index entries per page, thus increasing the total number of pages required to hold the entire index. Therefore, fewer index entries are transferred into memory with each I/O, resulting in more I/Os being needed to process an index with a small page size. Further, because SAS indexes are stored in a balanced binary tree configuration, greater numbers of index pages require more levels in an index. More index levels require more time and computer power to traverse when an index search takes place.

On the other hand, large index page sizes mean more index entries are stored on each index page, thereby decreasing the total number of index pages needed to store the entire index. More index entries are transferred with each I/O for indexes with large index pages because more index entries are stored on each page. Large index page sizes help decrease the number of index levels, which has a positive effect on the number of I/Os needed to read the index during an index search. Therefore, you want to maximize the index page size by specifying a large number for IBUFSIZE. In doing so, however, you should realize that a larger IBUFSIZE requires more computer memory. There is always the tradeoff between saving I/O and using more memory.

The one hidden disadvantage to specifying a large index page size occurs when there are many updates to the index. The updates may cause index page splits and merges as SAS rebalances the index structure. That could result in wasted space on some index pages. So, large index page sizes can be more advantageous for indexed SAS data sets that have few, if any, updates. You should factor this in your decision to override the default IBUFSIZE of 4096 bytes with a larger one.

This is the general format for the IBUFSIZE option:

IBUFSIZE = MAX | *n* | *n*K | *hex*

The various settings for this option are as follows:

- **MAX**   Sets the index page size to the maximum possible number, which is 32,767 bytes.

- *n*   Sets the index page size to a specific number of bytes. For example, *n* could be 4096 or 32767.

- *n*K   Sets the index page size to a multiple number of kilobytes (1,024 bytes). A value of 4K sets the index page size to 4096 bytes (4 * 1024).

- *hex*   Sets the index page size using a hexadecimal value. For example, specifying 7000X would set the index page size to 28,672 bytes, because 7000 in hexadecimal is equivalent to 28,672 in decimal notation.

The default value for IBUFSIZE is 4096 bytes. You should consider overriding the default by setting the value of IBUFSIZE to 32767 bytes on all operating systems except z/OS. On z/OS, set IBUFSIZE to 27648 bytes, which is half-track blocking and provides optimal disk space utilization. These are all-around good values that promote good index performance and good usage of disk space.[1]

---

[1] These author-recommended values have not been subjected to rigorous testing with many differently sized SAS data sets across all of the computer platforms that SAS currently runs on. You should experiment with them and with other values of IBUFSIZE to determine the optimal settings for your own applications.

When you specify IBUFSIZE=32767 (or 27648), SAS takes into account a number of host-specific factors (such as minimum optimal I/O block size) and then computes an index file page block size as close as possible to the value you specified. Though you specify IBUFSIZE=32767 (or 27648), more than likely your index file page size will be just slightly under that size.

To illustrate the point that larger values of IBUFSIZE decrease the number of index pages, consider what happens when a simple index is built on variable STATE in the INDEXLIB.PRODINDX data set, which has 2,304,000 observations. The index is first created with an IBUFSIZE of 4096 bytes in effect and then created with an IBUFSIZE of 32767 bytes. Table 5.1 compares the *number of index file pages* that can be found in the *engine/host-dependent information* section of a CONTENTS procedure listing for each index that was created.

Table 5.1 Comparing Index File Page Sizes

Index File Page Size	Number of Index File Pages
4096	4578
32767	581

By specifying an IBUFSIZE of 32767, the number of index pages was reduced by about 87%. As mentioned previously, this helps reduce the number of index levels and helps reduce the number of I/Os needed during index searches. You should seriously consider specifying an IBUFSIZE of 32767 (or 27648 for z/OS applications) in your SAS programs that create indexes.

The IBUFNO System Option

The IBUFNO system option specifies the number of index page buffers that are allocated in computer memory for each SAS index that is used in a program.[2] A *buffer* is an area in memory equal to the size of an index page. When I/Os bring index pages into memory, they are stored in index buffers. It is only when the index pages are actually in the buffers within computer memory that SAS has access to the entries stored on them.

You can control the number of buffers set aside for each SAS index by manipulating the value of IBUFNO. You should control the number of index buffers because larger IBUFNO values promote better index performance. Better performance is possible

---

[2] The IBUFNO option is not a documented option in SAS Version 9.1.3. As of this writing, it is scheduled to be a fully documented option in SAS Version 9.2.

because having more index buffers allows index pages at all levels of the index (that is, pages with root node entries, pages with branch node entries, and pages with leaf node entries) to be stored in the index buffers. Chances are very good that, with an increased number of index buffers, a particular index search already has many of the index pages it needs resident in memory and thus does not have to read as many index pages into memory from disk.

Alternately, smaller numbers of index buffers mean that those buffers are constantly being overwritten with new index pages being read in from disk. Because there are fewer index buffers available, the likelihood is very low that an index search already has a needed index page in an index buffer. Lower values of IBUFNO inadvertently cause more I/Os due to the greater frequency of index page reads from disk.

This is the general format for the IBUFNO option:

IBUFNO = *n*

In the format, above, *n* may be any integer between one and the maximum number that can be physically allocated by your operating system. The default value of IBUFNO is two. However, during index processing, SAS may dynamically adjust that number upward to account for the number of index levels, the open mode (input or update), and the number of logical opens.

It is difficult to give a guideline for what the optimal value of IBUFNO should be because it is dependent on the overall size of an index. For very large indexes, larger values of IBUFNO should promote good index performance. For smaller indexes, lower IBUFNO values suffice. *The author commonly sets the value for IBUFNO to 10 in his programs and has experienced modest performance gains.* However, this has not been subjected to rigorous testing with many different sized SAS data sets across all of the computer platforms that SAS currently runs on. You should experiment with this option to determine what value is optimal for your own SAS applications.

You should be sure that you override the default value of IBUFNO with your own value at a place in the program well before the DATA or PROC step that actually uses the index. When doing so, you should realize that an increased number of index buffers requires increased amounts of computer memory. The amount of memory needed is equal to the value of IBUFNO times the *index file page size*. Be certain that you have enough memory available to absorb larger values of IBUFNO.

The MSGLEVEL System Option

MSGLEVEL is not really an index option, per se. Rather, it is an option that controls the level of detail for messages written to the SAS log. MSGLEVEL reports MERGE statement warnings, which SORT product was used, when Cross-Environment Data Access (CEDA) engines were used to read a data set, and SAS index usage, among other things. However, if you do not specify MSGLEVEL=I, no index usage messages will be written to your SAS log. Therefore, you should *always* have MSGLEVEL=I specified in SAS programs that use indexes.

The general format for MSGLEVEL is as follows:

OPTIONS MSGLEVEL = N | I

These are the only two allowable values of MSGLEVEL:

- N This setting is the default and allows only NOTE, WARNING, and ERROR messages to be written to the SAS log.
- I This setting prints additional SAS INFO messages that pertain to index usage, merge processing, sort utilities, and CEDA usage, as well as the regular SAS NOTE, WARNING, and ERROR messages.

When MSGLEVEL=I is in effect, SAS surfaces index-related notes to the SAS log. If WHERE expression processing is used, the following information is given:

- When an index is used, a message is written to the SAS log specifying the name of the index.
- When an index is not used, but one exists that could optimize one or more conditions in the WHERE expression, SAS sometimes writes a message with a suggestion of what you can do to get SAS to use the index to the SAS log.[3]
- When the IDXWHERE or IDXNAME options (see Chapter 14, "Overriding Default Index Usage") could positively affect index processing but are not used, a message displaying the option and its suggested value is written to the SAS log.

If BY statement processing is used with an index, a message is written to the SAS log specifying the name of the index.

---

[3] This is stated in the SAS online documentation, and SAS developers have verified the existence of such messages. However, the author has never experienced these particular index messages. So, do not be surprised if you do not normally see them in circumstances where SAS does not use an index to optimize a WHERE expression in your programs.

Here are some examples of important index-related messages written to the SAS log
when MSGLEVEL=I has been specified:

- For an index created in a DATA step[4]:

   ```
   NOTE: Simple index state has been defined.
   ```

- For an index used in a WHERE expression:

   ```
   INFO: Index STATE selected for WHERE clause optimization.
   ```

- For an index used for BY statement processing:

   ```
   INFO: Index STATE selected for BY clause processing.
   ```

To see just how informative and valuable MSGLEVEL=I can be, look at the log of a
simple SAS program where the default MSGLEVEL=N has been specified:

```
      options msglevel=N;
10
11    data indexlib.prodindx(index=(state));
12    set  indexlib.prodsale;
13    run;
NOTE: There were 2304000 observations read from the data set
      INDEXLIB.PRODSALE.
NOTE: The data set INDEXLIB.PRODINDX has 2304000 observations and
      12 variables.
NOTE: DATA statement used:
      real time            45.31 seconds
      cpu time             6.73 seconds

14
15    data withindx;
16    set  indexlib.prodindx(where=(state eq 'Quebec'));
17    run;
```

(continued on next page)

---

[4] SAS *always* writes an index creation message to the log when an index is created with the DATASETS
procedure.

(continued)

```
NOTE: There were 115200 observations read from the data set
      INDEXLIB.PRODINDX.
      WHERE state='Quebec';
NOTE: The data set WORK.WITHINDX has 115200 observations and 12
      variables.
NOTE: DATA statement used:
      real time           0.48 seconds
      cpu time            0.20 seconds
```

In the SAS log above, the first DATA step creates a simple index based on STATE. The second DATA step uses STATE in a WHERE data set option to read observations with a specific value from the newly indexed SAS data set. The notes from the first SAS log do not tell you whether or not the SAS index was successfully created. The notes from the second SAS log do not tell you whether or not the index was used to retrieve observations from the WITHINDX SAS data set. For all you know, the index may not have been created in the first DATA step and may not have been used in the second DATA step.

This is in sharp contrast to a SAS log from the same simple program where MSGLEVEL=I has been specified:

```
20     options msglevel=I;
21
22     data indexlib.prodindx(index=(state));
23     set  indexlib.prodsale;
24     run;

NOTE: There were 2304000 observations read from the data set
      INDEXLIB.PRODSALE.
NOTE: The data set INDEXLIB.PRODINDX has 2304000 observations and
      12 variables.
NOTE: Simple index state has been defined.
NOTE: DATA statement used:
      real time           2:10.54
      cpu time            6.60 seconds

25
26     data withindx;
27     set  indexlib.prodindx(where=(state eq 'Quebec'));
```

(continued on next page)

(continued)

```
INFO: Index STATE selected for WHERE clause optimization.
28    run;
NOTE: There were 115200 observations read from the data set
      INDEXLIB.PRODINDX.
      WHERE state='Quebec';
NOTE: The data set WORK.WITHINDX has 115200 observations and 12
      variables.
NOTE: DATA statement used:
      real time              0.96 seconds
      cpu time               0.20 seconds
```

In this SAS log the third NOTE statement for the first DATA step reports that a "Simple index state has been defined." An INFO SAS note in the second DATA step reports an "Index STATE selected for WHERE clause optimization." This is the level of detail that lets you know exactly what is happening to your indexes in your SAS programs. That is why you should *always* specify MSGLEVEL=I in your SAS programs that create and use SAS indexes.

Summary

This chapter provided a discussion of the six options that affect SAS indexes. Three of the options, NOMISS, UNIQUE, and UPDATECENTILES, are specified in either a DATA step or a PROC step. The NOMISS option specifies that index entries *are not* to be built for observations with missing values in the key variable(s). The UNIQUE option specifies that the index key variable values must be unique for each observation of your SAS data set. And the UPDATECENTILES option specifies when centiles are to be recomputed after changes have been made to an index.

Three other index-related options, IBUFSIZE, IBUFNO, and MSGLEVEL=I, must be specified in OPTIONS statements. The IBUFSIZE system option specifies the size that SAS uses for the index file page size (block size) for all new SAS indexes. The IBUFNO system option specifies the number of index page buffers that are allocated in computer memory for each SAS index that is used in a program. Finally, setting the MSGLEVEL system option equal to I compels SAS to write index creation and usage messages to the SAS log.

Chapter 6

Identifying Index Characteristics

Introduction

When you approach an unfamiliar SAS data set that you have to process, one of the first things that you should do is determine whether the data set has one or more indexes. If you find an index built on a variable, or variables, that you intend to either subset using a WHERE expression or order via a BY statement, then you can streamline the performance of your SAS program. But where can you find definitive information that tells you that the SAS data set is indexed and the true nature of those indexes? This chapter presents the sources of SAS index information. It tells you where to look for information on index characteristics and how to interpret that information.

What to Look for in the CONTENTS Procedure

It should come as no surprise that the CONTENTS procedure is your best source of information about SAS indexes. When you execute PROC CONTENTS for an indexed SAS data set, SAS writes several important index metrics in several sections of the CONTENTS output listing. You can peruse the listing to determine the characteristics of the index file as well as the characteristics of the various indexes that reside within it.

As a reminder, here is an example of how to execute the CONTENTS procedure for a SAS data library:

```
proc contents data=indexlib._all_ details;
run;
```

The example executes PROC CONTENTS for the INDEXLIB SAS data library. The output listing contains a Directory section, which describes the individual members (data sets, indexes, catalogs, etc.) of the library as well as detailed information about each individual SAS data set.

This an example of the Directory section of a CONTENTS procedure listing:

```
                    The CONTENTS Procedure

                          Directory

                    Libref        INDEXLIB
                    Engine        V9
                    Physical Name  C:\Data Files
                    File Name      C:\Data Files


              Member  Obs, Entries
    #  Name   Type    or Indexes  Vars  Label   File Size  Last Modified

    1  PRODCOMP  DATA    2304000     12           296125440  01Oct05:10:26:54
       PRODCOMP  INDEX         3                   56386560  01Oct05:10:26:54
    2  PRODINDX  DATA    2304000     12           296125440  01Oct05:11:08:08
       PRODINDX  INDEX         9                  224523264  01Oct05:11:08:06
    3  PRODSALE  DATA    2304000     12           298021888  26Feb05:14:43:18
    4  TRANCAN   DATA     460800      4            22475776  28Mar04:13:41:42
```

In the example, you can see that two of the SAS data sets, PRODCOMP and PRODINDX, have indexes, while two, PRODSALE and TRANCAN, do not. The PRODCOMP index file contains three indexes, while the PRODINDX index file contains nine. If you were looking through this CONTENTS procedure listing for the first time, this would be good news. It means that indexes exist for these data sets. This fact should prompt you to look at the individual data set entries to determine which variables are index key variables that you can use to improve the performance of your application programs.

Here is an example output listing for the INDEXLIB.PRODINDX SAS data set with the index metrics annotated. The annotated metrics are described in the text following the CONTENTS listing.

```
                          The CONTENTS Procedure

Data Set Name   INDEXLIB.PRODINDX                Observations          2304000
Member Type     DATA                             Variables             12
Engine          V9                               Indexes               9      ❶
Created         Sat, Feb 26, 2005 01:53:40 PM    Integrity Constraints 1
Last Modified   Saturday, October 01, 2005 11:08:07 AM Observation Length 128
Protection                                       Deleted Observations  0
Data Set Type                                    Compressed            NO
Label                                            Sorted                NO
Data Representation  WINDOWS_32
Encoding             wlatin1  Western (Windows)


                    Engine/Host Dependent Information

              Data Set Page Size          32768
              Number of Data Set Pages    9037
              First Data Page             1
              Max Obs per Page            255
              Obs in First Data Page      237
              Index File Page Size        32256      ❷
              Number of Index File Pages  6961       ❸
              Number of Data Set Repairs  1
              Last Repair                 12:54 Sunday, August 14, 2005
              File Name                   C:\Data Files\prodindx.sas7bdat
              Release Created             9.0101M3
              Host Created                XP_PRO


              Alphabetic List of Variables and Attributes

     #    Variable    Type    Len    Format      Informat    Label

     4    ACTUAL      Num      8     DOLLAR12.2              Actual Sales
     1    COUNTRY     Char    10     $CHAR10.                Country
     3    COUNTY      Char    20     $CHAR20.                County
    10    DAYMONYR    Num      8     DATE7.      MONYY.      Day/Month/Year
    11    MONTH       Num      8                            Month
     5    PREDICT     Num      8     DOLLAR12.2              Predicted Sales
     6    PRODTYPE    Char    10     $CHAR10.                Product Type
```

(continued on next page)

(continued)

```
      7     PRODUCT      Char     10    $CHAR10.              Product
      9     QUARTER      Num       8    8.                    Quarter
     12     SEQNUM       Num       8                          Sequence Number
      2     STATE        Char     22    $CHAR22.              State/Province
      8     YEAR         Num       8    4.                    Year


              Alphabetic List of Integrity Constraints

                       Integrity
             #         Constraint      Type            Variables

             1         month_seqnum    Primary Key     MONTH SEQNUM


              Alphabetic List of Indexes and Attributes        ❹
```

#	Index	Unique Option	NoMiss Option	Owned by IC	# of Unique Values	Variables
1	COUNTRY_STATE		YES		16	COUNTRY STATE
2	COUNTY				6	
3	PRODUCT				4	
4	SEQNUM	YES	YES		2304000	
5	STATE		YES		16	
6	STATE_PRODUCT				64	STATE PRODUCT
7	YEAR		YES		14	
8	YEAR_AND_QUARTER				56	YEAR QUARTER
9	month_seqnum	YES		YES	2304000	MONTH SEQNUM

❶ **Indexes** specifies the number of indexes that are available for this particular SAS data set. The value can range from 0, meaning that there are no indexes, to any practical number. When the value is 0, the CONTENTS procedure listing does not contain the section titled "Alphabetic List of Indexes and Attributes." If the value is greater than 0, then the "Alphabetic List of Indexes and Attributes" section of the listing is created and gives you information on the individual SAS indexes that are available for your use.

In the example, above, the value for Indexes is 9, meaning that there are 9 indexes associated with this SAS data set.

❷ **Index File Page Size** is the size, in bytes, of the physical page that index entries are stored on. As discussed in the "How Indexes Are Structured" section in Chapter 1, "Introduction to Indexes," when an index is created, index entries are stored on their own index pages in an index file. The index file is a separate physical file structure from the SAS data set although it is logically related to it. The value of the IBUFSIZE system option that is currently in effect sets the index file page size when the first index is created for a SAS data set. (See "The IBUFSIZE System Option" in Chapter 5, "Index-Related Options," for a more thorough discussion of this option.) Once an index is created, its page size never changes. If additional indexes are added to a SAS data set, they use the same index file page size as the first index that was created. SAS adds additional index pages as necessary when index pages fill up with index entries.

In the example above, the index file page size is 32,256 bytes. The default index file page size is 4096, so you can conclude that the default was overridden via the IBUFSIZE system option when the first index was created.

❸ **Number of Index File Pages** tells you the number of index file pages that currently exist in the index file. The index pages are filled with root node, branch node, and leaf node entries for all indexes created for this particular SAS data set. As more entries are added to the index, the number of index file pages increases.

If several indexes are created for this data set, SAS puts them in the same index file and keeps track of which pages they occupy. As you add more indexes, the total number of index file pages increases. When indexes are removed, the index pages are placed on an *available space chain* for use if or when a new page for any of the remaining indexes, or a new index, is needed.

If you multiply the number of index file pages by the index file page size, you can determine the total amount of disk space needed to store the index. You might want to do this if you have to copy the data set and its index file elsewhere and are interested in determining the total amount of space needed for the new copies. You would calculate the size of the index, calculate the size of the SAS data set, and then add the sizes together to get the total space allocation that is required.

The number of index file pages in the example CONTENTS procedure listing is 6,961. Multiplying that figure by the index file page size (32,256) gives you a total index file size of 224,534,016 bytes or about 214 megabytes.

❹ **Alphabetic List of Indexes and Attributes** gives you detailed information about each individual index created for a SAS data set. It presents up to seven columns that describe the individual indexes:

- **#** This is a simple sequence number and has no real meaning. It does not describe the order in which indexes were created, but rather the order in which they are placed in the CONTENTS procedure listing. Because they are placed there in alphabetic order of the index name, this number could change for any given index when a new index is created and inserted into its proper order.

  This example has nine sequence numbers.

- **Index** This column specifies the name of the index. If it is a simple index, the index name is the name of the variable that was used to create the index. If it is a composite index, this is the name that was supplied as the composite index name. The indexes are listed in alphabetic order. Consequently, simple and composite indexes may be interspersed throughout the list.

  In this example, there are nine indexes listed in alphabetic order.

- **Unique Option** This column specifies whether or not an index was created using the UNIQUE option. (See "The UNIQUE Option" section in Chapter 5, "Index-Related Options," for more information on this option.) The values are either YES, meaning that the index is unique, or blank, meaning that it is not unique. If no indexes in a particular SAS data set are unique, then this column is not present in the "Alphabetic List of Indexes and Attributes." If there are one or more unique indexes, then this column will be there.

  This example reports that only the SEQNUM simple index has unique values.

- **NoMiss Option** This column reports whether the NOMISS option was specified when a particular index was created. (See "The NOMISS Option" section in Chapter 5, "Index-Related Options," for more information on this option.) The value in the listing is either YES, meaning that the NOMISS option is in effect, or blank, meaning that it is not.

  If no indexes in a particular SAS data set were created with the NOMISS option, then this column is not present in the "Alphabetic List of Indexes and Attributes."

  In this example, only the COUNTRY_STATE, SEQNUM, STATE, and YEAR indexes have the NOMISS option enabled.

- **Owned by IC** This column indicates that an index is owned by an integrity constraint.[1] Integrity constraints are sets of data validation rules specified by users to restrict the data values that can be stored for a variable in a SAS data set. They are created via the SQL procedure, the DATASETS procedure, or in the SAS Component Language (SCL).

  When users create *unique*, *primary key*, and *foreign key* integrity constraints, SAS creates an index for the variables involved and marks the index as being owned by an integrity constraint. If a SAS data set index already exists for the variables involved in the integrity constraint, SAS marks the existing index as being owned by an integrity constraint. Indexes that have a value of *YES* for Owned by IC are indexes with integrity constraints assigned to them.[2]

  This column is found only in an "Alphabetic List of Indexes and Attributes" when integrity constraints exist for a data set. When one or more integrity constraints exist, the CONTENTS procedure listing also includes an "Alphabetic List of Integrity Constraints," as in the example above.

  This example contains a single integrity constraint. It is created from the MONTH_SEQNUM composite index, is UNIQUE, and has 2,304,000 entries.

- **# of Unique Values** This is a very interesting column that reports the number of unique index values in the SAS data set. If it is for a simple index, this is the number of unique values that a particular variable holds within the SAS data set. If it is for a composite index, it represents the number of unique values that the particular combination of the component variable values has in the SAS data set. The greater the number of unique values, the more discriminant is the particular index. (For a discussion of *discriminant* see the "Proposed Index Key Variable Discriminant" section in Chapter 3, "Index Variable Selection Considerations.") It is usually good to see larger values in this column. The closer this number gets to the total number of observations in the SAS data set, the more powerful is the index for retrieving small subsets of data.

---

[1] The topic of integrity constraints falls well outside of the scope of this book. You can find more information about them in the SAS Online Documentation.

[2] Indexes owned by integrity constraints have the same structure and utility as those created by DATA steps or by the DATASETS and SQL procedures. They can also be used for other purposes, such as WHERE and BY processing.

In this example, we have the number of unique values ranging from a poor value of 4 to an ideal value of 2,304,000, the total number of observations in the SAS data set. The values for STATE_PRODUCT and YEAR_AND_QUARTER, which are 64 and 56 respectively, have to be regarded with caution. Though they may seem like more discriminant indexes, you cannot be sure without more information. For example, STATE_PRODUCT might have 63 unique variables within the entire SAS data set with a unique combination of STATE/PRODUCT and 2,303,937 observations which share the 64th combination of STATE/PRODUCT. That certainly would not be a very discriminant variable! More information can be found by looking at the centiles portion of the CONTENTS procedure listing. (Centiles are discussed in detail in Chapter 4, "Index Centiles.")

- **Variables** This column is present only if there are one or more composite indexes associated with the SAS data set. It lists the variables that make up the composite index in the order that they were specified. This is a very important column for determining which indexes are composite indexes and for understanding the composition of composite indexes. You can use this information to create WHERE and BY statements in your SAS programs that use the composite indexes.

   In the example, you can see that the COUNTRY_STATE index is a composite index created from variables COUNTRY and STATE. STATE_PRODUCT is a composite index created from STATE and PRODUCT. YEAR_AND_QUARTER is a composite index created from variables YEAR and QUARTER. Finally, the MONTH_SEQNUM index, owned by an integrity constraint, is created from the MONTH and SEQNUM variables.

Though this text recommends using the CONTENTS procedure, the same information can be gleaned from executing the DATASETS procedure. Here is an example of using PROC DATASETS to get a CONTENTS listing:

```
proc datasets library=indexlib;
  contents data=prodindx;
quit;
```

The example code above produces a CONTENTS listing identical to the one found earlier in this section.

What to Look for in the SAS Windowing Environment Session

You can obtain index information for SAS data sets from within the SAS windowing environment. To do this, you need to invoke SAS Explorer. The following displays show how you can navigate through SAS Explorer to find index information in SAS running on the Windows operating system.

Display 6.1 SAS Explorer First View

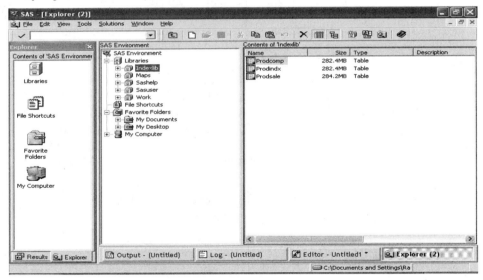

In Display 6.1, you can see the contents of the INDEXLIB SAS data library. There are three SAS data sets in that library, two of which have indexes. SAS Explorer does not show you the indexes. To determine if a SAS data set is indexed, you must do the following:

1. Single click on the data set to highlight it.

2. Right-click on the highlighted data set.

3. Click **Properties** at the bottom of the drop-down list.

4. On the top of the Properties window, click the **Indexes** tab. This displays all of the indexes for this SAS data set.

The following displays illustrate the process of getting to index information.

Display 6.2 Selecting Properties of the INDEXLIB.PRODINDX
           SAS Data Set

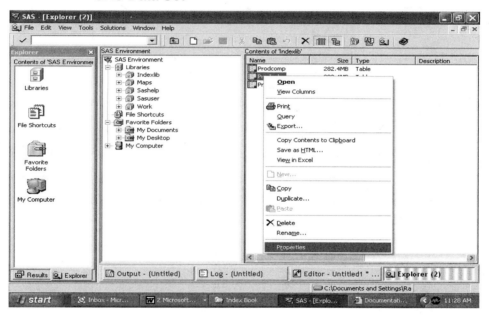

Display 6.3 The Properties Window for the INDEXLIB.PRODINDX
SAS Data Set.

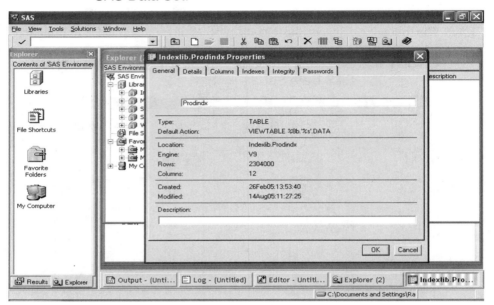

DIsplay 6.4 Index Information for the INDEXLIB.PRODINDX SAS Data Set (1 of 2, left scroll).

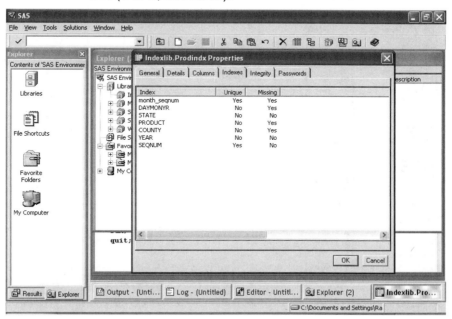

Display 6.5 Index Information for the INDEXLIB.PRODINDX SAS Data Set (2 of 2, right scroll).

If you look at Displays 6.4 and 6.5, you can see that the information is very similar to that found in a CONTENTS procedure listing. The only column not found in the displays that is found in a CONTENTS procedure listing is # of Unique Values. Unfortunately this is an important piece of information that is very helpful.

Displays 6.4 and 6.5 indicate that there is an integrity constraint for the MONTH_SEQNUM index. To get more information about the MONTH_SEQNUM integrity constraint, click the **Integrity** tab on the Properties window.

DIsplay 6.6 Integrity Constraint Information for the
INDEXLIB.PRODINDX SAS Data Set

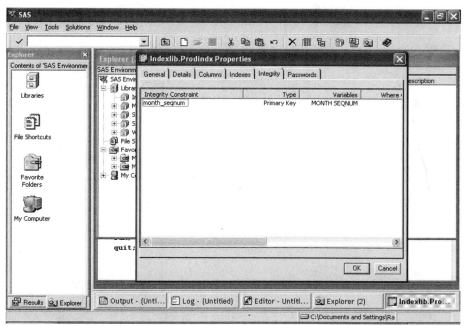

The Integrity tab reveals that the MONTH_SEQNUM index is a *primary key* integrity constraint. You can find more information about integrity constraints in the SAS Online Documentation.

What to Look for on Your Operating System

Because SAS indexes are stored in separate files on most operating systems, it is relatively straightforward to identify them. You simply look in the directory where a SAS data set is stored and look for entries that have the sas7bndx suffix. The SAS data set has the sas7bdat suffix, and its index file has the same base file name, but is followed by the sas7bndx suffix. For example, you might see PRODINDX.sas7bdat and PRODINDX.sas7bndx, a SAS data set and its index data set, respectively, in the same directory. PRODINDX is the base name of the SAS files; the suffixes tell you which is the data file and which is the index file.

Display 6.7 illustrates executing the **ls −l** command on a Linux server to display the contents of a Linux directory, which contains SAS files.

Display 6.7 List of SAS Files in a Linux Directory

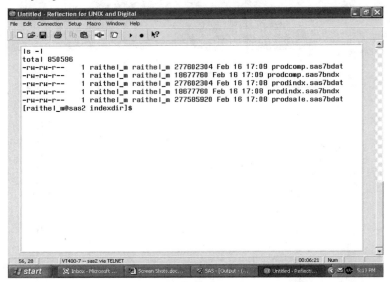

In the example, there are five files in the directory; three are SAS data sets and two are SAS index files. There is the PRODCOMP SAS data set and index, the PRODINDX SAS data set and index, and the PRODSALE SAS data set. If you needed additional information about the nature of the indexes, you would have to use SAS to generate a CONTENTS procedure listing.

Display 6.8 is a similar example of looking at a directory via Windows Explorer on a workstation running the Windows XP operating system.

Display 6.8 SAS Files in Windows Explorer on a Windows XP
Workstation

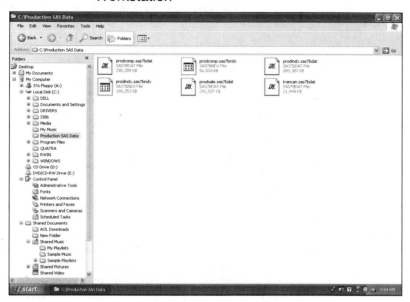

You can see that the **C:\Production SAS Data** directory contains six files. Four
are SAS data sets and two are indexes. They are the same data sets and indexes found in
the Linux example above except that these are on a Windows workstation.

You should be able to determine how best to check for SAS indexes on the operating
systems that you use. On some, you use the **dir** command. On other systems, it may be
the **ls -l** command. On still other host platforms, you invoke a GUI interface to see
what files a directory holds. The point is that on *almost* all operating systems, the index
file is visible in the directory that holds the SAS data set.

The one exception is the z/OS[3] operating system. Under z/OS, a SAS data library is a
single OS data set with an organization of Physical Sequential (PS) and a record format
of Fixed Standard (FS). Within that OS data set, SAS places SAS data sets, SAS indexes,
SAS catalogs, etc. When you are in native TSO or are in ISPF, you see only a single OS
data set that looks pretty much like any other fixed-length Physical Sequential data

---

[3] This is also true of earlier versions of z/OS such as OS/390 and MVS.

set. However, when you invoke SAS and use the LIBNAME statement to allocate that data set as a SAS data library, you can see the various SAS files stored within the OS data set. Consequently, under z/OS the only way that you can see if a SAS data set is indexed is to invoke SAS and check using either the SAS Display Manager or the CONTENTS procedure.

The exception to this exception is when you use the Hierarchical File System (HFS) on z/OS. Under HFS, SAS files are stored individually as they are in native UNIX environments. Therefore, SAS data sets have the sas7bdat suffix, and their index files have the same base file name but are followed by the sas7bndx suffix.

Summary

This chapter discussed three sources of SAS index information. The first source is a CONTENTS procedure listing that provides very detailed information about the number of indexes, the size of the index file, and the specifics of each index. The second source is SAS Explorer in the SAS Display Manager. SAS Explorer also enables you to determine the specific properties of indexes associated with a SAS data set. Finally, the chapter discussed how you can tell whether or not index files exist on your host system by using a GUI or by using operating system commands.

Chapter 7

Creating Indexes with the INDEX Data Set Option

Introduction

The INDEX data set option enables you to create new indexes at the same time that you create new SAS data sets. You can use the INDEX data set option in a DATA step or in the output DATA statement of a SAS procedure. When making an index in a DATA step or PROC step, SAS builds the index after the data set has been finalized and is being closed. After the step finishes processing, you have a complete SAS index immediately available to use to process subsets of the new SAS data set.

Here is an example of creating an index in a DATA step and creating one in a PROC step:

```
data indexlib.prodindx(index=(seqno /unique /nomiss));
set  indexlib.prodsale;
run;

proc sort
     data=indexlib.prodsale
     out=indexlib.state_county(index=(state));
       by state county;
run;
```

There are two things that you should know when considering whether you should create an index in a DATA or PROC step. The first is that the step will consume more CPU time and I/Os to execute because of the overhead processing that is done to create the index. This will increase your computer charges if you pay for CPU time and I/Os. Because of the increase in I/Os needed to create the index, your DATA step or PROC step will take longer to execute. This consideration should not be a showstopper because it will take some computer overhead to create the index no matter what tool is used to create it. You should be aware that the DATA step or procedure takes more computer resources and time to execute when an index is being produced than it would if one were not being made.

The second thing you should know when considering whether to create an index using the INDEX data set option is that your index will not be as efficient as it could be if the data set is not sorted in ascending index key variable order. SAS indexes are far more efficient when their SAS data sets have been sorted into ascending index key variable order, as discussed in Chapter 3, "Index Variable Selection Considerations." Unless the input data set was presorted by the index key variable(s), or the PROC step being executed uses a BY or CLASS statement to sort the output data set by the index key variable(s), the resulting SAS data set will probably not be sorted in ascending index key variable(s) order. Consequently, an index built from a DATA or PROC step under these circumstances will not be as efficient as one created by the DATASETS or the SQL procedures from a sorted SAS data set. Be careful to either make sure that the input data set is sorted by the index key variable(s) or use a BY or CLASS statement to sort the output SAS data set into index key variable order when creating an index in a PROC step.

It is not possible to sort a single SAS data set by every variable that is used to create simple and composite indexes. A sorted SAS data set can only have one sort sequence, that is, one or more variables by which it is sorted. For this reason when you are creating multiple indexes, you must choose the sort sequence that will be the most advantageous for both future index usage and for future BY processing of the data set. Then sort the SAS data set by that variable, or sequence of variables, before creating your indexes.

General Format of the INDEX Data Set Option

This section describes the general format of how a simple and a composite index can be created with the INDEX data set option. A definition of simple and composite indexes is provided in Chapter 1, "Introduction." The index options *unique* and *nomiss*, which are found in the text below, are described in Chapter 5, "Index-Related Options," so they will not be discussed in this chapter.

Simple Index Format

This is the format for creating a simple index in a DATA step:

DATA *data-set-name*(INDEX=(*variable-name* </UNIQUE> </NOMISS>));

As you can see, the index creation information is specified in the DATA statement. *Data-set-name* is the name of the new SAS data set that is created in the DATA step. Notice that *data-set-name* is followed by a set of parentheses, wherein the INDEX option specifies that an index is to be created. The inner set of parentheses, following the INDEX option, describes the particular characteristics of the new index. *Variable-name* is the name of a variable in the SAS data set that you intend to use as the index key variable. This variable must exist in the new (output) SAS data set, *data-set-name,* for the DATA step to complete successfully. *Variable-name* may be followed by the closing parenthesis if you do not intend to specify one of the index options. If you do intend to specify index options, then *variable-name* is followed by a slash (/) and the index option of your choice. If you intend to use several index options, each must be preceded by a slash. You may specify index options in any order.

This is the format for creating a simple index in a PROC step:

… OUT= *data-set-name*(INDEX=(*variable-name* </UNIQUE> </NOMISS>));

The exact format of the output statement varies, depending on the SAS procedure that is specified. However, the format of the INDEX data set option does not vary. It follows the same formatting rules as discussed above for the DATA step.

Composite Index Format

This is the format for creating a composite index in a DATA step:

> DATA *data-set-name*(INDEX=(*index-name*=(*var1 var2 etc.*))</UNIQUE>
>   </NOMISS>));

In the composite index format above, the INDEX option is enclosed in parentheses directly after *data-set-name*, the name of the new SAS data set being created. *Index-name* is an index name of your own choosing. It may be from 1 to 32 characters long and must follow the normal SAS variable naming conventions.[1] The only other restriction on *index-name* is that it cannot be the name of a variable that will exist in the new output SAS data set. *Index-name*= is followed by a set of parentheses that contain the two or more variables that will be used to create the composite index. The variables are listed in the order that you choose, each separated by one or more spaces. After the parenthetical variable list, you may choose to specify index options. If so, a slash (/) must precede each option. If not, then the ending parenthesis follows.

This is the general format for creating a composite index in a PROC step:

> … OUT= *data-set-name*(INDEX=(*index-name*=(*var1 var2 etc.*))</UNIQUE>
>   </NOMISS>));

The exact format of the output statement depends on the specific SAS procedure that is used. But, the format of the INDEX data set option for specifying a composite index follows the same rules as discussed for the DATA step.

---

[1] In the examples in this book, the author commonly fashions composite index names from the full name of the variables that make up the composite index. For example, composite index COUNTRY_STATE comprises the COUNTRY and STATE variables. This is simply a good naming convention and is not meant to imply that composite indexes must be named after their constituent variables. A composite index built from COUNTRY and STATE can just as easily be named CNTY_ST.

Example 7.1: Creating a Simple SAS Index in a DATA Step

This is an example of SAS code that creates a simple SAS index in a DATA step:

```
data indexlib.prodindx(index=(seqno /unique /nomiss));
set  indexlib.prodsale;
run;
```

In this example we are creating a simple index based on the variable SEQNO. The UNIQUE option tells SAS that each observation in the PRODINDX data set will have a unique value of SEQNO. (If that turns out not to be the case, the step above ends with an error condition and the data set is created, but the index is not.) By using the NOMISS option, we are specifying that SAS should not create index entries for observations that have missing values for SEQNO. Here is the SAS log for the program:

```
212   data indexlib.prodindx(index=(seqnum /unique /nomiss));
213   set  indexlib.prodsale;
214   run;


NOTE: There were 2304000 observations read from the data set
      INDEXLIB.PRODSALE.
NOTE: The data set INDEXLIB.PRODINDX has 2304000 observations and
      12 variables.
NOTE: Simple index seqnum has been defined.
NOTE: DATA statement used:
      real time             1:52.31
      cpu time              6.01 seconds
```

In the SAS log the third NOTE statement reads "Simple index seqnum has been defined." This is confirmation that the index has been successfully built by the DATA step.

This is what the "Alphabetic List of Indexes and Attributes" looks like for the simple index created by this SAS DATA step if you run the CONTENTS procedure:

```
                        The CONTENTS Procedure

        -----Alphabetic List of Indexes and Attributes-----

                                                    # of
                            Unique      Nomiss     Unique
             #    Index     Option      Option     Values

             1    SEQNUM    YES         YES        2304000
```

Note that the data set has a single simple index built on the variable SEQNUM. The index is using both the UNIQUE and the NOMISS options. There are 2,304,000 unique values of SEQNUM in the INDEXLIB.PRODINDX SAS data set, the same figure as the number of observations in the data set. That is further verification that the values of SEQNUM are unique throughout the INDEXLIB.PRODINX SAS data set.

Example 7.2: Creating Multiple Simple SAS Indexes in a DATA Step

You can create two or more simple SAS indexes in a DATA step. Here is an example of SAS statements that create four distinct indexes in a DATA step:

```
data indexlib.prodindx(index =(seqnum /unique /nomiss
                               state / nomiss
                               county
                               year / nomiss));
set   indexlib.prodsale;
run;
```

In this example an index is being created for SEQNUM, STATE, COUNTY, and YEAR. As in the previous example, the index for SEQNUM specifies the UNIQUE and NOMISS options. Both STATE and YEAR will be created with the NOMISS option in effect while COUNTY will not use that option. Notice that within the inner parentheses, each index variable is either followed by its particular options, each of which is preceded by a slash (/), or is followed by the next index variable.

Here is the SAS log for the execution of this example:

```
227   data indexlib.prodindx(index=(seqnum /unique /nomiss
228                                 state /nomiss
229                                 county
230                                 year /nomiss));

231   set  indexlib.prodsale;
232   run;

NOTE: There were 2304000 observations read from the data set
      INDEXLIB.PRODSALE.
NOTE: The data set INDEXLIB.PRODINDX has 2304000 observations and
      12 variables.
NOTE: Simple index year has been defined.
NOTE: Simple index county has been defined.
NOTE: Simple index state has been defined.
NOTE: Simple index seqnum has been defined.
NOTE: DATA statement used:
      real time            1:46.64
      cpu time             20.29 seconds
```

The SAS log has four separate NOTEs specifying that each simple SAS index has been defined. When creating multiple simple SAS indexes in a DATA step, you should always look for the NOTEs in the SAS log and verify that they have been successfully created.

This is what the "Alphabetic List of Indexes and Attributes," from the CONTENTS procedure looks like after the DATA step has successfully executed:

```
                    The CONTENTS Procedure

        -----Alphabetic List of Indexes and Attributes-----

                                                       # of
                          Unique       Nomiss        Unique
            #   Index     Option       Option        Values

            1   COUNTY                                   6
            2   SEQNUM    YES          YES         2304000
            3   STATE                  YES              16
            4   YEAR                   YES              14
```

All three of the simple indexes that were specified in the DATA step are shown in the CONTENTS procedure listing. Note that they are listed in alphabetic order, not the order (SEQNUM, STATE, COUNTY, YEAR) that they were specified in the DATA step where they were created.

Example 7.3: Creating a Composite SAS Index in a DATA Step

This is an example of creating a composite SAS index in a DATA step:

```
data indexlib.prodcomp(index=(country_state=(country state) /
                                             nomiss));
set  indexlib.prodsale;
run;
```

In the example, index COUNTRY_STATE is being created as a composite of variables COUNTRY and STATE. The NOMISS option was specified; therefore, no index entries are created for observations where both COUNTRY and STATE have missing values.

Here is the SAS log for this DATA step:

```
168  data indexlib.prodcomp(index=(country_state=(country state) /
                                         nomiss));
169  set  indexlib.prodsale;
170  run;


NOTE: There were 2304000 observations read from the data set
INDEXLIB.PRODSALE.
NOTE: The data set INDEXLIB.PRODCOMP has 2304000 observations and 11
variables.
NOTE: Composite index country_state has been defined.
NOTE: DATA statement used:
      real time           58.04 seconds
      cpu time            7.46 seconds
```

As you can see, the third NOTE states that the composite index COUNTRY_STATE has been successfully defined by the DATA step.

Here is what the "Alphabetic List of Indexes and Attributes" from a CONTENTS procedure listing of the INDEXLIB.PRODCOMP SAS data set looks like:

```
                    The CONTENTS Procedure


        -----Alphabetic List of Indexes and Attributes-----


                                    # of
                         Nomiss   Unique
    #     Index          Option   Values    Variables
    --------------------------------------------------------
    1     country_state   YES         16    COUNTRY STATE
```

You can see that the data set now has a single composite index, named COUNTRY_STATE, that the index uses the NOMISS option, that there are sixteen unique values for the COUNTRY_STATE composite index, and that the COUNTRY_STATE composite index is built from variables COUNTRY and STATE.

Example 7.4: Creating Multiple Composite SAS Indexes in a DATA Step

Multiple composite indexes may also be created for a new SAS data set in a DATA step. Here is an example of creating three new composite indexes:

```
data indexlib.prodcomp(index=(country_state=(country state) /
                                        nomiss
                              year_and_quarter=(year quarter)
                              state_product=(state product)));
set  indexlib.prodsale;
run;
```

In this example, composite indexes COUNTRY_STATE, YEAR_AND_QUARTER, and STATE_PRODUCT are created. Notice that, unlike creating multiple simple indexes, each composite index name is followed by parentheses in which the variables for that particular index are specified. After the parentheses, index options may be listed, each preceded by a slash (/).

Here is the SAS log from the execution of the DATA step above:

```
335   data indexlib.prodcomp(index=(country_state=(country state) /
      nomiss
336                                    year_and_quarter=(year quarter)
337                                    state_product=(state product)));
338   set  indexlib.prodsale;
339   run;


NOTE: There were 2304000 observations read from the data set
INDEXLIB.PRODSALE.
NOTE: The data set INDEXLIB.PRODCOMP has 2304000 observations and 11
variables.
NOTE: Composite index state_product has been defined.
NOTE: Composite index year_and_quarter has been defined.
NOTE: Composite index country_state has been defined.
NOTE: DATA statement used:
      real time            1:20.81
      cpu time             17.85 seconds
```

The creation of each composite index is listed in a separate NOTE in the SAS log. This makes it is easy to tell whether or not they were successfully created.

Here is the "Alphabetic List of Indexes and Attributes" from PROC CONTENTS for data set INDEXLIB.PRODCOMP:

```
                      The CONTENTS Procedure


      -----Alphabetic List of Indexes and Attributes-----


                                  # of
                        Nomiss  Unique
     #     Index        Option   Values   Variables
     ------------------------------------------------------------
     1     country_state  YES        16   COUNTRY STATE
     2     state_product             64   STATE PRODUCT
     3     year_and_quarter          56   YEAR QUARTER
```

All three of the composite indexes created in the example DATA step are listed along with their options, the number of unique values, and the variables that make up each composite index.

Example 7.5: Creating a Simple Index in a SAS Procedure

In this example, a simple index is created in a SAS procedure:

```
proc summary data=indexlib.prodsale;
      class country state county prodtype product;
      var   actual predict;
output out=templib.sum_products(index=(_type_)) sum=;
run;
```

The SUMMARY procedure is being executed to produce an output SAS data set named SUM_PRODUCTS in the TEMPLIB SAS data library. The INDEX data set option dictates that an index be created for the variable _TYPE_.

Here is the SAS log from executing this SUMMARY procedure:

```
91    proc summary data=indexlib.prodsale;
92         class country state county prodtype product;
93         var   actual predict;
94    output out=templib.sum_products(index=(_type_)) sum=;
95    run;


NOTE: There were 2304000 observations read from the data set
INDEXLIB.PRODSALE.
NOTE: The data set TEMPLIB.SUM_PRODUCTS has 264 observations and 9
variables.
NOTE: Simple index _type_ has been defined.
NOTE: PROCEDURE SUMMARY used:
      real time          5.89 seconds
      cpu time           1.48 seconds
```

The log shows that the simple index named _TYPE_ has been defined. Note that with only 264 observations and nine variables, it is rather doubtful that an index is warranted for the SUM_PRODUCTS SAS data set. It will probably always be more efficient for SAS to read the entire data set sequentially. However, the point of this example is not the viability of the index, but how a simple index can be created in the output SAS data set from a SAS procedure.

Here is the "Alphabetic List of Indexes and Attributes" from PROC CONTENTS for data set TEMPLIB.SUM_PRODUCTS:

```
        -----Alphabetic List of Indexes and Attributes-----

                                     # of
                                    Unique
                #      Index        Values
                       _____

                1      _TYPE_          32
```

You can see that a simple index was created for variable _TYPE_ and that it contains 32 unique values. Because neither the UNIQUE nor the NOMISS option was used when the index was created, neither the UNIQUE option nor the NOMISS option columns are present in the "Alphabetic List of Indexes and Attributes" for the _TYPE_ index.

Example 7.6: Creating a Composite Index in a SAS Procedure

This is an example of creating a composite index in a SAS procedure:

```
proc sort
    data=indexlib.prodsale
    out=templib.prodindx(index=(coun_stat_cnty=(country state
                                                county) /
                                                nomiss));
        by country state county;
run;
```

In this SORT procedure, data set INDEXLIB.PRODSALE is input to the sort, and the data set TEMPLIB.PRODINDX is created as the sorted output SAS data set. A composite index named COUN_STAT_CNTY is created from the COUNTRY, STATE, and COUNTY variables.

The log from running this SORT procedure looks like this:

```
68    proc sort
69        data=indexlib.prodsale
70        out=templib.prodindx(index=(coun_stat_cnty=(country state
                                              county) /nomiss));
71        by country state county;
72    run;


NOTE: SAS sort was used.
NOTE: There were 2304000 observations read from the data set
INDEXLIB.PRODSALE.
NOTE: The data set TEMPLIB.PRODINDX has 2304000 observations and 12
variables.
NOTE: Composite index coun_stat_cnty has been defined.
NOTE: PROCEDURE SORT used:
      real time              6:53.17
      cpu time               15.04 seconds
```

The NOTE in the SAS log shows that the COUN_STAT_CNTY composite index was successfully created.

This is what the "Alphabetic List of Indexes and Attributes" from PROC CONTENTS for data set INDEXLIB.PRODSALE looks like:

```
                  The CONTENTS Procedure


        -----Alphabetic List of Indexes and Attributes-----


                                    # of
                         Nomiss   Unique
        #    Index       Option   Values      Variables
        _____

        1    coun_stat_cnty   YES      20      COUNTRY STATE COUNTY
```

You can see the entry for the COUN_STAT_CNTY composite index. The CONTENTS listing shows that the NOMISS option was enabled, that there are 20 unique values for the composite index, and that the composite index is made from the COUNTRY, STATE, and COUNTY variables.

Example 7.7: Creating Simple and Composite SAS Indexes in a SAS Procedure

In this example, both simple and composite indexes are created in the same SAS procedure:

```
proc sort
   data=indexlib.prodsale
   out=templib.prodindx(index=(seqnum / unique
                               daymonyr / nomiss
                               coun_stat_cnty = (country state
                                                 county) / nomiss
                               prodtype_product = (prodtype
                                                   product)));
   by country state county;
run;
```

As in Example 7.6, data set INDEXLIB.PRODSALE is input to the sort; data set TEMPLIB.PRODINDX is created as the sorted output SAS data set. However, in this example, two simple indexes are created, one from the SEQNUM variable and one from DAYMONYR. The first is created using the UNIQUE option; the latter using the NOMISS option. A composite index named COUN_STAT_CNTY is created from the COUNTRY, STATE, and COUNTY variables with the NOMISS option enabled. Finally, the PRODTYPE_PRODUCT composite index is created from the PRODTYPE and PRODUCT variables.

This is the SAS log from executing the SORT procedure:

```
96    proc sort
97        data=indexlib.prodsale
98        out=templib.prodindx(index=(seqnum / unique
99                                    daymonyr / nomiss
100                                   coun_stat_cnty = (country state
                                                       county) / nomiss
101                                   prodtype_product = (prodtype
                                                         product)));

102       by country state county;
103   run;

NOTE: SAS sort was used.
```

(continued on next page)

(continued)

```
NOTE: There were 2304000 observations read from the data set
      INDEXLIB.PRODSALE.
NOTE: The data set TEMPLIB.PRODINDX has 2304000 observations and 12
      variables.
NOTE: Composite index prodtype_product has been defined.
NOTE: Composite index coun_stat_cnty has been defined.
NOTE: Simple index daymonyr has been defined.
NOTE: Simple index seqnum has been defined.
NOTE: PROCEDURE SORT used:
      real time              5:35.09
      cpu time              28.10 seconds
```

The log shows that four indexes—two composite and two simple—were successfully created by the SORT procedure for the TEMPLIB.PRODINDX output SAS data set. Now, that new SAS data set can be processed by any one of those indexes.

Here is the "Alphabetic List of Indexes and Attributes" from a CONTENTS procedure listing of the new TEMPLIB.PRODINDX SAS data set.

```
                    The CONTENTS Procedure

       -----Alphabetic List of Indexes and Attributes-----

                                        # of
                      Unique   Nomiss   Unique
    #    Index        Option   Option   Values   Variables
    _____

    1    DAYMONYR                YES       168
    2    SEQNUM        YES              2304000
    3    coun_stat_cnty          YES        20   COUNTRY STATE COUNTY
    4    prodtype_product                    4   PRODTYPE PRODUCT
```

The CONTENTS listing provides the specifics on the four indexes that were created. Notice that two of the indexes, COUN_STAT_CNTY and PRODTYPE_PRODUCT, have very few unique values. This means that they are not particularly discriminant and will probably not be very effective indexes. However, they do illustrate how both composite and simple indexes can be created within the same SAS procedure, which is the point of this particular example.

Summary

The INDEX data set option is a handy tool for creating new indexes at the same time that you create new SAS data sets. The INDEX data set option can be used in a DATA step or in the output DATA statement of a SAS procedure. When it is used, SAS first creates the new data set and then builds the index (or indexes) before closing the data set at the end of the execution of a DATA or PROC step. You can create multiple simple and composite indexes in the same DATA or PROC step using the INDEX data set option.

Chapter 8

Creating Indexes with the DATASETS Procedure

Introduction

The DATASETS procedure is a good tool to use to create indexes for existing SAS data sets. You may use it to build indexes immediately after a DATA step or procedure has created a SAS data set instead of creating the index within the DATA or PROC step. Or you may use the DATASETS procedure long after a SAS data set has been created, when it becomes apparent to you that a new index would give processing of that data set a performance boost.

The DATASETS procedure is also a practical device to use to add additional indexes to a SAS data set that already contains one or more indexes. (The SQL procedure can also be used to add new indexes to existing SAS data sets. See Chapter 9, "Creating Indexes with the SQL Procedure," for more information.) This is so because PROC DATASETS builds the new index and adds it to the SAS data set's existing index file. If you were to use a DATA or PROC step, you would have to rebuild the data set and its original indexes in order to add new ones.

An advantage to using the DATASETS procedure is that it is the only index-creating tool that enables you to modify the value of the UPDATECENTILES option at index creation time. The UPDATECENTILES option specifies what percentage of index key variable values may change before SAS recomputes an index's centiles. The default of 5% is usually adequate, but you may have a good reason to set it to another value at index creation time. If so, then you must use PROC DATASETS to create the index. (The UPDATECENTILES option is fully discussed in Chapter 4, "Index Centiles," and in Chapter 5, "Index-Related Options.")

The simplicity of using the DATASETS procedure and its obvious presence in a SAS program make it a more "self documenting" place to create SAS indexes. You can easily spot the DATASETS procedure (that is creating one or more indexes) in your SAS program, while index creation in a DATA step may be more subtle and less easy to catch at a glance. Many SAS programmers elect to use the DATASETS procedure to create SAS indexes, rather than creating them in DATA steps. There is no performance or time penalty for using either method, that is, creating an index in a DATA step versus creating the index in a DATASETS procedure that follows the DATA step that created a SAS data set.

General Format of DATASETS Procedure Code

This section describes the general format of how a simple and a composite index may be created with the DATASETS procedure. You can find the definitions of simple and composite indexes in Chapter 1, "Introduction to Indexes." The UNIQUE, NOMISS, and UPDATECENTILES index options used in the text below are all thoroughly discussed in Chapter 5, "Index-Related Options."

Simple Index Format

This is the general format for creating a simple index in a DATASETS procedure:

```
PROC DATASETS LIBRARY=libref;
   MODIFY SAS-data-set;;
     INDEX CREATE variable-name / UNIQUE NOMISS
     UPDATECENTILES = ALWAYS | 0 | NEVER | 101 | integer;
   RUN;
QUIT;
```

The LIBRARY option specifies the *libref* of the SAS data library containing the SAS data set for which you want to build an index. The MODIFY statement contains the name of the *SAS-data-set* that is to be indexed. The INDEX CREATE statement names the specific variable, *variable-name*, that is to be used in the creation of a simple index. If you need to specify options, *variable-name* is followed by a single slash (/) and then by any combination of the UNIQUE, NOMISS, and UPDATECENTILES options.

Composite Index Format

This is the general format for using the DATASETS procedure to create a composite index:

```
PROC DATASETS LIBRARY=libref;
   MODIFY SAS-data-set;
     INDEX CREATE index-name=(var1, var2, ...) / UNIQUE NOMISS
     UPDATECENTILES = ALWAYS | 0 | NEVER | 101 | integer;
   RUN;
QUIT;
```

The SAS library and data set are identified in the first two DATASETS procedure statements. The INDEX CREATE statement begins by specifying an *index-name*, followed by a parenthetical list of two or more variables. The *index-name* is the user-chosen name for the composite index and may be any valid SAS variable name as long as it is not the name of a variable that exists in the data set.[1] The index variables *(var1, var2, ...)* are listed in order of importance with a blank space separating each of them. If there are any options that must be specified, they follow the parenthetical variable list, separated by a single slash (/). You can specify one or more index options, and they may appear in any order.

Example 8.1: Creating a Simple SAS Index

The following SAS code creates a simple SAS index for an existing SAS data set using the DATASETS procedure:

```
proc datasets library=indexlib;
  modify prodindx;
    index create seqnum /nomiss unique updatecentiles=10;
  run;
quit;
```

This DATASETS procedure creates a simple index based on the variable SEQNUM. The NOMISS index option specifies that SAS should not create index entries for observations that have missing values for SEQNUM. The UNIQUE option specifies that all values of SEQNUM are unique for each observation in the INDEXLIB.PRODINDX SAS data set. Finally, the UPDATECENTILES option is used to change the setting so that index centiles are updated when ten percent of the values of SEQNUM have been modified in the INDEXLIB.PRODINDX data set.

---

[1] In the examples in this book, the author commonly fashions composite index names from the full name of the variables that make up the composite index. For example, composite index COUNTRY_STATE has the COUNTRY and STATE variables. This is a good naming convention and is not meant to imply that composite indexes must be named for their constituent variables. A composite index built from COUNTRY and STATE can just as easily be named CNTY_ST.

This is the SAS log generated from executing the DATASETS procedure above:

```
12    proc datasets library=indexlib;
                                     -----Directory-----
Libref:          INDEXLIB
Engine:          V9
Physical Name:   C:\Data Files
File Name:       C:\Data Files


             #   Name     Memtype   File Size   Last Modified

             1   PRODCOMP  DATA      297255936   08JAN2007:17:41:45
             2   PRODINDX  DATA      298021888   09JAN2007:10:40:06
             3   PRODSALE  DATA      298034176   08JAN2007:11:42:33
             4   TRANCAN   DATA       22475776   28MAR2007:13:41:42
13      modify prodindx;
14         index create seqnum /nomiss unique updatecentiles=10;
NOTE: Simple index SEQNUM has been defined.
15         run;
16    quit;
```

The log shows the typical output of the DATASETS procedure, showing the state of the INDEXLIB SAS data library *before* any modification has taken place. The NOTE in the log states that the "Simple index SEQNUM has been defined" to let you know that the index was successfully built.

Here is what the "Alphabetic List of Indexes and Attributes" for INDEXLIB.PRODINDX looks like after the index has been created:

```
                    The CONTENTS Procedure

          -----Alphabetic List of Indexes and Attributes-----
                                                     # of
                            Unique     Nomiss      Unique
             #   Index      Option     Option      Values

             1   SEQNUM     YES        YES         2304000
```

You can see that there is a simple index created from SEQNUM with the UNIQUE and NOMISS options enabled. The listing also shows that there are 2,304,000 unique values of SEQNUM in the INDEXLIB.PRODINDX SAS data set.

Example 8.2: Creating Multiple Simple SAS Indexes

Sometimes you may want to create more than one index for an existing SAS data set. It is fairly easy to do so using the DATASETS procedure. Here is an example of creating four SAS indexes for the INDEXLIB.PRODINDX SAS data set:

```
proc datasets library=indexlib;
  modify prodindx;
    index create seqnum /nomiss unique updatecentiles=10;
    index create state / nomiss;
    index create county;
    index create year /nomiss;
  run;
quit;
```

In this DATASETS procedure example, there is one INDEX CREATE statement per index. Each one states the name of the variable that is to have an index built for it, followed by a slash (/), and then by options if there are any index options.

This is the SAS log from executing the DATASETS procedure, above:

```
41    proc datasets library=indexlib;
                                    -----Directory-----
Libref:         INDEXLIB
Engine:         V9
Physical Name: C:\Data Files
File Name:     C:\Data Files


        #  Name      Memtype   File Size  Last Modified

        1  PRODCOMP  DATA      297255936  08JAN2007:17:41:45
        2  PRODINDX  DATA      298034176  09JAN2007:10:53:14
        3  PRODSALE  DATA      298034176  08JAN2007:11:42:33
        4  TRANCAN   DATA       22475776  28MAR2007:13:41:42
```

(continued on next page)

(continued)

```
42      modify prodindx;
43          index create seqnum /nomiss unique updatecentiles=10;
NOTE: Simple index SEQNUM has been defined.
44          index create state / nomiss;
NOTE: Simple index STATE has been defined.
45          index create county;
NOTE: Simple index COUNTY has been defined.
46          index create year /nomiss;
NOTE: Simple index YEAR has been defined.
47      run;
48   quit;
```

In the SAS log, you can see that there are four separate NOTE statements saying that each one of the simple SAS indexes has been defined by the execution of the DATASETS procedure.

Here is what the "Alphabetic List of Indexes and Attributes" from a CONTENTS procedure listing of INDEXLIB.PRODINDX looks like after the DATASETS procedure creates the indexes:

```
                  The CONTENTS Procedure

      -----Alphabetic List of Indexes and Attributes-----
                                                # of
                       Unique      Nomiss      Unique
       #     Index     Option      Option      Values

       1     COUNTY                                 6
       2     SEQNUM     YES         YES       2304000
       3     STATE                  YES            16
       4     YEAR                   YES            14
```

You can see that INDEXLIB.PRODINDX contains four indexes that use various index options. You can use one or more of these indexes in your SAS applications that access this data set.

Example 8.3: Creating a Composite SAS Index

In this example, a composite SAS index is created using the DATASETS procedure:

```
proc datasets library=indexlib;
  modify prodcomp;
    index create country_state=(country state) / nomiss;
  run;
quit;
```

The PROC DATASETS statement points to the libref, INDEXLIB, of the SAS data
library that contains the SAS data set that will have an index added to it. The MODIFY
statement specifies the SAS data set within the SAS data library that is to be indexed.
The INDEX CREATE statement specifies that composite index COUNTRY_STATE is
to be created from variables COUNTRY and STATE and that the NOMISS option is to
be in effect.

This is the SAS log from the execution of the DATASETS procedure in the example:

```
439   proc datasets library=indexlib;
                                      -----Directory-----
Libref:         INDEXLIB
Engine:         V9
Physical Name: C:\Data Files
File Name:      C:\Data Files

              #   Name      Memtype    File Size   Last Modified

              1   PRODCOMP  DATA       277586944   12DEC2006:12:21:08
              2   PRODINDX  DATA       277586944   12DEC2006:11:07:15
              3   PRODSALE  DATA       277574656   27MAR2006:18:59:10
              4   TRANCAN   DATA        22475776   28MAR2006:13:41:42
440     modify prodcomp;
441        index create country_state=(country state);
NOTE: Composite index country_state has been defined.
442     run;
443   quit;
```

The log notes that composite index COUNTRY_STATE has been defined.

Here is the "Alphabetic List of Indexes and Attributes" from the CONTENTS procedure output for data set INDEXLIB.PRODCOMP after the COUNTRY_STATE composite index was created in the DATASETS procedure:

```
                      The CONTENTS Procedure


        -----Alphabetic List of Indexes and Attributes-----
                                       # of
                            Nomiss    Unique
        #    Index          Option    Values     Variables
        -------------------------------------------------------
        1    country_state    YES         16     COUNTRY STATE
```

The "Alphabetic List of Indexes and Attributes" shows that the COUNTRY_STATE index has the NOMISS option enabled, has sixteen unique values, and is composed of the COUNTRY and STATE variables.

Example 8.4: Creating Multiple Composite SAS Indexes

The DATASETS procedure is a great tool for creating multiple composite SAS indexes. Here is an example of creating three SAS indexes with varying options for a single SAS data set in the same execution of the DATASETS procedure:

```
proc datasets library=indexlib;
  modify prodcomp;
    index create country_state=(country state) / nomiss;
    index create year_and_quarter=(year quarter) /
          updatecentiles = 10;
    index create state_product=(state product);
  run;
quit;
```

In the example, each composite index is specified on a separate INDEX CREATE statement. The NOMISS option is specified for the COUNTRY_STATE index, the UPDATECENTILES option is specified for the YEAR_AND_QUARTER index, and no option is specified for the STATE_PRODUCT index.

This is the SAS log for the execution of the DATASETS procedure:

```
539  proc datasets library=indexlib;
                                   -----Directory-----
Libref:          INDEXLIB
Engine:          V9
Physical Name: C:\Data Files
File Name:       C:\Data Files


          #  Name      Memtype   File Size   Last Modified

          1  PRODCOMP  DATA      277586944   12DEC2007:12:35:32
          2  PRODINDX  DATA      277586944   12DEC2007:11:07:15
          3  PRODSALE  DATA      277574656   27MAR2007:18:59:10
          4  TRANCAN   DATA       22475776   28MAR2007:13:41:42
540    modify prodcomp;
541      index create country_state=(country state) / nomiss;
NOTE: Composite index country_state has been defined.
542      index create year_and_quarter=(year quarter) / updatecentiles = 10;
NOTE: Composite index year_and_quarter has been defined.
543      index create state_product=(state product);
NOTE: Composite index state_product has been defined.
544    run;

545  quit;

NOTE: PROCEDURE DATASETS used:
      real time            1:40.28
      cpu time             17.34 seconds
```

The output shows that each INDEX CREATE statement is followed by a NOTE specifying the composite index has been defined. You should always check for these NOTEs to ensure that each of the indexes that you specified in the DATASETS procedure has been successfully created.

The CONTENTS for INDEXLIB.PRODCOMP contains this "Alphabetic List of Indexes and Attributes":

```
                          The CONTENTS Procedure

           -----Alphabetic List of Indexes and Attributes-----
                                          # of
                                Nomiss   Unique
        #     Index             Option   Values    Variables
        -------------------------------------------------------
        1     country_state     YES          16    COUNTRY STATE
        2     state_product                  64    STATE PRODUCT
        3     year_and_quarter               56    YEAR QUARTER
```

Note that all of the indexes specified in the DATASETS procedure are listed along with their attributes. Though UPDATECENTILES = 10 was specified for the YEAR_AND_QUARTER index, it is not displayed in the "Alphabetic List of Index and Attributes" section of the CONTENTS procedure listing. To get centile information, you must specify the CENTILES option on the PROC CONTENTS statement. That produces a separate centiles section of the CONTENTS procedure listing. Centiles are fully discussed in Chapter 4, "Index Centiles."

Summary

The DATASETS procedure enables you to create indexes for existing SAS data sets. You can create one or more simple and/or composite indexes for a SAS data set with the DATASETS procedure. You can even produce simple and composite indexes for a specific SAS data set in the same execution of the DATASETS procedure. Because PROC DATASETS stands out in your SAS program code, it may be a better device, in terms of documenting where indexes are actually being produced, to use to create indexes in your SAS programs.

Chapter 9

Creating Indexes with the SQL Procedure

Introduction

The SQL procedure is an ideal tool for SAS programmers who are more comfortable with SQL programming than with traditional SAS DATA step and procedure step programming. The terminology for SAS data set objects is different for users of SAS SQL, being more in keeping with mainstream SQL programming. In SAS SQL parlance, a SAS data set is a *table*, an observations is a *row*, and a variable is a *column*. You can create a new index for a column or for multiple columns in the same SQL procedure where a SAS table is first created. Or, you can use PROC SQL to create one or more new indexes for an existing SAS table.

One of the shortcomings of the SQL procedure is that it does not allow you to specify the NOMISS index option. You may specify the UNIQUE index option, but attempting to specify NOMISS results in a syntax error. If you are interested in having the index built with the NOMISS option in effect, then you must either use the index DATA set option or the DATASETS procedure. This is necessary because NOMISS can *only* be specified when an index is first constructed. It is not something that can be added later. (See Chapter 5, "Index-Related Options," for a thorough discussion of the NOMISS and UNIQUE index options.)

General Format of SQL Procedure Code

This section discusses the general format of how simple and composite indexes may be created with the SQL procedure. A definition of simple and composite indexes is provided in Chapter 1, "Introduction to Indexes."

Simple Index Format

Here is the format for creating a simple index with the SQL procedure:

```
PROC SQL;
    CREATE <UNIQUE> INDEX column-name ON table-name;
QUIT;
```

In the CREATE INDEX statement, the UNIQUE option is entirely optional. If used, it must be placed between the CREATE and INDEX keywords. *Column-name* is the name of the column in the SAS table that is used to build a simple index. *Table-name* is the name of the SAS table that is having a new index built for it.

Composite Index Format

This is the format for creating a composite index with the SQL procedure:

```
PROC SQL;
    CREATE <UNIQUE> INDEX index-name ON table-name
        (column-name1<,column-name2>...);
QUIT;
```

In the format, above, *index-name* is the name of the new composite index. You are responsible for choosing *index-name*; you can choose any valid SAS column name not already in use in the table.[1] The *table-name* is followed by parentheses containing the list of columns that are to make up the composite index. Each *column-name* is separated from the next one by a comma.

Flexibility of Using the SQL Procedure to Create Indexes

As mentioned in the introduction to this chapter, the SQL procedure can be used to create indexes for existing SAS tables as well as for new ones. This makes the SQL procedure more flexible as an index-creating tool than either the INDEX data set option or the DATASETS Procedure. The INDEX data set option can only be used when creating indexes for new SAS data sets. The DATASETS procedure can only be used to create indexes for existing SAS data sets. The SQL procedure has the index-creating functionality of both of the other tools and can be used in many different ways.

You can use the SQL procedure to create the following:

- a simple index for an existing SAS table or for a new SAS table
- multiple simple indexes for an existing SAS table or for a new SAS table
- a composite index for an existing SAS table or for a new SAS table

---

[1] In the examples in this book, the author commonly creates composite index names from the full name of the variables that make up the composite index. For example, composite index COUNTRY_STATE uses the COUNTRY and STATE variables. This is a good naming convention and is not meant to imply that composite indexes must be named for their constituent variables. A composite index built from COUNTRY and STATE can just as easily be named CNTY_ST.

- multiple composite indexes for an existing SAS table or for a new SAS table
- combinations of simple and composite indexes for an existing SAS table or for a new SAS table

From this list, you can see that you can use the SQL procedure in any situation in which you need to create an index. The one exception is if you need to use the NOMISS option, which the SQL procedure does not support. Several of these situations are illustrated in the following examples.

Example 9.1: Creating a Simple Index for an Existing SAS Table

In this example, the SQL procedure is used to create a simple index on an existing SAS table:

```
proc sql;
    create unique index seqnum on indexlib.prodindx;
quit;
```

This code specifies that a simple index be built for the SEQNUM column in the INDEXLIB.PRODINDX SAS table. For this to execute correctly, the INDEXLIB.PRODINDX table must already exist and must contain a column named SEQNUM. Additionally, the values for SEQNUM must be unique for each row found in the INDEXLIB.PRODINDX table.

Here is the SAS log from executing the SQL procedure, above:

```
11   proc sql;
12   create unique index seqnum on indexlib.prodindx;
NOTE: Simple index seqnum has been defined.
13   quit;
NOTE: PROCEDURE SQL used:
      real time           28.40 seconds
      cpu time            3.90 seconds
```

The NOTE in the SAS log states that the "Simple index seqnum has been defined." This is your feedback that the index has been successfully created by the SQL procedure.

Here is what the "Alphabetic List of Indexes and Attributes" from a PROC CONTENTS listing of INDEXLIB.PRODINDX looks like after the index is built:

```
                    The CONTENTS Procedure

        -----Alphabetic List of Indexes and Attributes-----

                                              # of
                                 Unique      Unique
             #      Index        Option      Values
                               _____

             1      SEQNUM        YES        2304000
```

This is further proof that a simple index was created for column SEQNUM in SAS table INDEXLIB.PRODCOMP. You can see that the UNIQUE option is in effect for this index.

Example 9.2: Creating a Simple Index for a New SAS Table

This is an illustration of how a simple index can be formed within the SQL procedure when a table is created first:

```
proc sql;
   create table indexlib.prodindx as
   select * from indexlib.prodsale;
   create unique index seqnum on indexlib.prodindx;
quit;
```

In the example, table INDEXLIB.PRODINDX is to be created from table INDEXLIB.PRODSALE. After that, a new simple index, based on SEQNUM, is to be created for the new table.

This is what the SAS log for the execution of this SQL procedure looks like:

```
63    proc sql;
64    create table indexlib.prodindx as
65    select * from indexlib.prodsale;
NOTE: Table INDEXLIB.PRODINDX created, with 2304000 rows and 12
      columns.

66    create unique index seqnum on indexlib.prodindx;
NOTE: Simple index seqnum has been defined.
67    quit;
NOTE: PROCEDURE SQL used:
      real time                1:25.75
      cpu time                 6.03 seconds
```

The first NOTE indicates that table INDEXLIB.PRODINDX has been created. The second NOTE states that a simple index, based on SEQNUM, has been produced. This is a handy way of creating an index that you know will be used to process a table in subsequent invocations of the SQL procedure within a SAS program.

Example 9.3: Creating Multiple Simple Indexes for an Existing SAS Table

This execution of the SQL procedure creates multiple simple indexes for columns on an existing SAS data set:

```
proc sql;
   create unique index seqnum on indexlib.prodindx;
   create index county on indexlib.prodindx;
   create index state on indexlib.prodindx;
   create index year on indexlib.prodindx;
quit;
```

This code creates a simple index for the SEQNUM, COUNTY, STATE, and YEAR columns of the INDEXLIB.PRODINDX SAS table. Only the SEQNUM index has the UNIQUE option enabled; therefore, only unique values of SEQNUM may exist in the table.

The SAS log for the execution of the code looks like this:

```
105  proc sql;
106  create unique index seqnum on indexlib.prodindx;
NOTE: Simple index seqnum has been defined.
107  create index county on indexlib.prodindx;
NOTE: Simple index county has been defined.
108  create index state on indexlib.prodindx;
NOTE: Simple index state has been defined.
109  create index year on indexlib.prodindx;
NOTE: Simple index year has been defined.
110  quit;
NOTE: PROCEDURE SQL used:
      real time            1:55.36
      cpu time             17.14 seconds
```

The first four NOTES in the SAS log serve to verify that all four of the simple indexes have been successfully created for the INDEXLIB.PRODINDX table.

Example 9.4: Creating a Composite Index for an Existing SAS Table

In this example, a composite index is created for an existing SAS table:

```
proc sql;
   create index country_state on indexlib.prodcomp(country,
         state);
quit;
```

In this example, composite index COUNTRY_STATE is being created from columns COUNTRY and STATE for the INDEXLIB.PRODCOMP SAS table. The UNIQUE option is not used; therefore, duplicate combinations of COUNTRY/STATE may exist within the SAS table.

The log for the execution of the code looks like this:

```
147  proc sql;
148  create index country_state on indexlib.prodcomp(country, state);
NOTE: Composite index country_state has been defined.
149  quit;
NOTE: PROCEDURE SQL used:
      real time             1:08.37
      cpu time              5.54 seconds
```

The NOTE in the log reports that a composite index, named COUNTRY_STATE, has been defined for the SAS table.

A CONTENTS procedure listing for the INDEXLIB.PRODCOMP SAS table reports the following in the "Alphabetic List of Indexes and Attributes":

```
                      The CONTENTS Procedure

          -----Alphabetic List of Indexes and Attributes-----

                                    # of
                                   Unique
          #     Index              Values    Variables

          1     country_state        16      COUNTRY STATE
```

Because the UNIQUE option was not specified, the listing does not contain a column labeled Unique. Additionally, because the NOMISS option cannot be specified in the SQL procedure, the listing does not contain a column labeled Nomiss.

Example 9.5: Creating a Composite Index for a New SAS Table

This is an example of creating a composite index for a newly produced SAS table:

```
proc sql;
   create table indexlib.prodcomp as
   select * from indexlib.prodsale;
   create index country_state on indexlib.prodcomp(country,
                                                   state);
   quit;
```

In the example, above, SAS table INDEXLIB.PRODCOMP is created from table INDEXLIB.PRODSALE. Then composite COUNTRY_STATE is formed from the COUNTRY and STATE columns.

The SAS log for this example looks like this:

```
230  proc sql;
231  create table indexlib.prodcomp as
232  select * from indexlib.prodsale;
NOTE: Table INDEXLIB.PRODCOMP created, with 2304000 rows and 12
columns.

233  create index country_state on indexlib.prodcomp(country, state);
NOTE: Composite index country_state has been defined.
234  quit;
NOTE: PROCEDURE SQL used:
     real time          1:52.21
     cpu time           9.32 seconds
```

The first NOTE reports that the INDEXLIB.PRODCOMP table has been successfully created by the SQL procedure. The second NOTE states that the COUNTRY_STATE composite index has been effectively created by the procedure.

A CONTENTS procedure listing for the INDEXLIB.PRODCOMP SAS table will look the same as that in Example 9.4.

Example 9.6: Creating Multiple Composite Indexes for an Existing SAS Table

Multiple composite indexes may be created for an existing SAS table via the SQL procedure. Here is an example where three are created:

```
proc sql;
    create index country_state on indexlib.prodcomp(country,
                                                    state);
    create index year_and_quarter on indexlib.prodcomp(year,
                                                       quarter);
    create index state_product on indexlib.prodcomp(state,
                                                    product);
quit;
```

In this example, we are creating the COUNTRY_STATE composite index, built from COUNTRY and STATE; the YEAR_AND_QUARTER composite index, built from YEAR and QUARTER; and the STATE_PRODUCT composite index built from STATE and PRODUCT. All of these are being built for SAS table INDEXLIB.PRODCOMP.

Here is the log for this SQL procedure:

```
274  proc sql;
275  create index country_state on indexlib.prodcomp(country, state);
NOTE: Composite index country_state has been defined.
276  create index year_and_quarter on indexlib.prodcomp(year,
quarter);
NOTE: Composite index year_and_quarter has been defined.
277  create index state_product on indexlib.prodcomp(state, product);
NOTE: Composite index state_product has been defined.
278  quit;
NOTE: PROCEDURE SQL used:
      real time            1:36.64
      cpu time             16.78 seconds
```

The NOTEs in the SAS log indicate that each composite index has been successfully created.

Here is the "Alphabetic List of Indexes and Attributes" from a CONTENTS procedure listing:

```
                        The CONTENTS Procedure

               -----Alphabetic List of Indexes and Attributes-----

                                          # of
                                         Unique
               #     Index               Values    Variables

               1     country_state         16      COUNTRY STATE
               2     state_product         64      STATE  PRODUCT
               3     year_and_quarter      56      YEAR  QUARTER
```

All three composite indexes and their attributes appear in the CONTENTS listing.

Summary

The SQL procedure can be used to create indexes for both existing and new SAS tables. You can create simple indexes based on a single-table column or composite indexes built from two or more columns. You may also create any combination of simple and/or composite indexes for an existing SAS table, or for a new SAS table, in the same SQL procedure. If you are more comfortable with SQL programming than with traditional SAS DATA step and procedure step programming, you will find creating SAS indexes no trouble at all.

Chapter 10

Using Indexes with a WHERE Expression

Introduction

The WHERE expression can be used to select a subset of observations from a SAS data set that is being used as input to a DATA step or a PROC step. WHERE expressions can be found in WHERE statements in DATA and PROC steps, in the WHERE data set option used in DATA and PROC steps, and in the WHERE clause used in the SQL procedure.

The general format of the WHERE expression is as follows:

WHERE *where-expression*;

In the WHERE statement, WHERE data set option, and WHERE clause, *where-expression* can be any valid SAS language arithmetic or logical expression. Only thirteen forms of the WHERE expression enable SAS to use an existing simple index. They are described in the section, "Rules for SAS Using a Simple Index," later in this chapter. There are four conditions that must be met for SAS to use a composite index. They are discussed in the section, "Rules for SAS Using Compound Index Optimization," later in this chapter.

Here are two examples of WHERE expressions in DATA steps:

```
data Florida;
    set indexlib.prodindx(where=(state='Florida'));
run;


data Florida;
    set indexlib.prodindx;

    where state = 'Florida';

run;
```

Both of the DATA steps in this example produce the same results. The only difference between them is the placement of the WHERE expression. The first DATA step uses a WHERE data set option, while the second uses a WHERE statement. If SAS data set INDEXLIB.PRODINDX contains a simple index built from the STATE variable, SAS would use it to subset the data set and return all observations where STATE is equal to Florida for both DATA steps.

Here are two examples of using WHERE expressions in SAS procedures:

```
proc sort in=indexlib.prodindx(where=(state='Florida'))
   out=Florida;
   by  product;
run;

proc summary nway data=indexlib.prodindx;
   class product;
   var actual predict;
   where state='Florida';
   output out=Florida sum=;
run;
```

In both procedures, the WHERE expression is used to make sure that only observations with STATE equal to Florida are actually input to the procedure. PROC SORT uses the WHERE data set option; PROC SUMMARY uses the WHERE statement. The selected observations are then either sorted or summarized by the respective procedures above. If there is an index for the variable STATE, SAS considers using it to optimize WHERE expression processing for both of the procedures.

This final example illustrates the WHERE clause:

```
proc sql;
   create table Florida as
   select * from indexlib.prodindx
   where state eq 'Florida';
quit;
```

In the example, the WHERE clause is used by PROC SQL to select only observations from table INDEXLIB.PRODINDX where STATE is equal to Florida. PROC SQL uses indexes to optimize WHERE clauses when the conditions for using them are right. Therefore, the example code might use an index to return the subset of observations where STATE equals Florida if an index exists for the STATE column in the INDEXLIB.PRODINDX table.

When a WHERE expression contains index key variables, SAS investigates the possibility of optimizing resource overhead by using an index. SAS decides which index, if any, can be used by asking the following questions:

1. In the WHERE expression, are any of the variables key variables in a simple index?

2. In the WHERE expression, are any of the variables the first key variable in a composite index?

3. Would using an index return a subset of observations that fulfills the selection criteria specified in the WHERE expression?

4. Given the estimated number of observations that would be returned via an index, would using the index be more efficient than sequentially reading the entire data set?

When the answers to questions 1, 3, and 4 are "yes," SAS utilizes a simple index to subset the data. When the answers to questions 2, 3, and 4 are "yes," SAS uses a composite index to subset the data. If more than one index satisfies those conditions, SAS selects the index that returns the smallest number of observations. If no indexes satisfy the conditions (1, 3, and 4 for a simple index; or 2, 3, and 4 for a composite index), the data set is read sequentially.

SAS does not use a simple or composite index to optimize a WHERE expression in cases where that expression conflicts with a BY statement specified in the same DATA step or procedure. This is explained in more detail in the section "Conflicts between the BY Statement and the WHERE Expression," found in Chapter 11, "Using Indexes with a BY Statement."

Rules for SAS Using a Simple Index

As mentioned earlier, there are thirteen specific forms of the WHERE expression that allow SAS to use an existing simple index. If you do not use any one of these forms in your WHERE expression, then SAS *absolutely cannot* exploit an existing simple index and optimize your data retrieval. The thirteen forms are as follows:

1. Normal relational operators

   ```
   where year > 2000;

   where year gt 2000;
   ```

2. Normal relational operators with NOT

   ```
   where actual ^> predict;

   where actual not gt predict;
   ```

3. CONTAINS operator

   ```
   where state contains 'North';
   ```

4. Comparison operator with the colon modifier

   ```
   where state =: 'North';
   ```

5. TRIM function

```
where trim(state) = 'North Carolina'
```

6. Range conditions with upper and lower bounds or range conditions that use the BETWEEN-AND operator

```
where 1999 < year < 2005;
```

```
where year between 1999 and 2005;
```

7. Pattern-matching operators LIKE and NOT LIKE

```
where state like 'North %';
```

```
where country like '%Republic%';
```

8. IS MISSING and IS NULL operators

```
where county is missing;
```

```
where county is null;
```

9. SUBSTR function when it is of the form

```
where substr(argument,position,<n>) = 'value';
```

In this substring form, the following must be true for an index to be used:

1. The value of *position* must be 1.

2. The value of *<n>* must be less than or equal to the length of *argument*.

3. The value of *<n>* must be equal to the length of *value*

Here is an example using these rules:

```
where substr(state,1,5) = 'North';
```

10. IN operator

```
where product in ('BED', 'CHAIR');
```

11. Series of OR operations using the same index variable

```
where product = 'BED' or product = 'CHAIR' or
      product = 'DESK';
```

12. Equal to truncated string operator in PROC SQL

```
where state eqt 'New';
```

13. Any WHERE clause composed of two or more of the above ten forms connected via AND

```
where (product in('BED', 'CHAIR')) and (county is missing);
```

You can find more information on the specifics of WHERE expressions by consulting the current version of the *SAS Language Reference: Dictionary* or SAS online documentation.

Rules for SAS Using Compound Index Optimization

SAS uses what is known as *compound optimization* to use a composite index in a WHERE expression. Compound optimization may occur when several variables of a composite index are specified in a WHERE expression and are joined together with logical operators such as AND or OR. If the conditions are right, then SAS uses compound optimization to exploit the composite index in order to subset the data. The following conditions must be true for compound optimization to occur:

1. At least the first two key variables in the composite index must be used in the WHERE condition[1]:

```
where country eq 'U.S.A' and state eq 'Texas' and year
lt 2005;
```

---

[1] SAS compares the WHERE variables, one-by-one, from left-to-right, with the variables in an existing composite index. SAS stops when it reaches the end of the shortest list of matching variables. If two or more of the WHERE variables match two or more of the variables in the composite index, then SAS may use that composite index.

2. The conditions are connected using the AND logical operator:

```
where country eq 'U.S.A' and state eq 'Texas';
```

3. Any conditions using the OR logical operator must specify the same variable and use the EQ operator:

```
where country eq 'U.S.A' and (state eq 'Florida' or state
eq 'Texas');
```

4. At least one condition must be the EQ or IN operator:

```
where country eq 'U.S.A' and state in('Florida', 'Texas');
```

In these examples assume that composite index COUNTRY_STATE, composed of COUNTRY and STATE, was built for SAS data set INDEXLIB.PRODINDX. SAS automatically recognizes that the conditions are right for using compound optimization and uses the COUNTRY_STATE composite index to optimize WHERE expression processing.

You may recall that you, the programmer, are responsible for providing a name for a composite index. Though a composite index retains the specific name that you gave it, that name can *never* be used in a WHERE expression. For example, consider the aforementioned composite index COUNTRY_STATE used *incorrectly* in the following DATA step code:

```
data Florida;
   set indexlib.prodindx;

   where country_state = 'U.S.A.Florida';

run;
```

The errant code in this example produces this SAS error message:

```
ERROR: Variable country_state is not on file INDEXLIB.PRODINDX.
```

The error is generated because COUNTRY_STATE is the name of a composite index and not a variable name. SAS data set INDEXLIB.PRODINDX does not know anything about a variable named COUNTRY_STATE. Therefore, the DATA step is terminated with a SAS error. Keep in mind that composite index names may never be used in WHERE expressions.

Example 10.1: Using a WHERE Expression in a DATA Step with a Simple Index

This is an example of a WHERE expression in a DATA step using a simple index.

```
options msglevel=I;
data canada_sales;
   set  indexlib.prodindx;

   where state in('British Columbia', 'Ontaria', 'Quebec',
      'Saskatchewan');

run;
```

This example uses simple index WHERE expression form #10 discussed in the previous section, "Rules for SAS Using a Simple Index." It creates data set CANADA_SALES from observations in INDEXLIB.PRODINDX that have specific values for STATE. Here is the SAS log generated from executing this DATA step:

```
22    options msglevel=I;
23    data canada_sales;
24    set  indexlib.prodindx;
25
26    where state in('British Columbia', 'Ontaria', 'Quebec',
      'Saskatchewan');
INFO: Index STATE selected for WHERE clause optimization.
27
28    run;

NOTE: There were 345600 observations read from the data set
      INDEXLIB.PRODINDX.
      WHERE state in ('British Columbia', 'Ontaria', 'Quebec',
      'Saskatchewan');
NOTE: The data set WORK.CANADA_SALES has 345600 observations and
      12 variables.
NOTE: DATA statement used:
      real time           8.26 seconds
      cpu time            0.81 seconds
```

Because there is a simple index built for variable STATE, SAS uses it. You can see the informational note (INFO), "Index STATE selected for WHERE clause optimization," in the SAS log. The combination of having a SAS index based on STATE, and using a proper form of the WHERE expression, allows SAS to use the index to return the subset.

Example 10.2: Using a WHERE Expression in a DATA Step with a Composite Index

In the following example, a WHERE expression is used in a DATA step to precipitate compound optimization of a composite index.

```
options msglevel=I;
data sample1;
   set  indexlib.prodcomp;

   where country eq "U.S.A." and (state = "Florida" or state =
      "Texas");

run;
```

The WHERE clause adheres to condition #3 for compound optimization as discussed in the section "Rules for SAS Using Compound Index Optimization," above. Therefore, SAS determines whether there is a composite index available that meets the specified criteria. This is the SAS log generated by this example:

```
28    options msglevel=I;
29    data sample1;
30    set  indexlib.prodcomp;
31
32    where country eq "U.S.A." and (state = "Florida" or state
      = "Texas");
INFO: Index country_state selected for WHERE clause optimization.
33
34    run;


NOTE: There were 230400 observations read from the data set
      INDEXLIB.PRODCOMP.
      WHERE (country='U.S.A.') and state in ('Florida',
      'Texas');
```

(continued on next page)

(continued)

```
NOTE: The data set WORK.SAMPLE1 has 230400 observations and 12
      variables.
NOTE: DATA statement used:
      real time             3.50 seconds
      cpu time              0.43 seconds
```

The SAS log clearly states that index COUNTRY_STATE was used for WHERE clause optimization. There is nothing in the INFO message indicating that COUNTRY_STATE is a composite index, though it is in this example. The fact that COUNTRY_STATE suddenly appears in the log though it is not found in the WHERE statement is a clear sign that it is a composite index.

Example 10.3: Using a WHERE Expression in a PROC Step with a Simple Index

Here is an example of a SAS procedure using a WHERE data set option to exploit a simple index and return observations that have a range of values.

```
proc summary nway data=indexlib.prodindx(where=(1999 < year <
      2004));
      class product;
      var actual predict;
output out=sales2000_2003 sum=;
run;
```

In the example, the WHERE data set option is used to feed only the observations where YEAR is between 1999 and 2004 (2000, 2001, 2002, and 2003) directly into PROC SUMMARY. Because the WHERE expression uses simple index form #6 discussed in the section "Rules for SAS Using a Simple Index," SAS uses the simple index built for variable YEAR. The log for executing this procedure looks like this:

```
42    proc summary nway data=indexlib.prodindx(where=(1999 <
      year < 2004));
INFO: Index YEAR selected for WHERE clause optimization.
43        class product;
44        var actual predict;
45    output out=sales2000_2003 sum=;
46    run;
```

(continued on next page)

(continued)

```
NOTE: There were 576000 observations read from the data set
      INDEXLIB.PRODINDX.
      WHERE ((year>1999 and year<2004));
NOTE: The data set WORK.SALES2000_2003 has 4 observations and 5
      variables.
NOTE: PROCEDURE SUMMARY used:
      real time          0.82 seconds
      cpu time           0.82 seconds
```

The INFO note in the SAS log reports that the YEAR index was used. Using the index to select only the required observations from INDEXLIB.PRODINDX and to send them into PROC SUMMARY saves computer resources and program execution time.

Example 10.4: Using a WHERE Expression in a PROC Step with a Composite Index

Composite indexes can be effectively used to improve the performance of SAS procedures. In this example, observations from SAS data set INDEXLIB.PRODCOMP are subset through the use of an index and passed to PROC UNIVARIATE:

```
proc univariate data=indexlib.prodcomp
   (where=(year = 2005 and quarter = 1 and actual > 1000));
run;
```

This WHERE expression adheres to compound optimization condition #1, discussed in the section "Rules for SAS Using Compound Index Optimization." There is a composite index, named YEAR_AND_QUARTER, that was constructed from the YEAR and QUARTER variables in SAS data set INDEXLIB.PRODCOMP. Because both variables are the first two listed in the WHERE expression, SAS can use the YEAR_AND_QUARTER composite index to fetch observations. Once it has each observation in computer memory, SAS determines if the final condition (ACTUAL > 1000) is true. If so, it passes the observation to PROC UNIVARIATE; if not, the observation is discarded.

Here is the SAS log from this execution of PROC UNIVARIATE:

```
56      proc univariate data=indexlib.prodcomp(where=(year = 2005 and
        quarter = 1 and actual >
56 ! 1000));
INFO: Index year_and_quarter selected for WHERE clause optimization.
57      run;


NOTE: PROCEDURE UNIVARIATE used:
        real time           2.51 seconds
        cpu time            0.10 seconds
```

The INFO note in the SAS log provides assurance that the YEAR_AND_QUARTER composite index was indeed used by PROC UNIVARIATE.

Example 10.5: Using a WHERE Expression in PROC SQL with a Simple Index

PROC SQL exploits a simple index through a WHERE expression whenever it can. In this example, a new table named BED_SALES is being created from a subset of rows found in table INDEXLIB.PRODINDX. The subset is based on the value "BED" in column PRODUCT.

```
proc sql;
    create table bed_sales as
    select * from indexlib.prodindx
    where product eq "BED";
quit;
```

In this example, PROC SQL uses simple index WHERE expression form #1 discussed in the section, *"Rules for SAS Using a Simple Index."* Using the WHERE clause, SAS exploits a simple index created for the PRODUCT column in the INDEXLIB.PRODINDX table.

This is what the SAS log looks like:

```
78    proc sql;
79    create table bed_sales as
80    select * from indexlib.prodindx
81    where product eq "BED";
INFO: Index PRODUCT selected for WHERE clause optimization.
NOTE: Table WORK.BED_SALES created, with 576000 rows and 12 columns.

82    quit;
NOTE: PROCEDURE SQL used:
      real time            2.53 seconds
      cpu time             1.01 seconds
```

The SAS log has the reassuring INFO note that the PRODUCT index was used for WHERE clause optimization.

Example 10.6: Using a WHERE Expression in PROC SQL with a Composite Index

PROC SQL also engages in compound optimization when it has the opportunity to take advantage of a composite index in a WHERE expression. Here is a simple example:

```
proc sql;
   create table first_half_2005 as
   select * from indexlib.prodcomp
   where year eq 2005 and quarter in(1, 2);
quit;
```

The SQL code above uses a WHERE clause that specifies criteria for the values of the YEAR and QUARTER columns. Table INDEXLIB.PRODCOMP has composite index YEAR_AND_QUARTER; SAS uses that index to return the subset rows to the new table, FIRST_HALF_2005.

```
93    proc sql;
94    create table first_half_2005 as
95    select * from indexlib.prodcomp
96    where year eq 2005 and quarter in(1, 2);
INFO: Index year_and_quarter selected for WHERE clause optimization.
NOTE: Table WORK.FIRST_HALF_2005 created, with 57600 rows and 12
      columns.

97    quit;
NOTE: PROCEDURE SQL used:
      real time            1.73 seconds
      cpu time             0.18 seconds
```

The WHERE expression conformed to compound optimization condition #2, discussed in the section "Rules for SAS Using Compound Index Optimization." That is why SAS used the composite index and noted it in the INFO message in the SAS log.

Summary

WHERE expressions can be used to select a subset of observations from an indexed SAS data set. WHERE expressions can be found in WHERE statements in DATA and PROC steps, in WHERE data set options in DATA and PROC steps, and in WHERE clauses in PROC SQL. If the WHERE expression satisfies one of the thirteen rules for using a simple index and an appropriate index is available, SAS may use it to optimize WHERE expression processing. Similarly, if a WHERE expression uses one of the four rules for compound index optimization and there is an appropriate index available, SAS may decide to use that index. WHERE expressions that do not meet the rules for simple and compound index optimization cannot cause SAS to use an index.

Chapter 11

Using Indexes with a BY Statement

Introduction

The BY statement is one of the four SAS statements that you may use to take advantage of SAS indexes. BY statements are used to return observations from a SAS data set in a specified sort order. When indexes exist for a data set accessed with a BY statement *and the data is not sorted in BY statement variable order*, SAS automatically determines if one of the indexes can be used. If an index can be used, then SAS uses it to return observations in ascending index key value sequence. As a result, you end up with output data that is sorted in order of the variables listed in the BY statement.

Where two or more indexes satisfy a BY statement's index selection criteria, SAS chooses the index that provides ordering for the largest number of BY variables. The observations are then returned in ascending BY variable value order using that index.

The general format of the BY statement is as follows:

BY <descending> VARLIST <notsorted>;

In the form above, VARLIST is a list of one or more data set variables that are to be used to order the observations being returned. The DESCENDING option states that the observations are to be returned in descending VARLIST variable value order. The NOTSORTED option declares that observations with the same VARLIST BY values are to be grouped together within the data set. But within those groups the observations are not sorted into either ascending or descending order.

SAS *will not* consider using an index to perform BY statement processing if any of the following conditions are true:

- The data is already sorted in descending order of the variables in the BY statement
- The DESCENDING option is used in the BY statement.
- The NOTSORTED option is used in the BY statement.
- The NOMISS option was used when the data set's indexes were created. You can read about the NOMISS option in the "Data Step and Procedure Options" section of Chapter 5, "Index-Related Options."

NOTE: Do not confuse the BY statement, used in DATA and PROC steps, with the ORDER BY statement used in PROC SQL. With PROC SQL SAS does not optimize the ORDER BY statement by using indexes. Consequently, only a BY statement in a DATA or PROC step can take advantage of SAS indexes.

SAS uses different rules to determine if it can use an index with a BY statement for simple and for composite indexes. The following sections describe these rules.

Rules for SAS Using a Simple Index

SAS uses a simple index to facilitate BY statement processing when either of the following conditions is true:

- VARLIST has a single variable that is the key variable in a simple index.
- VARLIST has two or more variables. The *first* variable in VARLIST is the key variable in a simple index, *and* the other VARLIST variables are in ascending sort sequence within the indexed SAS data set.

To understand the second condition, consider a SAS data set with a simple index created for the variable STATE. If a BY statement reads BY STATE PRODUCT, SAS attempts to use the STATE index. However, if the data is not sorted into ascending PRODUCT order within each STATE, SAS produces an error message that looks something like this:

```
ERROR: Data set INDEXLIB.PRODINDX is not sorted in ascending
       sequence. The current by-group has Product = CHAIR and
       the next by-group has PRODUCT = BED.
```

You should be cautious when attempting to use a simple index for BY processing when you have multiple variables in the BY statement. If the data is not ordered in ascending sequential order of the subsequent, non-index variables, you will get a SAS error.

Rules for SAS Using a Composite Index

SAS uses a composite index to facilitate BY statement processing when either of the following conditions is true:

- VARLIST is a single variable that is the *first* key variable in a composite index.
- VARLIST is made up of two or more variables that match the first two or more key variables in a composite index. If there are additional variables in VARLIST that do not match the index variables, they must be in ascending sort sequence within the indexed SAS data set.

In the second condition described above, SAS compares the BY variables, one by one from left to right, with the variables in an existing composite index. (Note that SAS is comparing the variable names, not the variable values.) SAS stops when it reaches the end of the shortest list of matching variables. If several of the BY variables match several of the variables in the composite index, then that composite index may be used.

For example, consider a composite index built from COUNTRY/STATE/PRODUCT and a BY statement that reads:

```
by country state year;
```

SAS would match the first two variables in the BY statement with the first two variables in the composite index. If the data within COUNTRY/STATE was in ascending order by YEAR, then SAS would use the composite index to order the observations.

Using an Index Via a BY Statement to Avoid a Sort

You can use a BY statement to avoid having to sort your data to an output data set. Sometimes using an index is more efficient, but sometimes it is not. If there is no WHERE expression to subset the data, SAS returns the entire data set by first going to the index for each observation. This is likely to be more computer-resource intensive and slower than a PROC SORT. The fact that observations are returned in ascending order is a side effect, not a design goal for SAS indexes. Using an index to supply the BY statement ordering is a convenience and may be faster than a SORT under certain circumstances, especially when a WHERE expression is used to subset the amount of data read from the indexed SAS data set.

Whether using an index via a BY statement is more efficient than a sort depends on the characteristics of the particular SAS data set and the index involved. Issues such as the size of the SAS data set, the size of the index, the data set page size, the index file page size, the size of a subset produced via a WHERE expression (if applicable), and the number of BY variables are all factors. It is difficult to formulate a rule of thumb. Therefore, you should consider experimenting to determine what is the most efficient way to order observations output from your SAS data sets in a particular BY sequence.

Here is an example where using an index to facilitate BY statement processing is actually faster than performing a sort:

```
proc sort data=indexlib.prodindx out=prodindx;
    by county;
run;

proc print data=prodindx noobs;
    by county;
    id county;
    var county daymonyr prodtype predict actual;
    title1 "All Observations By county";
run;
```

In the example, SAS data set INDEXLIB.PRODINDX is sorted by COUNTY and output to a temporary SAS data set. Then, PROC PRINT is used to create a report. The data set was sorted to a temporary SAS data set to avoid having to re-sort INDEXLIB.PRODINDX just for this particular report. However, the report needed to be created in COUNTY order.

Here is the SAS log from executing the program:

```
110   proc sort data=indexlib.prodindx out=prodindx;
111       by county;
112   run;


NOTE: SAS sort was used.
NOTE: There were 2304000 observations read from the data set
      INDEXLIB.PRODINDX.
NOTE: The data set WORK.PRODINDX has 2304000 observations and 12
      variables.
NOTE: PROCEDURE SORT used:
      real time            4:21.56
      user cpu time        3.26 seconds
      system cpu time      7.18 seconds
      Memory                         2166k
```

(continued on next page)

(continued)

```
113
114  proc print data=prodindx noobs;
115       by county;
116       id county;
117  var county daymonyr prodtype predict actual;
118  title1 "All Observations By county";
119  run;


NOTE: There were 2304000 observations read from the data set
      WORK.PRODINDX.
NOTE: PROCEDURE PRINT used:
      real time            22.76 seconds
      user cpu time        15.74 seconds
      system cpu time      0.76 seconds
      Memory                          136k
```

You can see that PROC SORT and PROC PRINT together took about 4:44 minutes of real time, 19 seconds of user CPU time, 8 seconds of system CPU time, and 2302 kilobytes of memory. In general terms, that is not a lot of computer resources. However, the sort is not necessary, considering that INDEXLIB.PRODINDX is an indexed SAS data set.

The sort could be avoided by exploiting the simple index built on COUNTY by using the BY statement in PROC PRINT:

```
proc print data=indexlib.prodindx noobs;
     by county;
     id county;
     var county daymonyr prodtype predict actual;
     title1 "All Observations By county";
run;
```

The SAS log for this simplified program looks like this:

```
76    proc print data=indexlib.prodindx noobs;
77        by county;
INFO: Index COUNTY selected for BY clause processing.
NOTE: An index was selected to execute the BY statement.
      The observations will be returned in index order rather than
      in physical order.  The
      selected index is for the variable(s):
 COUNTY
78        id county;
79    var county daymonyr prodtype predict actual;
80    title1 "All Observations By county";
81    run;

NOTE: There were 2304000 observations read from the data set
      INDEXLIB.PRODINDX.
NOTE: PROCEDURE PRINT used:
      real time              57.68 seconds
      user cpu time          17.62 seconds
      system cpu time        1.74 seconds
      Memory                             148k
```

This program used about 58 seconds of real time, 18 seconds of user CPU time, 2 seconds of system CPU time, and 148 kilobytes of memory.

It may be more efficient to use an existing index when its key variables coincide with the BY variables that you are going to use in a DATA or PROC step. This can help you to eliminate unnecessary SORT procedures, slimming down your SAS programs and diminishing the computer resources that they consume when executing.

Conflicts between the BY Statement and the WHERE Expression

There are instances when a BY statement's attempt to use an index can come into conflict with a WHERE expression's attempt. This conflict can happen when observations (returned via an index with a WHERE expression) violate the order specified in a BY statement. When a DATA or a PROC step specifies both a BY statement and a WHERE expression, SAS looks for an index that can satisfy the requirements of both. If one cannot be found, the BY statement takes precedence and an index that facilitates BY statement processing is used.

In this example, the BY and WHERE expressions do not come into conflict:

```
data canada;
set  indexlib.prodcomp;
where country='Canada' and state in('British Columbia',
                'Ontario', 'Quebec', 'Saskatchewan');
    by country state;
run;
```

The composite index COUNTRY_STATE satisfies both the WHERE statement and the BY statement. SAS then uses that index to subset the data and to order the variables in the new CANADA SAS data set. Here is the SAS log from executing the DATA step, above:

```
44    data canada;
45    set  indexlib.prodcomp;
46    where country='Canada' and state in('British Columbia',
   ! 'Ontario', 'Quebec', 'Saskatchewan');
INFO: Index country_state selected for WHERE clause
      optimization.
47       by country state;
48    run;


INFO: Index country_state selected for BY clause processing.
NOTE: There were 345600 observations read from the data set
      INDEXLIB.PRODCOMP.
      WHERE (country='Canada') and state in ('British Columbia',
      'Ontario', 'Quebec',
      'Saskatchewan');
NOTE: The data set WORK.EXTRACT has 345600 observations and 12
      variables.
NOTE: DATA statement used:
      real time             5.78 seconds
      cpu time              0.46 seconds
```

The SAS log has an INFO note saying that the WHERE statement used index COUNTRY_STATE for its optimization and an INFO note saying that the BY statement used COUNTRY_STATE. Therefore, there is no conflict between the two statements, and both use the same composite index.

The WHERE and BY statements *do* conflict in this next example:

```
data extract;
   set  indexlib.prodcomp;
   where year = 2000 and quarter = 1;
   by country state;
run;
```

The INDEXLIB.PRODCOMP SAS data set has a composite index named YEAR_AND_QUARTER that can satisfy the WHERE expression and a composite index named COUNTRY_STATE that can satisfy the BY statement. But the order of the observations returned by the YEAR_AND_QUARTER index conflicts with the order specified in the BY statement. Therefore, that index is not used. Take a look at the SAS log for this DATA step:

```
36    data canada;
37    set  indexlib.prodcomp;
38    where year = 2000 and quarter = 1;
INFO: Index year_and_quarter selected for WHERE clause
      optimization.
39       by country state;
40    run;


INFO: Use of index year_and_quarter for WHERE clause
      optimization cancelled.
INFO: Index country_state selected for BY clause processing.
NOTE: There were 28800 observations read from the data set
      INDEXLIB.PRODCOMP.
      WHERE (year=2000) and (quarter=1);
NOTE: The data set WORK.EXTRACT has 28800 observations and 12
      variables.
NOTE: DATA statement used:
      real time          45.90 seconds
      cpu time            2.65 seconds
```

You can see that SAS originally selects the YEAR_AND_QUARTER composite index to optimize the WHERE expression. However, when SAS finally registers the conflict with the BY statement's needs, it cancels the use of that index. The BY statement takes precedence over the WHERE statement when it comes to exploiting the available indexes.

The point of this discussion is that you must be careful when you are using a BY statement with a WHERE expression to exploit SAS indexes. It is not something that should be avoided. You merely need to understand the rules and code your SAS programs accordingly. Exercising caution ensures that the use of one does not cancel out the use of the other.

Example 11.1: Using a BY Statement in a DATA Step to Exploit a Simple Index

This example uses a BY statement in a DATA step to exploit a simple index:

```
data canada;
    set indexlib.prodindx(where=(state in('British Columbia'
                                          'Ontario' 'Quebec'
                                          'Saskatchewan')));
        by state;
run;
```

The DATA step creates data set CANADA by extracting observations from INDEXLIB.PRODINDX that match the WHERE clause criteria. Because there is a simple index based on STATE, SAS uses it in the WHERE and BY statements and outputs observations to the CANADA data set in ascending STATE value sequence. Consequently, the new CANADA SAS data set is sorted into STATE order.

SAS used the STATE index for BY statement processing because of the following:

- The INDEXLIB.PRODINDX data set is not already sorted by STATE.
- Neither the DESCENDING nor NOTSORTED options were used in the BY statement.
- The STATE index was not created with the NOMISS option.

Here is the SAS log for this DATA step:

```
3    data canada;
4    set  indexlib.prodindx(where=(state in('British Columbia'
  !                                         'Ontario' 'Quebec'
  !                                         'Saskatchewan')));
INFO: Index STATE selected for WHERE clause optimization.
5          by state;
6    run;


INFO: Index STATE selected for BY clause processing.
NOTE: There were 460800 observations read from the data set
      INDEXLIB.PRODINDX.
      WHERE state in ('British Columbia', 'Ontario', 'Quebec',
      'Saskatchewan');
NOTE: The data set WORK.CANADA has 460800 observations and 12
      variables.
NOTE: DATA statement used:
      real time            14.95 seconds
      user cpu time        0.71 seconds
      system cpu time      0.35 seconds
      Memory                            181k
```

In the SAS log, the second INFO statement states that the STATE index was selected for BY clause processing. This affirms that SAS exploited this simple index.

Example 11.2: Using a BY Statement in a DATA Step to Exploit a Composite Index

Here is an example of a DATA step that uses a BY statement to employ a composite index.

```
data newyears;
set  indexlib.prodcomp;
        by year;
run;
```

SAS data set INDEXLIB.PRODCOMP has a composite index named YEAR_AND_QUARTER that is built from the YEAR and QUARTER variables. The BY statement specifies that data be returned from INDEXLIB.PRODCOMP ordered by YEAR, which is the first variable in the composite index. Therefore, SAS uses the YEAR_AND_QUARTER composite index to build the NEWYEARS SAS data set with observations ordered by ascending YEAR value.

In this example, SAS was able to use the YEAR_AND_QUARTER composite index to facilitate BY statement processing because of the following:

- The INDEXLIB.PRODCOMP data set is not already sorted by YEAR.

- The YEAR_AND_QUARTER composite index exists, and the first variable in the index matches the first variable in the BY statement.

- Neither the DESCENDING nor NOTSORTED options were used in the BY statement.

- The YEAR_AND_QUARTER index was not created with the NOMISS option enabled.

This is the SAS log for the DATA step:

```
36    data newyears;
37    set  indexlib.prodcomp;
38           by year;
39    run;


INFO: Index year_and_quarter selected for BY clause processing.
NOTE: There were 2304000 observations read from the data set
      INDEXLIB.PRODCOMP.
NOTE: The data set WORK.NEWYEARS has 2304000 observations and 12
      variables.
NOTE: DATA statement used:
      real time            1:18.68
      user cpu time        3.12 seconds
      system cpu time      1.54 seconds
      Memory                        173k
```

The INFO message in the log clearly states that SAS selected the index YEAR_AND_QUARTER for BY clause processing. Thus, you do not need to have every variable in a composite index specified in a BY statement for that composite index to be utilized. You must simply have the first one or more variables in the BY statement match the first one or more variables in the composite index.

Example 11.3: Using a BY Statement in a PROC Step to Exploit a Simple Index

BY statements can be used in SAS procedures to facilitate the use of simple indexes. This is an example of using a BY statement to provide data to PROC RANK.

```
proc rank data=indexlib.prodindx(where=(year between 2000 and
                                        2005))
          out=studyears;
    by year;
    var    year    actual;
    ranks  yearank actualrank;
run;
```

In this example, the RANK procedure is being fed observations with a year value between 2000 and 2005 from SAS data set INDEXLIB.PRODINDX. The BY statement causes SAS to use the YEAR index to pass those observations to the RANK procedure in ascending YEAR value order.

SAS is able to use the YEAR index because of the following:

- The INDEXLIB.PRODINDX data set is not already sorted by YEAR.
- Neither the DESCENDING nor NOTSORTED options were used in the BY statement.
- The YEAR index was not created with the NOMISS option.

The log for this program looks like this:

```
135  proc rank data=indexlib.prodindx(where=(year between 2000 and
                                             2005))
136             out=studyears;
INFO: Index YEAR selected for WHERE clause optimization.
137     by year;
INFO: Index YEAR selected for BY clause processing.
NOTE: An index was selected to execute the BY statement.
      The observations will be returned in index order rather than
      in physical order.  The selected index is for the variable(s):
YEAR
```

(continued on next page)

(continued)

```
138        var    year    actual;
139        ranks  yearank actualrank;
140     run;


NOTE: There were 806400 observations read from the data set
      INDEXLIB.PRODINDX.
      WHERE ((year>=2000 and year<=2005));
NOTE: The data set WORK.STUDYEARS has 806400 observations and 14
      variables.
NOTE: PROCEDURE RANK used:
      real time          16.01 seconds
      user cpu time      6.49 seconds
      system cpu time    0.84 seconds
      Memory                        5554k
```

The SAS log has both an INFO and a NOTE message reporting on the use of the YEAR index. The BY statement's use of the index to order input variables is more efficient than having the RANK statement sort them once it has read them all from the INDEXLIB.PRODINDX SAS data set.

Example 11.4: Using a BY Statement in a PROC Step to Exploit a Composite Index

This PROC PRINT uses a composite index for BY statement processing.

```
proc print data=indexlib.prodcomp;
     by state product;
     var   state product daymonyr predict actual;
     sum                 daymonyr predict actual;
run;
```

This program prints all observations from the INDEXLIB.PRODCOMP SAS data set in ascending STATE/PRODUCT order because of the variables in the BY statement. The BY statement makes use of the STATE_PRODUCT composite index, which is built from the STATE and PRODUCT variables. It does so because of the following:

- The INDEXLIB.PRODCOMP data set is not already sorted in STATE/PRODUCT order.

- The STATE_PRODUCT index exists and has the same order of variables as the BY statement.

- Neither the DESCENDING nor NOTSORTED options are used in the BY statement.

- The STATE_PRODUCT index was not created with the NOMISS option.

Consider the log for this SAS procedure:

```
44    proc print data=indexlib.prodcomp;
45        by state product;
INFO: Index state_product selected for BY clause processing.
NOTE: An index was selected to execute the BY statement.
      The observations will be returned in index order rather than
      in physical order.  The selected index is for the variable(s):
 STATE
 PRODUCT
46        var  state product daymonyr predict actual;
47        sum                daymonyr predict actual;
48     run;


NOTE: There were 2304000 observations read from the data set
      INDEXLIB.PRODCOMP.
NOTE: PROCEDURE PRINT used:
      real time           1:13.54
      user cpu time       20.04 seconds
      system cpu time     2.15 seconds
      Memory                         175k
```

The SAS log has an INFO message stating that the STATE_PRODUCT index was selected for BY clause processing. There is a second NOTE statement that describes the use of the index to return observations in index order rather than physical order for the variables STATE and PRODUCT. Consequently, the report that is output from PROC PRINT is *sorted* into ascending order of STATE and PRODUCT even though the INDEXLIB.PRODCOMP SAS data set is not sorted by STATE and PRODUCT. If the STATE_PRODUCT composite index had not existed for that data set, SAS would have produced an error for the use of that particular BY statement because the data set is not stored in STATE and/or PRODUCT order.

Summary

BY statements can use indexes to return observations from SAS data sets in a specified sort order. They may be used in a DATA step or in a SAS procedure. SAS considers using an index to facilitate BY statement processing when the

- data is not already sorted in descending order of the variables in the BY statement
- DESCENDING and NOTSORTED options are not used in the BY statement
- NOMISS option was not used when the index was created.

When these conditions are true and SAS can use an index, the result is output data that is sorted in order of the variables listed in the BY statement.

Returning observations using a BY statement and an index may not be as efficient as using the SORT procedure to order the observations. This is more likely to be the case when the entire SAS data set is to be input, ordered in a particular BY variable sequence, and output. It is less likely to be the case when a WHERE expression is used to subset a data set's observations in concert with ordering done with the BY statement. Ultimately, the performance depends on factors specific to the SAS data set, index, and output variable sort order that is required.

Chapter **12**

Using Indexes with the KEY Option on a MODIFY Statement

Introduction

The KEY option on a MODIFY statement can be used to update an indexed *master* SAS data set by matching it with observations from a *transaction* SAS data set. The transaction data set is read from beginning to end. SAS uses the transaction variable (or variables) specified in the KEY option to search the master data set's index to determine if there is a matching value in the master data set. When a match is found, the observation in the master SAS data set is either replaced or removed, depending on the needs of the program. If a match is not found, the transaction observation can be appended to the master data set if that is what you want to do, or it can be disregarded.

The general format of the KEY option on a MODIFY statement is as follows:

MODIFY *master-SAS-data-set* KEY=*index-variable(s)* /UNIQUE <*other MODIFY statement options*>;

In the MODIFY statement, *master-SAS-data-set* is an indexed SAS data set. The KEY option is followed by a single variable if the index match is to be made via a simple index or the *composite index name* if the match is to be carried out through a composite index. Other MODIFY statement options that have no effect at all on the use of indexes are not specified in the general format above.

Here is an example of the KEY option on a MODIFY statement:

```
data indexlib.prodfile;
set  indexlib.tranfile;
modify  indexlib.prodfile key=seqnum;

select (_iorc_);
  when(%sysrc(_sok)) do; /* A match was found, update master */
      actual  = newactual;
      predict = newpredict;
      replace;
  end;
```

```
   when (%sysrc(_dsenom)) do; /* No match was found */
      _error_ = 0;
   end;
   otherwise do;
       length errormessage $200.;
       errormessage = iorcmsg();
       put "ATTENTION: unknown error condition: "
              errormessage;
   end;
 end;
 run;
```

In this example, master data set INDEXLIB.PRODFILE is being updated by matching observations from transaction data set INDEXLIB.TRANFILE. Note that the same SAS data set, INDEXLIB.PRODFILE *must* be specified in both the DATA statement and the MODIFY statement for this to work properly.

The KEY option on the MODIFY statement for INDEXLIB.PRODFILE uses the simple index based on SEQNUM. When an observation is read from INDEXLIB.TRANFILE, the value of SEQNUM is matched against the SEQNUM simple index in INDEXLIB.PRODFILE through the KEY option on the MODIFY statement. The SELECT statement logic determines whether or not a match is found. When a match is found, the values of ACTUAL and PREDICT are updated to values found in the transaction observation. Then the master data set observation is replaced (updated) in the INDEXLIB.PRODFILE SAS data set. If a match is not found, the _ERROR_ automatic variable is set back to zero so that no messages are written to the SAS log.

Here is what the SAS log for this DATA step looks like:

```
453   data indexlib.prodfile;
454   set  indexlib.tranfile;
455   modify  indexlib.prodfile key=seqnum;
456
457   select (_iorc_);
458       when(%sysrc(_sok)) do;       /* A match was found, update
          master */
459           actual  = newactual;
460           predict = newpredict;
461           replace;
462       end;
463       when (%sysrc(_dsenom)) do; /* No match was found */
464           _error_ = 0;
465       end;
```

(continued on next page)

(continued)

```
466       otherwise do;
467           length errormessage $200.;
468           errormessage = iorcmsg();
469           put "Unknown error condition: " errormessage;
470       end;
471   end;
472
473   run;


NOTE: There were 11 observations read from the data set
      INDEXLIB.TRANFILE.
NOTE: The data set INDEXLIB.PRODFILE has been updated.   There were
      9 observations rewritten, 0
      observations added and 0 observations deleted.
NOTE: DATA statement used:
      real time            0.01 seconds
      user cpu time        0.00 seconds
      system cpu time      0.00 seconds
      Memory                          162k
```

The log indicates that 11 observations were read from INDEXLIB.TRANFILE and that 9 observations were rewritten to the EXTRACT SAS data set. That means that 9 out of the 11 observations in INDEXLIB.TRANFILE matched the value of SEQNUM in 1 or more of the observations in the INDEXLIB.PRODFILE SAS data set.

The log also states how many observations were added and how many observations were deleted through the use of the KEY option on the MODIFY statement. In this case, no observations were added or deleted because the DATA step did not specify that observations were to be deleted or output to the master data set. However, when program logic allows for the addition or deletion of observations, the values for those two fields in the NOTE in the SAS log may be other than zero. Therefore, it is important to check this NOTE in the SAS log.

Determining When There Is a Match

The example in the previous section introduces the _IORC_ automatic variable, which SAS uses to store the return code for each I/O operation (index search) attempted through the KEY option on the MODIFY statement. When you perform a key search operation,

SAS stores a numeric value in the _IORC_ automatic variable that specifies whether the I/O operation is successful. Because the numeric values are subject to change in different versions of the software, SAS provides mnemonic values—surfaced via the %SYSRC macro—that specify the outcome of the attempted I/O operation. *You* are responsible for checking the mnemonic value of _IORC_ to determine the outcome of an attempted index search. You must then write your DATA step program logic according to what you want to have happen when a match occurs or when a match does not occur.

The two mnemonic values that SAS uses for the KEY option on the MODIFY statement are as follows:

_sok

> SAS returns this mnemonic value when a matching observation is found in the master data set, based on the KEY variable values specified in the transaction observation. This means that the I/O operation was successful.

_dsenom

> SAS returns this mnemonic value when no matching observation is found in the master data set, based on the KEY variable values supplied by the transaction observation. This means that the I/O operation was *not* successful.

You should use the SYSRC autocall macro to test the value of _IORC_. Here, again, is the example DATA step from the previous section:

```
data indexlib.prodfile;
set  indexlib.tranfile;
modify  indexlib.prodfile key=seqnum;

select (_iorc_);
  when(%sysrc(_sok)) do; /* A match was found, update master */
      actual  = newactual;
      predict = newpredict;
      replace;
  end;
  when (%sysrc(_dsenom)) do; /* No match was found */
      _error_ = 0;
  end;
  otherwise do;
      length errormessage $200.;
      errormessage = iorcmsg();
      put "ATTENTION: unknown error condition: "
            errormessage;
  end;
end;

run;
```

The SELECT statement examines the value of _IORC_. The %SYSRC autocall macro is used in the WHEN statements to surface the mnemonic value of _IORC_ in order to determine whether or not the I/O attempt was successful. The first WHEN statement specifies that when the value of _IORC_ is equal to "_sok" (meaning that a matching observation has been found in INDEXLIB.PRODFILE), SAS should assign new values to ACTUAL and PREDICT and then update the observation in INDEXLIB.PRODFILE. The second WHEN statement states that when the value of _IORC_ is equal to "_dsenom" (meaning that no matching observation was found in INDEXLIB.PRODFILE), the _ERROR_ automatic variable is to be set to zero. In this case, no observation is updated in the master SAS data set. The OTHERWISE statement is executed in the rare case that SAS returns an unexpected I/O message. If this should happen, that message is written to the SAS log so that it may be investigated further.

When SAS does not find a match while using the KEY option on a MODIFY statement, it sets the _ERROR_ automatic variable equal to 1. If you do not set _ERROR_ back to 0, SAS writes a non-fatal error message to the SAS log. That error message is a dump of the values of all variables in the transaction observation, the variable values of the last master observation written to the Program Data Vector (PDV), and the current values of all SAS automatic variables (_N_, _ERROR_, _IORC_). When there are hundreds or thousands of non-matching transactions, the SAS log becomes loaded with the dump of the mismatched transaction information, extending its size.

Some programmers find it helpful to have non-matching transaction information dumped to the SAS log because it documents the mismatches. Others find it obnoxious because they prefer not to have unnecessary error messages written to the SAS log. This text takes the latter position and offers SAS code examples that suppress the non-match error messages.

Here is an example of a SAS log from a simple DATA step that uses the KEY option on a MODIFY statement and does not reset the _ERROR_ automatic variable back to 0 when there is a mistake:

```
474   data indexlib.prodfile;
475   set  indexlib.tranfile;
476   modify  indexlib.prodfile key=seqnum;
477
478   select (_iorc_);
479     when(%sysrc(_sok)) do; /* A match was found, update master */
480         actual  = newactual;
481         predict = newpredict;
482         replace;
483     end;
```

(continued on next page)

(continued)

```
484        otherwise;
485   end;
486
487   run;


STATE=Arizona SEQNUM=10171987 newactual=0 newpredict=0 COUNTRY=
COUNTY=  ACTUAL=. PREDICT=.
PRODTYPE=  PRODUCT=  YEAR=. QUARTER=. DAYMONYR=. MONTH=. _ERROR_=1
          _IORC_=1230015 _N_=1
STATE=Massachusetts SEQNUM=4271955 newactual=1000 newpredict=1000
COUNTRY=U.S.A. COUNTY=
ACTUAL=$9,999.00 PREDICT=$9,999.00 PRODTYPE=FURNITURE PRODUCT=BED
YEAR=1995 QUARTER=1
DAYMONYR=01JAN95 MONTH=1 _ERROR_=1 _IORC_=1230015 _N_=11
NOTE: There were 11 observations read from the data set
INDEXLIB.TRANFILE.
NOTE: The data set INDEXLIB.PRODFILE has been updated.  There were 9
      observations rewritten, 0
      observations added and 0 observations deleted.
NOTE: DATA statement used:
      real time             0.03 seconds
      user cpu time         0.00 seconds
      system cpu time       0.01 seconds
      Memory                          162k
```

In the example, there are no observations in INDEXLIB.PRODFILE with the value of SEQNUM equal to 10171987 and 4271955. Because the _ERROR_ automatic variable was not set back to 0 within the DATA step, the 2 mismatched observations in INDEXLIB.TRANFILE generated errors and were written to the SAS log.

This example shows how important it is to query the _IORC_ automatic variable to determine the success of individual index match attempts. You should *always* use the _IORC_ automatic variable to do the following:

1. Determine the success of the attempted index match.

2. Perform the required action when there is a match:

   ▪ Replace (update) the master data set observation, or
   ▪ Remove (delete) the master data set observation.

3. Perform the required action when there is not a match:

- Output (append) the transaction observation to the master data set, or

- Do nothing.

4. Set the _ERROR_ automatic variable back to 0 when there is a mismatch.

5. Write an error message to the log when SAS does not return either the _sok or the _dsenom mnemonic.

You can use the following SAS code template to check the value of _IORC_ in DATA steps when you update a master data set with a transaction data set via the KEY option on a MODIFY statement:

```
select (_iorc_);
   when(%sysrc(_sok)) do;      /* A match was found */
      <<replace or remove>>;
   end;
   when (%sysrc(_dsenom)) do; /* No match was found */
      <<output or do nothing>>;
      _error_ = 0;
   end;
   otherwise do;
       length errormessage $200.;
       errormessage = iorcmsg();
       put "ATTENTION: unknown error condition: "
              errormessage;
   end;
end;
```

This _IORC_ return code check enables you to properly update your master SAS data set and keep your SAS log free from annoying mismatch errors.

How the Master SAS Data Set Can Be Updated

The KEY option on a MODIFY statement enables you to update an indexed master SAS data set in three ways. You can update an existing observation, remove an existing observation, or add a new observation to the master data set. Obviously, what you decide to do depends on the needs of your particular SAS application. The following sections discuss the specifics of each type of update.

Updating Matching Master Data Set Observations

You can update one or more variables in a master data set observation after a match is made with a transaction observation. This is done by assigning new values to the master data set variables. You may decide to set a master data set variable equal to a variable in the transaction observation, perform a computation that updates a master data set variable, or perform some other operation on a master data set variable. Once you have completed updating the variables of interest on a master data set observation, you *must* specifically replace the updated master data set observation using the REPLACE statement.

There are several important things that you must remember when updating a master data set observation:

- If you do not specifically assign a new value to a variable in the master data set observation, that variable is not updated.

- No new variables are *added* to the master data set. Therefore, you do not need to be concerned when the transaction data set has variables not found in the master data set. The master data set *is not* modified to include variables found only in the transaction data set.

- Other than the index key variable(s), variables in the transaction data set observation must have names that differ from those on the master data set observation. This is necessary because SAS creates one entry in the PDV for each distinct variable name found among all open SAS data sets. When it reads a transaction observation, it loads the variable values from that observation into entries in the PDV. When SAS reads a master observation through a successful index key search, it loads the entries in the PDV with the variable values found in the master data set observation. If there are same-named variables, SAS overlays the values from the transaction observation with those from the same-named variables in the master data set observation. That is why it is necessary to have different variable names for transaction data set variables that are used to update the master data set observation.

- After updating all of the variables in the master data set observation, you *must* execute the REPLACE statement to update the observation in the master data set. Failure to do so results in absolutely no change to the observation in the master data set.

Here is an example of updating a master data set's observations when a match is found:

```
data indexlib.prodfile;
set  indexlib.tranfile;
modify  indexlib.prodfile key=seqnum;

select (_iorc_);
   when(%sysrc(_sok)) do; /* A match was found, update master */
        actual  = newactual;
        predict = newpredict;
        replace;
   end;
   when (%sysrc(_dsenom)) do; /* No match was found */
        _error_ = 0;
   end;
   otherwise do;
        length errormessage $200.;
        errormessage = iorcmsg();
        put "ATTENTION: unknown error condition: "
                errormessage;
   end;
end;

run;
```

Notice that specific variable assignments are made when a match is made. Also, notice that the variables in the transaction data set (NEWACTUAL and NEWPREDICT) have names that differ from those in the master data set. Finally, you can see that the REPLACE statement is executed after all of the master data set variables are assigned new values. The REPLACE statement replaces the observation in the master SAS data set and precipitates a note in the SAS log that reads something like this:

```
NOTE: The data set INDEXLIB.PRODFILE has been updated.  There
      were 9 observations rewritten, 0 observations added and 0
      observations deleted.
```

You should always check the SAS log when attempting to update master data set transactions to determine how many observations were *rewritten*. Those are the observations that were updated by your program using the KEY option on the MODIFY statement.

Removing Matching Master Data Set Observations

Sometimes the object of performing an index match with a transaction data set is to delete the observations with corresponding index key variable values from the master data set. This can easily be done with the REMOVE statement. When the REMOVE statement is executed, it deletes the matching observation from the master SAS data set.

Here is an example of using the REMOVE statement:

```
data indexlib.prodfile;
set  indexlib.tranfile;
modify  indexlib.prodfile key=seqnum;

select (_iorc_);
  when(%sysrc(_sok)) do; /* A match was found, update master */
      remove;
  end;
  when (%sysrc(_dsenom)) do; /* No match was found */
                             _error_ = 0;
  end;
  otherwise do;
      length errormessage $200.;
      errormessage = iorcmsg();
      put "ATTENTION: unknown error condition: "
              errormessage;
  end;
end;

run;
```

In this example, observations in transaction data set INDEXLIB.TRANFILE are matched against the INDEXLIB.PRODFILE master SAS data set via the SEQNUM simple index. When a match is found, the matching observation in INDEXLIB.PRODFILE is deleted via the REMOVE statement.

Here is the log from executing this program:

```
488   data indexlib.prodfile;
489   set  indexlib.tranfile;
490   modify  indexlib.prodfile key=seqnum;
491
492   select (_iorc_);
493      when(%sysrc(_sok)) do; /* A match was found, update master */
494         remove;
495      end;
496      when (%sysrc(_dsenom)) do; /* No match was found */
497         _error_ = 0;
498      end;
499      otherwise do;
500         length errormessage $200.;
501         errormessage = iorcmsg();
502         put "ATTENTION: unknown error condition: "
503            errormessage;
504      end;
505   end;
506
507   run;

NOTE: There were 11 observations read from the data set
      INDEXLIB.TRANFILE.
NOTE: The data set INDEXLIB.PRODFILE has been updated.  There were
      0 observations rewritten, 0 observations added and 9
      observations deleted.
NOTE: DATA statement used:
      real time              0.00 seconds
      user cpu time          0.00 seconds
      system cpu time        0.00 seconds
      Memory                             162k
```

It is important to notice that the log states how many observations were deleted. In this instance, 9 observations were deleted. Thus, we know then that 9 index matches were made and that the master SAS data set was properly updated.

Adding Observations to the Master Data Set

You can use the transaction data set to add new observations to the master SAS data set. When you do so, you have a choice of adding a new observation when there is an index match or when there is not an index match for a particular transaction data set observation. The only restriction is that if there is a match and the index is a unique index, SAS does not let you add the transaction observation to the master data set.

Here is an example of adding observations using the OUTPUT statement:

```
data indexlib.prodfile;
set  indexlib.tranfile;
modify  indexlib.prodfile key=seqnum;

select (_iorc_);
  when(%sysrc(_sok)) do; /* A match was found, update master */
      remove;
  end;
  when (%sysrc(_dsenom)) do; /* No match was found */
  output;
  _error_ = 0;
  end;
  otherwise do;
      length errormessage $200.;
      errormessage = iorcmsg();
      put "ATTENTION: unknown error condition: "
            errormessage;
  end;
end;

run;
```

This DATA step matches observations from the INDEXLIB.TRANFILE against the INDEXLIB.PRODFILE using the SEQNUM simple index. When the DATA step finds a match, the observation in INDEXLIB.PRODFILE is deleted via the REMOVE statement. When it does not find a match, the observation in the INDEXLIB.TRANFILE transaction file is appended to INDEXLIB.PRODFILE via the execution of the OUTPUT statement.

This is the log from the execution of this DATA step:

```
508   data indexlib.prodfile;
509   set  indexlib.tranfile;
510   modify  indexlib.prodfile key=seqnum;
511
512   select (_iorc_);
513      when(%sysrc(_sok)) do; /* A match was found, update master */
514         remove;
515      end;
516      when (%sysrc(_dsenom)) do; /* No match was found */
517      output;
518      _error_ = 0;
519      end;
520      otherwise do;
521         length errormessage $200.;
522         errormessage = iorcmsg();
523         put "ATTENTION: unknown error condition: "
524            errormessage;
525      end;
526   end;
527
528   run;

NOTE: There were 11 observations read from the data set
      INDEXLIB.TRANFILE.
NOTE: The data set INDEXLIB.PRODFILE has been updated.  There were
      0 observations rewritten, 2 observations added and 9
      observations deleted.
NOTE: DATA statement used:
      real time           0.01 seconds
      user cpu time       0.01 seconds
      system cpu time     0.00 seconds
      Memory                         162k
```

Notice that the second NOTE reports that two observations were added to INDEXLIB.PRODFILE. This affirms that non-matching transaction observations were truly added to the master SAS data set.

Working with Duplicate Key Variable Values

All of the examples in the previous sections have assumed that both the master and transaction data sets have observations with unique key variable values. This means that no two observations in INDEXLIB.PRODINDX or in INDEXLIB.TRANFILE have the same value for SEQNUM. In reality, however, there are four possibilities for the relationship of duplicate and unique key variable values between the master and transaction SAS data sets.

Unique Index Key Variable Values in Both the Master and the Transaction SAS Data Sets

This is the best situation because it is the easiest to program. You are assured that a given transaction either finds a match on a key variable value in the master data set or it does not. You do not have to do any special traversing of either SAS data set or any special error handling. You can create simple SAS DATA step code to handle either a match or a mismatch. "Example 12.1: Unique Index Key Variable Values in Both SAS Data Sets," provides an example of how to handle this situation.

Unique Key Variable Values in the Master SAS Data Set and Duplicate Key Variable Values in the Transaction SAS Data Set

Whenever the key variable value in the transaction SAS data set changes value, SAS starts a new index search at the very beginning of the index. When there are two consecutive transactions with the same key variable value, SAS does not start its search at the beginning of the master data set's index for the second transaction. It starts its search from the current index record forward, towards the end of the index. Because the master data set index has unique values, it will not find a match as it traverses onward from the current index record. Subsequent transaction observations with the same key variable value will result in a "match not found" condition and will not be used to update the master SAS data set.

Here is a more graphic example of the problem. Consider this portion of a master SAS data set that is to be updated, via an index built for SEQNUM, by a very small transaction SAS data set containing 2 observations:

Master SAS Data Set

SEQNUM	STATE	ACTUAL	PREDICT
11111	Arizona	$112,955	$110,000
22222	**Arizona**	**$101,787**	**$100,000**
33333	Arizona	$ 97,467	$200,000

Transaction SAS Data Set

SEQNUM	STATE	NEWACTUAL	NEWPREDICT
22222	Arizona	$200,453	$200,000
22222	Arizona	$450,250	$350,000

The first transaction observation finds a match on SEQNUM = 22222 in the master SAS data set. The corresponding master data set observation has its ACTUAL and PREDICT variables updated to $200,453 and $200,000, respectively. When the second transaction attempts to make a match through the KEY option on the MODIFY statement, the KEY variable has the same value, SEQNUM=22222, as in the previous index search. Because the key variable value did not change, SAS does not start its index search back at the beginning of the index. Rather, it starts searching for SEQNUM=22222 in subsequent index records. The first value it sees is SEQNUM=33333. SAS does not find a match for the second transaction observation. The result is that the second transaction observation is not used to update the master SAS data set.

The fix for this situation is to use the UNIQUE option on the MODIFY statement. The UNIQUE option directs SAS to go back to the beginning of the index for *every* index search. This enables every transaction with a duplicate index key value to be matched with the corresponding master SAS data set transaction. "Example 12.2: Duplicate Index Key Variable Values in the Transaction SAS Data Set," illustrates the SAS code you can use in this type of situation.

Duplicate Index Key Variable Values in the Master SAS Data Set and Unique Key Variable Values in the Transaction SAS Data Set

By default, an index search returns the first master data set observation with the specified index key variable value. If there are master data set observations with duplicate index key variable values, only the first one will be updated by the transaction observation.

This is probably not what you want to happen. More than likely, you want *all* master data set observations with the matching index key variable value to be updated by the corresponding transaction observation.

Here is an example of this situation:

Master SAS Data Set

SEQNUM	STATE	ACTUAL	PREDICT
22222	**Arizona**	**$112,955**	**$110,000**
22222	Arizona	$101,787	$100,000
22222	Arizona	$ 97,467	$200,000

Transaction SAS Data Set

SEQNUM	STATE	NEWACTUAL	NEWPREDICT
22222	Arizona	$450,250	$350,000
33333	Arizona	$200,453	$200,000

In the example, the first master data set observation with SEQNUM equal to 22222 is matched, updated, and replaced by the first transaction observation. This results in ACTUAL equaling $450,250 and PREDICT equaling $350,000 in the master SAS data set. Subsequent master data set observations with SEQNUM equal to 2222 are not matched and updated by the first transaction observation. Instead, SAS reads the second transaction observation and attempts to make a match for SEQNUM = 33333.

You can force SAS to continue to read subsequent master data set observations with duplicate key variable values by using a DO loop. The DO loop directs SAS to continue to use the index to return master data set observations with the same key variable value. The DO loop does this until SAS cannot find another match in the index. This technique is illustrated in "Example 12.3: Duplicate Index Key Variable Values in the Master SAS Data Set."

Duplicate Index Key Variable Values in Both the Master and the Transaction SAS Data Sets

This is the trickiest of all possible update situations. In this situation, you want to have all master data set observations with a specific index key variable value updated by all transaction data set observations containing that same value. Some master data set observations might be unique and have duplicate corresponding transaction data set observations. Alternately, some transaction data set observations might be unique and have duplicate corresponding master data set observations. Or there could be multiple master and transaction data set observations with the same index key variable values.

Here is an example of this type of situation:

Master SAS Data Set

Observation	SEQNUM	STATE	ACTUAL	PREDICT
2046	22222	Arizona	$112,955	$110,000
2047	22222	Arizona	$101,787	$100,000
2048	22222	Arizona	$ 97,467	$200,000

Transaction SAS Data Set

Observation	SEQNUM	STATE	NEWACTUAL	NEWPREDICT
1	22222	Arizona	$450,250	$350,000
2	22222	Arizona	$200,453	$200,000
3	33333	Arizona	$321,453	$300,000

In this example, the intent of a SAS program is to update the value of ACTUAL in the master data set by adding the value of NEWACTUAL from the transaction SAS data set. The three master data set observations would have ACTUAL equal to the following:

- observation 2046: $112,955 + $450,250 + $200,453 = $763,658
- observation 2047: $101,787 + $450,250 + $200,453 = $752,490
- observation 2048: $ 97,467 + $450,250 + $200,453 = $748,170

In order to achieve these results you must control both how SAS searches the index and how it traverses the transaction SAS data set. This requires that you do the following:

- Pre-sort the transaction data set by the index key variable(s).
- Use BY statement processing for the transaction data set.
- Use a DO loop to read the master data set (through the index) for all observations with a given key variable value.
- Use a dummy key value to go back to the top of the index when the next transaction has the same key value as the current one.

This technique (Moorman and Warner 1999, pp. 20-21) is demonstrated in "Example 12.4: Duplicate Index Key Variable Values in Both the Master and the Transaction SAS Data Sets."

No matter what the character of your two data sets, you should always sort your transaction SAS data set into ascending order of the key variable(s) value(s). This promotes good performance by increasing the possibility that the index file pages and the data set page that are needed to satisfy the next index match are currently held in memory in an index buffer and data buffer, respectively. Sorting the transaction file before using the KEY option on a MODIFY statement increases the possibility that you can avoid too many costly I/Os.

Example 12.1: Unique Index Key Variable Values in Both SAS Data Sets

In this example, the master data set has a simple index that is built from the SEQNUM variable. All observations in the master SAS data set have unique key variable values. The observations in the transaction SAS data set also have unique values for SEQNUM. The goal of this DATA step is to update the master SAS data set's observations with those with matching values of SEQNUM in the transaction data set.

```
data indexlib.prodfile;
set  indexlib.tranfile;
modify  indexlib.prodfile key=seqnum;

select (_iorc_);
  when(%sysrc(_sok)) do; /* A match was found, update master */
      actual = newactual;
      predict = newpredict;
      replace;
  end;
  when (%sysrc(_dsenom)) do; /* No match was found */
      _error_ = 0;
  end;
  otherwise do;
      length errormessage $200.;
      errormessage = iorcmsg();
      put "ATTENTION: unknown error condition: "
              errormessage;
  end;
end;

run;
```

The MODIFY statement tells SAS that INDEXLIB.PRODFILE, the SAS data set named in the DATA statement, should be modified instead of being overwritten. The KEY option on the MODIFY statement for INDEXLIB.PRODFILE specifies that the SEQNUM simple index is to be used to search for observations in the master SAS data set. The _IORC_ automatic variable is queried to determine the success of the attempted index key variable value match. When a match is found, the values of ACTUAL and PREDICT are updated in the master data set observation. The updated master data set observation is rewritten to the master SAS data set via the REPLACE statement. If no match is found, the _ERROR_ automatic variable is reset so that no errors are written to the SAS log and nothing further is done with the mismatched transaction observation.

Here is the SAS log from executing this example DATA step:

```
453  data indexlib.prodfile;
454  set  indexlib.tranfile;
455  modify  indexlib.prodfile key=seqnum;
456
457  select (_iorc_);
458     when(%sysrc(_sok)) do; /* A match was found, update master */
459          actual  = newactual;
460          predict = newpredict;
461          replace;
462     end;
463     when (%sysrc(_dsenom)) do; /* No match was found */
464          _error_ = 0;
465     end;
466     otherwise do;
467          length errormessage $200.;
468          errormessage = iorcmsg();
469          put "Unknown error condition: " errormessage;
470     end;
471  end;
472
473  run;


NOTE: There were 11 observations read from the data set
      INDEXLIB.TRANFILE.
NOTE: The data set INDEXLIB.PRODFILE has been updated.  There were
      9 observations rewritten, 0
      observations added and 0 observations deleted.
NOTE: DATA statement used:
      real time             0.01 seconds
      user cpu time         0.00 seconds
      system cpu time       0.00 seconds
      Memory                         162k
```

In the log, you can see that there were 11 observations read from INDEXLIB.TRANFILE, the transaction data set. The log states that 9 observations were rewritten to INDEXLIB.PRODINDX. This means that there were 9 observations in INDEXLIB.TRANFILE with SEQNUM values matching those in the master SAS data set. Therefore, the values of ACTUAL and PREDICT in the 9 master SAS data set observations were updated. Two INDEXLIB.TRANFILE observations did not have matches in the master SAS data set. They had no effect on the master SAS data set.

Notice that the SAS log does not contain any notes stating that an index was used. SAS normally writes index usage notes in the log when MSGLEVEL=I has been specified and it uses an index to optimize a WHERE or BY statement. No notes are necessary because the KEY option on a MODIFY statement *always* uses the specified index. This contrasts with WHERE and BY statements where SAS may or may not use an index, depending on its calculation as to whether doing so would be optimal.

You can use this example program to craft your own index searches when both the indexed master SAS data set and the transaction SAS data set contain unique index key variable values. In doing so, you must be certain that the index key variable values are unique in both data sets. Otherwise, you definitely will not get the results that you want.

Example 12.2: Duplicate Index Key Variable Values in the Transaction SAS Data Set

In this example, the master SAS data set has unique index key variable values, but the transaction data set does not. The transaction data set contains the following:

- 5 observations with SEQNUM = 501
- 4 observations with SEQNUM = 506
- 1 observation with SEQNUM = 10171897
- 1 observation with SEQNUM = 4271955

Only the first two SEQNUM values, 501 and 506, are found in the master SAS data set. The purpose of this DATA step is to update master data set observations with each matching transaction observation via the index. When there is not a match, the transaction observation is added to the master SAS data set.

Here is the SAS code:

```
data indexlib.prodfile;
set  indexlib.tranfile;
modify  indexlib.prodfile key=seqnum / unique;

select (_iorc_);
   when(%sysrc(_sok)) do; /* A match was found, update master */
       actual  = actual + newactual;
       predict = predict + newpredict;
       replace;
   end;
   when (%sysrc(_dsenom)) do; /* No match was found, add to master */
       actual  = newactual;
       predict = newpredict;
       output;
       _error_ = 0;
   end;
   otherwise do;
       length errormessage $200.;
       errormessage = iorcmsg();
       put "ATTENTION: unknown error condition: "
               errormessage;
   end;
end;

run;
```

The UNIQUE option on the MODIFY statement causes SAS to start its index search at the beginning of the SEQNUM simple index whenever a new observation is read from INDEXLIB.TRANFILE. Consequently, members of the transaction data set with duplicate SEQNUM values find a match in the master SAS data set whenever a matching value of SEQNUM exists. This would not be the case if the UNIQUE option was not used. (See "Unique Key Variable Values in the Master SAS Data Set and Duplicate Key Variable Values in the Transaction SAS Data Set" earlier in this chapter.)

Note the code when there is not a match. In that case, ACTUAL is set equal to NEWACTUAL, and PREDICT is set equal to NEWPREDICT before the observation is output. This is necessary because the transaction data set observation does not contain variables named ACTUAL and PREDICT. (Rather, it contains NEWACTUAL and NEWPREDICT.) If you did not assign values to ACTUAL and PREDICT before outputting to the master SAS data set, those variables would end up containing either missing values or some extraneous values left over in the Program Data Vector from a previously read master data set observation.

Here is the log for this DATA step:

```
871   data indexlib.prodfile;
872   set  indexlib.tranfile;
873   modify  indexlib.prodfile key=seqnum / unique;
874
875   select (_iorc_);
876      when(%sysrc(_sok)) do; /* A match was found, update master */
877           actual  = actual + newactual;
878           predict = predict + newpredict;
879           replace;
880      end;
881      when (%sysrc(_dsenom)) do; /* No match was found, add to
                                      master */
882           actual  = newactual;
883           predict = newpredict;
884           output;
885           _error_ = 0;
886      end;
887      otherwise do;
888           length errormessage $200.;
889           errormessage = iorcmsg();
890           put "ATTENTION: unknown error condition: "
891              errormessage;
892      end;
893   end;
894
895   run;


NOTE: There were 11 observations read from the data set
      INDEXLIB.TRANFILE.
NOTE: The data set INDEXLIB.PRODFILE has been updated.  There were
      9 observations rewritten, 2 observations added and 0 observations deleted.
      observations added and 0 observations deleted.
NOTE: DATA statement used:
      real time              0.01 seconds
      user cpu time          0.00 seconds
      system cpu time        0.01 seconds
      Memory                                 163k
```

The log states that 9 observations were rewritten. That accounts for the observation with SEQNUM = 501 being updated 5 times by transaction data set observations with the same SEQNUM value. Additionally, the observation with SEQNUM = 506 was updated 4 times by same-valued transaction observations. Two observations were added. Their SEQNUMs equal 10171987 and 4271955.

Example 12.3: Duplicate Index Key Variable Values in the Master SAS Data Set

In this example, there are duplicate index key variable values in the master SAS data set, but unique key variable values in the transaction data set. The master SAS data set has a non-unique composite index, named COUNTRY_STATE, that was built from the COUNTRY and STATE variables. The transaction data set contains only 1 observation for each of these 3 Country/State values: *U.S.A./Arizona*, *U.S.A./Florida*, and *U.S.A./Massachusetts*, as well as some other Country/State values. However, the master SAS data set contains the following:

- 11 observations where Country/State equals *U.S.A./Arizona*

- 40 observations where Country/State equals *U.S.A./Florida*

- 10 observations where Country/State equals *U.S.A./Massachusetts*

This poses a bit of a problem because an index search returns the first master data set observation with the specified index key variable value. When there are multiple master data set observations with duplicate index key variable values, only the first observation is updated by the transaction observation. You can overcome this problem by putting the MODIFY statement inside a DO loop.

Here is how this can be coded:

```
data indexlib.prodfile;
set  indexlib.tranfile;

do until (_iorc_=%sysrc(_dsenom));
   modify  indexlib.prodfile key=country_state;

   select (_iorc_);
       when(%sysrc(_sok)) do; /* A match was found, update master */
             actual = newactual;
             predict = newpredict;
             replace;
```

```
          end;
          when (%sysrc(_dsenom)) do; /* No match was found */
                _error_ = 0;
          end;
          otherwise do;
                length errormessage $200.;
                errormessage = iorcmsg();
                put "ATTENTION: unknown error condition: "
                      errormessage;
          end;
      end;
   end;
 end;
 run;
```

In the example, SAS first reads an observation from INDEXLIB.TRANFILE, the transaction SAS data set. The DO UNTIL statement forces SAS to repeatedly attempt to read observations from the master SAS data set via the COUNTRY_STATE composite index in order to find a match for the values of COUNTRY/STATE found in the transaction observation. When a match is found, the master data set observation is updated. SAS continues to attempt to find matching master observations, via the index, until a non-matching condition is found and *_IORC_= %sysrc(_dsenom)*. Then the DO UNTIL loop is satisfied, the next transaction observation is read, and the index search begins again.

Here is the SAS log from this DATA step:

```
1140  data indexlib.prodfile;
1141  set  indexlib.tranfile;
1142
1143  do until (_iorc_=%sysrc(_dsenom));
1144       modify  indexlib.prodfile key=country_state;
1145
1146       select (_iorc_);
1147          when(%sysrc(_sok)) do; /* A match was found, update
                                            master */

1148               actual = newactual;
1149               predict = newpredict;
1150               replace;
1151          end;
1152          when (%sysrc(_dsenom)) do; /* No match was found */
1153               _error_ = 0;
1154          end;
```

(continued on next page)

(continued)

```
1155            otherwise do;
1156                 length errormessage $200.;
1157                 errormessage = iorcmsg();
1158                 put "ATTENTION: unknown error condition: "
1159                     errormessage;
1160            end;
1161        end;
1162   end;
1163   run;


NOTE: There were 11 observations read from the data set
      INDEXLIB.TRANFILE.
NOTE: The data set INDEXLIB.PRODFILE has been updated.   There were
      61 observations rewritten,
      0 observations added and 0 observations deleted.
NOTE: DATA statement used:
      real time              0.01 seconds
      user cpu time          0.01 seconds
      system cpu time        0.00 seconds
      Memory                            165k
```

The log shows that 61 observations in INDEXLIB.PRODFILE were rewritten. That is consistent with our expectation of what SAS would update:

- 11 observations where Country/State equals U.S.A./Arizona
- 40 observations where Country/State equals U.S.A./Florida
- 10 observations where Country/State equals U.S.A./Massachusetts

Apparently, of the 11 observations in the INDEXLIB.TRANFILE SAS data set, only 3 of them had matches in the INDEXLIB.PRODFILE SAS data set. But they each had multiple matches within the master SAS data set.

Example 12.4: Duplicate Index Key Variable Values in Both the Master and the Transaction SAS Data Sets

The trickiest of all index updates takes place when both the master and the transaction data sets have observations with duplicate key variable values. These kinds of updates are tricky because every master observation with a given key variable value must be updated by every transaction observation with the same key variable value. You need a technique to help SAS keep track of where the key variable value is in both files when attempting to make the matches through the index.

The basic steps to the technique that you can use are as follows:

1. Use BY statement processing (with the NOTSORTED option) for the transaction data set.

2. Use a DO loop to read the master data set (through the index) for all observations with a given key variable value.

3. Use a dummy key value to go back to the top of the index to match master observations with the next transaction observation having a duplicate key value.

In this example, there are duplicate index key variable values in both the master and transaction SAS data sets. The master SAS data set has a non-unique composite index, named COUNTRY_STATE, that was built from the COUNTRY and STATE variables. The master SAS data set contains:

- 11 observations where Country/State equals U.S.A./Arizona
- 40 observations where Country/State equals U.S.A./Florida
- 10 observations where Country/State equals U.S.A./Massachusetts
- 939 observations with various other values for Country/State

The transaction SAS data set contains:

- 3 observations where Country/State equals U.S.A./Arizona
- 1 observations where Country/State equals U.S.A./Florida
- 3 observations where Country/State equals U.S.A./Massachusetts
- 4 observations with various Country/State values not found in the master data set

We would expect that there would be 103 observations *rewritten* to the master SAS data set after executing the example DATA step. The 103 rewritten observations would be for the following key variable value matches:

- Country/State equals U.S.A./Arizona: (3 transaction obs) * (11 master obs) = 33 updates
- Country/State equals U.S.A./Florida: (1 transaction obs) * (40 master obs) = 40 updates
- Country/State equals U.S.A./Massachusetts: (3 transaction obs) * (10 master obs) = 30 updates

The example SAS code follows this basic algorithm:

1. Read a transaction observation.

2. Attempt to match the transaction observation with a master observation through the index.

3. If there is a match, update the master observation and return to Step 2 to find the next master observation with the same key variable value.

4. If there is not a match, determine if this is the last transaction with this specific key variable value.

5. If it is the last transaction with that specific key variable value, return to Step 1.

6. If it is not the last transaction with that specific key variable value, set the key variable value to a nonsense value (to reset the index search back to the beginning) and go to Step 2. (This will fail, and then it will iterate and attempt to match the real value.)

Here is the example SAS code:

```
data indexlib.prodfile;
set  indexlib.tranfile;
  by notsorted country state;   ❶

flag = 0;  ❷

do until (_iorc_=%sysrc(_dsenom));   ❸

  if flag = 1 then country = input('0000'x,$10.);   ❹

  modify  indexlib.prodfile key=country_state;

  select (_iorc_);
      when(%sysrc(_sok)) do;      /* A match was found */  ❺
          actual = actual + newactual;
          predict = predict + newpredict;
          replace;
      end;
```

```
      when (%sysrc(_dsenom)) do; /* No match was found */  ❻
         _error_ = 0;
         if not last.country and not last.state and not flag
            then do;  ❼
               flag = 1;
               _IORC_ = 0;
         end;
      end;
      otherwise do;
            length errormessage $200.;
            errormessage = iorcmsg();
            put "ATTENTION: unknown error condition: "
               errormessage;
      end;
   end;
end;

run;
```

Here are the annotations for this example:

❶ The BY statement with the NOTSORTED option tells SAS that transaction observations with the same BY value are grouped together but are not necessarily sorted. This statement is necessary so that you can use the "last" automatic variable later in this DATA step. Using the NOTSORTED option enables you to avoid sorting the transaction data set. The BY statement in the example specifies that the transaction data set sort order is COUNTRY and STATE.

❷ The FLAG variable is used to indicate when you want to read the first master observation with a given key variable value after a transaction observation with a duplicate value is read.

❸ The DO UNTIL loop allows iterative reading of the master SAS data set via the index. As long as a match is found, this loop is executed. Multiple master data set observations are updated for a single transaction observation within this loop. When there is no longer a match on an index key variable value (that is, it has run out of matching master observations), this loop is exited.

❹ This IF statement takes care of the condition when a new transaction observation has the same key variable value as the previous one. The index search for the matching master transaction begins from where the index pointer is currently located and searches towards the end of the index. Consequently, it would miss all of the matching master transactions. You must fake out the index by setting the value of one of the key variable fields to '0000'x. This forces the index to search again starting from the top. The value, '0000'x, was chosen because it is *very* unlikely to occur in the variable COUNTRY. It has the added advantage that SAS can quickly determine that there is no matching entry by looking at only the very first index nodes.

❺ When a match is found, you update the master observation with values from the transaction observation.

❻ When no match is found, you reset _ERROR_ and check to see if this is the last transaction with the specific key variable values.

❼ This IF statement checks to see if this is the last transaction observation with a given key variable value. At this point, the previous transaction observation has been matched with all master observations that have the same key variable value. If this is a transaction observation with the same key variable value as the previous transaction observation, then you set the FLAG variable to 1 and _IORC_ to 0. You want to stay in the DO UNTIL loop and create a bogus value for COUNTRY to force the index to begin its search again at the beginning. Then you fall through the DO UNTIL loop, go back to the top of the DATA step and read a new transaction observation.

Here is the SAS log for this DATA step:

```
5     data indexlib.prodfile;
6     set  indexlib.tranfile;
7         by NOTSORTED country state;
8
9     flag = 0;
10
11    do until (_iorc_=%sysrc(_dsenom));
12
13        if flag = 1 then country = input('0000'x,$10.);
14
15        modify  indexlib.prodfile key=country_state;
16
17        select (_iorc_);
18            when(%sysrc(_sok)) do; /* A match was found, update
                                        master */
```

(continued on next page)

(continued)

```
19              actual = actual + newactual;
20              predict = predict + newpredict;
21              replace;
22          end;
23          when (%sysrc(_dsenom)) do; /* No match was found */
24              _error_ = 0;
25              if not last.country and not last.state and not flag
                then do;
26                  flag = 1;
27                  _IORC_ = 0;
28              end;
29          end;
30          otherwise do;
31              length errormessage $200.;
32              errormessage = iorcmsg();
33              put "ATTENTION: unknown error condition: "
34                  errormessage;
35          end;
36      end;
37  end;
38
39  run;


NOTE: There were 11 observations read from the data set
      INDEXLIB.TRANFILE.
NOTE: The data set INDEXLIB.PRODFILE has been updated.  There
      were 103 observations rewritten,
      0 observations added and 0 observations deleted.
NOTE: DATA statement used:
      real time            0.07 seconds
      user cpu time        0.00 seconds
      system cpu time      0.03 seconds
      Memory                        230k
```

As predicted, you can see that there were 103 observations rewritten to the
INDEXLIB.PRODFILE master SAS data set. Each one of the master observations was
updated by each one of the matching transaction observations.

Summary

The KEY option on a MODIFY statement provides a way for you to update an indexed *master* SAS data set by matching it with observations from a *transaction* SAS data set. SAS reads the transaction data set from beginning to end and uses the transaction variable(s) specified in the KEY option to search the master data set's index for a match. When a match is found, your program logic specifies whether the master data set observation is updated or deleted. When no match is found, you can either add the transaction observation to the master data set or disregard it. You can determine whether or not a match was made by querying the value of the _IORC_ automatic variable.

The programming logic that you use to update a master SAS data set via a transaction data set must account for one of four possibilities. The first is that there are only unique index key variable values in the observations in both the master and transaction data sets. The second is that there are unique index key variable values in the master data set but duplicate key variable values in the transaction data set. The third is that there are observations with duplicate index key variable values in the master SAS data set but unique ones in the transaction data set. Finally, the most complicated situation is when there are observations with duplicate index key variable values in both the master and transaction SAS data sets. The text explains the ramifications of each scenario and provides examples that show you how to craft DATA step logic to handle each situation.

Chapter **13**

Using Indexes with the KEY Option on a SET Statement

Introduction

The KEY option on a SET statement enables you to create a new SAS data set by matching observations from a *transaction* SAS data set with those from an indexed *master* SAS data set. The transaction data set is read from beginning to end. SAS uses the transaction observation variable(s) specified in the KEY option to search the master data set index to determine if there is a matching value in the master data set. When a match is found, the observation in the master SAS data set is written to the new SAS data set.

The general format of the KEY option on a SET statement is as follows:

> SET *master-SAS-data-set* KEY=*index-variable(s)* /UNIQUE *<other SET statement options>*;

In the SET statement, *master-SAS-data-set* is an indexed SAS data set. The KEY option is followed by a single variable if the index match is to be made via a simple index or by the *composite index name* if the match is to be carried out through a composite index. The UNIQUE option specifies that SAS should always start at the beginning of an index when doing the next index search. The UNIQUE option is used when there are duplicate transaction observations that must be matched to unique master data set observations. The UNIQUE option is discussed in more detail later in this chapter. SET statement options that have no effect at all on the use of indexes are not specifically noted in the general format above.

Here is a simple example of the KEY option on a SET statement:

```
data extract(drop=newactual newpredict);
set  indexlib.tranfile;
set  indexlib.prodfile key=seqnum;

length errormessage $200.;
drop errormessage;

select (_iorc_);
```

```
when(%sysrc(_sok)) do;       /* A match was found */
    output;
end;
when (%sysrc(_dsenom)) do; /* No match was found */
    _error_ = 0;
end;
otherwise do;
    errormessage = iorcmsg();
    put "ATTENTION: unknown error condition: "
            errormessage;
end;
end;

run;
```

In this example, a new data set named EXTRACT is being created by matching observations from the INDEXLIB.TRANFILE transaction data set with the INDEXLIB.PRODFILE master SAS data set. The KEY option on the SET statement for INDEXLIB.PRODFILE uses the simple index based on SEQNUM. When an observation is read from INDEXLIB.TRANFILE, the value of SEQNUM is matched against the SEQNUM simple index in INDEXLIB.PRODFILE through the KEY option on the SET statement. The SELECT statement logic determines whether or not a match is found. When a match is found, it is output to the EXTRACT SAS data set. If a match is not found, the _ERROR_ automatic variable is set back to 0 so that no messages are written to the SAS log.

Here is the SAS log for this DATA step:

```
825   data extract(drop=newactual newpredict);
826   set   indexlib.tranfile;
827   set   indexlib.prodfile key=seqnum;
828
829   length errormessage $200.;
830   drop errormessage;
831
832   select (_iorc_);
833      when(%sysrc(_sok)) do;       /* A match was found */
834          output;
835      end;
836      when (%sysrc(_dsenom)) do; /* No match was found */
837          _error_ = 0;
838      end;
839      otherwise do;
840          errormessage = iorcmsg();
```

(continued on next page)

(continued)

```
841           put "ATTENTION: unknown error condition: "
842              errormessage;
843       end;
844   end;
845
846   run;


NOTE: There were 11 observations read from the data set
      INDEXLIB.TRANFILE.
NOTE: The data set WORK.EXTRACT has 9 observations and 12 variables.
NOTE: DATA statement used:
      real time          0.01 seconds
      user cpu time      0.01 seconds
      system cpu time    0.00 seconds
      Memory                          169k
```

The log indicates that 11 observations were read from INDEXLIB.TRANFILE and that 9 observations were written to the EXTRACT SAS data set. That means that 9 out of the 11 observations in INDEXLIB.TRANFILE matched the values of SEQNUM in the INDEXLIB.PRODFILE SAS data set.

Determining When There Is a Match

The previous example implicitly introduced the _IORC_ automatic variable. SAS uses the _IORC_ automatic variable to store the return code for each I/O operation (index search) attempted through the KEY option on the SET statement. When you perform an index search, SAS stores a numeric value in the _IORC_ automatic variable that specifies whether or not the I/O operation was successful. These numeric values are subject to change in future releases of SAS. Therefore, mnemonic values that surface via the %SYSRC macro are provided to specify the outcome of the attempted I/O operation. You must check the mnemonic value of _IORC_ to determine the outcome of an attempted index search and then write your DATA step program logic according to what you want to do when a match is or is not found.

The two mnemonic values that SAS uses for the KEY option on the SET statement are as follows:

_sok

> This mnemonic value is returned when a matching observation is found in the master data set based on the KEY variable values specified in the transaction observation. The I/O operation was successful.

_dsenom

> This mnemonic value means that no matching observation was found in the master data set based on the KEY variable values supplied by the transaction observation. The I/O operation was not successful.

You must use the SYSRC autocall macro to test the value of _IORC_. Here again is the example DATA step from the previous section:

```
data extract(drop=newactual newpredict);
set   indexlib.tranfile;
set   indexlib.prodfile key=seqnum;

length errormessage $200.;
drop errormessage;

select (_iorc_);
  when(%sysrc(_sok)) do;     /* A match was found */
      output;
  end;
  when (%sysrc(_dsenom)) do; /* No match was found */
      _error_ = 0;
  end;
  otherwise do;
      errormessage = iorcmsg();
      put "ATTENTION: unknown error condition: "
            errormessage;
  end;
end;

run;
```

The SELECT statement tests the value of _IORC_. The %SYSRC autocall macro surfaces the mnemonic value of _IORC_ in order to determine whether or not the I/O attempt was successful. The first WHEN statement specifies that when the value of _IORC_ is equal to _sok (meaning that a match has been found), SAS should output the matching master data set observation to the new data set. The second WHEN statement states that when the value of _IORC_ is equal to _dsenom (meaning that no match was found), the _ERROR_ automatic variable is to be set to 0. In this case, no observation is written to the new EXTRACT SAS data set.

The OTHERWISE statement is executed only when SAS returns an unexpected I/O message. In the example, the IORCMSG() function is used to return the message associated with the unexpected (not _sok or _dsenom) mnemonic value of _IORC_. The variable ERRORMESSAGE is used in this situation to output the value to the log. A DROP statement is used in the DATA step to keep ERRORMESSAGE from ending up in every observation in the new EXTRACT SAS data set.

When SAS does not find a match while using the KEY option on a SET statement, it sets the _ERROR_ automatic variable to 1. If you do not set it back to 0 before the end of a DATA step, SAS prints a non-fatal error message in the SAS log. That error message is a dump of the values of all variables in the transaction observation, the variable values of the last master observation written to the Program Data Vector, and the current values of several SAS automatic variables (_N_, _ERROR_, and _IORC_). When there are hundreds or thousands of non-matching transactions, the SAS log can get quite long.

Some programmers find the dump of non-matching observation variable values to the SAS log helpful because it documents the mismatches. Others find it bothersome because they do not want to have unnecessary error messages written to the SAS log. The SAS code provided in this chapter shows examples that suppress the non-matching error messages.

Here is an example of a SAS log from a simple DATA step that uses the KEY option on a SET statement but does not use the _IORC_ automatic variable to check the results of index match attempts:

```
705    data extract;
706    set  indexlib.tranfile;
707    set  indexlib.prodfile key=seqnum;
708    run;


COUNTRY=U.S.A. STATE=Arizona COUNTY=  ACTUAL=$0.00 PREDICT=$0.00
PRODTYPE=FURNITURE
 PRODUCT=SOFA YEAR=1995 QUARTER=1 DAYMONYR=01JAN95 MONTH=1
 SEQNUM=10171987 ❶ _ERROR_=1
 _IORC_=1230015 _N_=1
 COUNTRY=U.S.A. STATE=Massachusetts COUNTY=  ACTUAL=$1,000.00
 PREDICT=$1,000.00
 PRODTYPE=FURNITURE PRODUCT=BED YEAR=1995 QUARTER=1 DAYMONYR=01JAN95
 MONTH=1 SEQNUM=4271955 ❶
 _ERROR_=1 _IORC_=1230015 _N_=11
```

(continued on next page)

(continued)

```
NOTE: There were 11 observations read from the data set
INDEXLIB.TRANFILE.
NOTE: The data set WORK.EXTRACT has 11 observations and 12 variables.
NOTE: DATA statement used:
      real time               0.03 seconds
      user cpu time           0.00 seconds
      system cpu time         0.01 seconds
      Memory                             166k
```

❶ In the example, there are no observations in INDEXLIB.PRODFILE with the value of SEQNUM equal to 10171987 or 4271955. Because the _ERROR_ automatic variable was not set back to 0 within the DATA step, the 2 mismatched observations in INDEXLIB.TRANFILE generated errors and were written to the SAS log.

Also, the _IORC_ automatic variable was not queried, and there is no DATA step logic that specifies what to do with matches and mismatches. For these reasons, the EXTRACT SAS data set includes the following:

- 9 matching observations from the master data set
- 2 mismatched observations from the transaction data set

Those are obviously not the results that you would want if you were going to the trouble of using the KEY option on a SET statement to subset observations in a master data set to build a new SAS data set. You would only want to include matches between the transaction and the master SAS data sets in the new EXTRACT SAS data set.

The previous example shows how important it is to query the _IORC_ automatic variable to determine the success of individual index match attempts. You should *always* use the _IORC_ automatic variable to do the following:

- Determine the success of the index match.
- Output observations that match.
- Set the _ERROR_ automatic variable back to 0 when there is a mismatch.
- Write an error message to the log when SAS does not return either the _sok or the _dsenom mnemonic.

Consequently, you should use the following template for _IORC_ return code checks.
The template should be used in all DATA steps where you subset a master data set with a
transaction data set via the KEY option on a SET statement:

```
length errormessage $200.;
drop errormessage;

select (_iorc_);
  when(%sysrc(_sok)) do;      /* A match was found */
      <<ACTION THAT YOU WANT TO TAKE>>;
  end;
  when (%sysrc(_dsenom)) do; /* No match was found */
      _error_ = 0;
  end;
  otherwise do;
      errormessage = iorcmsg();
      put "ATTENTION: unknown error condition: "
             errormessage;
  end;
end;
```

This _IORC_ return code check ensures that you include only matching observations in
your output SAS data set and that your SAS log is free from annoying errors about
mismatches.

NOTE: The DROP statement is necessary to keep the ERRORMESSAGE variable out
of the new data set created in the DATA step. ERRORMESSAGE is needed in
those rare instances when a non-traditional value of _IORC_ is encountered and
the SAS I/O message (IORCMSG()) must be written to the SAS log. The
ERRORMESSAGE variable should not become a variable in the new data set.

Variables Written to the New SAS Data Set

By default, the new SAS data set contains all variables found in both the transaction and
the master SAS data set. This is not usually an issue because transaction data sets contain
either of the following:

- only the variable or variables that are used on the KEY option to perform the
  index search
- all variables found in the master SAS data set

In either of these two cases, the new SAS data set will contain the same variables as the master SAS data set.

However, when the transaction data set contains variables not found in the master data set, those variables are written to the new SAS data set along with the variables found in the master SAS data set.

Consider the two SAS data sets used in the previous examples and the variables they contain:

INDEXLIB.PRODFILE

actual	county	country	daymonyr	month	predict
prodtype	product	quarter	seqnum	state	year

INDEXLIB.TRANFILE

month	newactual	newpredict	seqnum

Executing the following DATA step adds variables to the EXTRACT data set.

```
data extract;
set   indexlib.tranfile;
set   indexlib.prodfile key=seqnum;

length errormessage $200.;
drop errormessage;

select (_iorc_);
  when(%sysrc(_sok)) do;      /* A match was found */
      output;
  end;
  when (%sysrc(_dsenom)) do; /* No match was found */
      _error_ = 0;
  end;
  otherwise do;
      errormessage = iorcmsg();
      put "ATTENTION: unknown error condition: "
             errormessage;
  end;
end;

run;
```

The EXTRACT data set then contains the following variables:

EXTRACT

actual	county	country	daymonyr	month	predict
prodtype	product	quarter	seqnum	state	year
newactual	newpredict				

Notice that the variables NEWACTUAL and NEWPREDICT are now found in the new EXTRACT SAS data set. They contain the values found in the matching observations in the INDEXLIB.TRANFILE transaction SAS data set. All other variables in EXTRACT contain the values found in the INDEXLIB.PRODFILE master SAS data set.

To keep unwanted transaction data set variables from being written to the output SAS data set, use either the DROP statement or data set option or use the KEEP statement or data set option. Below are three examples that all achieve the same result, which is to disallow NEWACTUAL and NEWPREDICT from being written to the EXTRACT SAS data set. Here is the first example:

```
/* Example 1 */
data extract(drop = newactual newpredict);
set   indexlib.tranfile;
set   indexlib.prodfile key=seqnum;

length errormessage $200.;
drop errormessage;

select (_iorc_);
   when(%sysrc(_sok)) do;      /* A match was found */
      output;
   end;
   when (%sysrc(_dsenom)) do; /* No match was found */
      _error_ = 0;
   end;
   otherwise do;
      errormessage = iorcmsg();
      put "ATTENTION: unknown error condition: "
              errormessage;
   end;
end;

run;
```

Here is the second example:

```
/* Example 2 */
data extract;
set  indexlib.tranfile;
set  indexlib.prodfile key=seqnum;

length errormessage $200.;
drop errormessage;
drop newactual newpredict;

select (_iorc_);
  when(%sysrc(_sok)) do;      /* A match was found */
      output;
  end;
  when (%sysrc(_dsenom)) do; /* No match was found */
      _error_ = 0;
  end;
  otherwise do;
      errormessage = iorcmsg();
      put "ATTENTION: unknown error condition: "
            errormessage;
  end;
end;

run;
```

Here is the third example:

```
/* Example 3 */
data extract;
set  indexlib.tranfile(keep=month seqnum);;
set  indexlib.prodfile key=seqnum;

length errormessage $200.;
drop errormessage;

select (_iorc_);
  when(%sysrc(_sok)) do;      /* A match was found */
      output;
  end;
  when (%sysrc(_dsenom)) do; /* No match was found */
      _error_ = 0;
  end;
```

```
    otherwise do;
        errormessage = iorcmsg();
        put "ATTENTION: unknown error condition: "
                errormessage;
    end;
end;

run;
```

There are a number of places that you could choose to specify either DROP or KEEP to eliminate NEWACTUAL and NEWPREDICT from the new EXTRACT SAS data set. The examples show some, but not all, of the possibilities.

The important thing to keep in mind is that *you* are responsible for the variables output to the observations in the new SAS data set. When a match is found, SAS outputs the variables and values found in the matching master data set observation. If there are any variables in the transaction data set that do not occur in the master SAS data set, SAS outputs them and their values to the new observation. If you do not want variables that are found exclusively in the transaction data set to be output to the new data set, then you must specifically use DROP or KEEP statements (or options) to exclude them.

You should also consider that all variables *created* in the DATA step are written to the new SAS data set. That is why there is a DROP statement for ERRORMESSAGE in all of the examples. ERRORMESSAGE is used on the odd chance that a non-traditional value of _IORC_ is encountered and the SAS I/O message, IORCMSG(), must be written to the SAS log. However, because ERRORMESSAGE should not make its way into the new SAS data set, it is dropped. Be careful to make sure it is dropped in your own SAS programs if you use the _IORC_ return code check template that was proposed earlier in this chapter. Similarly, if you create other special-use variables that you do not want to keep, make sure to drop them because you don't want them to output to the new data set.

When a match is found using the KEY option on a SET statement, by default the entire master data set observation is written to the new data set. This ensures that the observations in the new data set will have all of the variable values found in the master data sets observations. This happens even when same-named variables in the transaction data set have values that differ from those of the matching observations in the master SAS data set.

If part of the intent in creating a new SAS data set from a transaction data set and a master data set is to update the matching observations, you must specifically do so in

your DATA step. Here is an example where the matching observations are updated
before being written to the new SAS data set:

```
data extract(drop = newactual newpredict);
set  indexlib.tranfile;
set  indexlib.prodfile key=seqnum;

length errormessage $200.;
drop errormessage;

select (_iorc_);
  when(%sysrc(_sok)) do;       /* A match was found */
      actual = newactual;
      predict = newpredict;
output;
  end;
  when (%sysrc(_dsenom)) do; /* No match was found */
      _error_ = 0;
  end;
  otherwise do;
      errormessage = iorcmsg();
      put "ATTENTION: unknown error condition: "
              errormessage;
  end;
end;

run;
```

In the example, when a match is found, ACTUAL is set to NEWACTUAL and
PREDICT is set to NEWPREDICT. This is done before the OUTPUT statement. The
result is that the observations from INDEXLIB.PRODFILE that are written to the
EXTRACT data set now contain new values for ACTUAL and PREDICT. These values
were in variables NEWACTUAL and NEWPREDICT, respectively, in the matching
observations of the INDEXLIB.TRANFILE transaction data set. Consequently, not only
has the new data set been produced by subsetting the master SAS data set, but the
observations have been updated with new values for two variables.

Working with Duplicate Key Variable Values

All of the examples in the previous sections worked on the assumption that both the
master and transaction data sets have observations with unique key variable values. That
means that no two observations in INDEXLIB.PRODINDX or INDEXLIB.TRANFILE
have the same value for SEQNUM. But this may not always be the case. There are four

possibilities for the relationship of duplicate key variable values between the master and transaction SAS data sets.

Unique Index Key Variable Values in Both the Master and the Transaction SAS Data Sets

This is the best situation because it is the easiest to program and provides the most predictable results. You are assured that a given transaction either finds a match on the key variable value in the master data set or it does not. You do not have to do any special traversing of either SAS data set or any special error handling. Matching observations are written to the new SAS data set; non-matching observations are not. You can create simple SAS DATA step code to handle either a match or a mismatch. "Example 13.1: Unique Index Key Variable Values in Both SAS Data Sets," provides an example of how to handle this situation.

Unique Key Variable Values in the Master SAS Data Set and Duplicate Key Variable Values in the Transaction SAS Data Set

Whenever the key variable value in the transaction SAS data set changes value, SAS starts a new index search at the very beginning of the index. When there are two consecutive transactions with the same key variable value, SAS does not start its search at the beginning of the master data set index for the second transaction. Instead, it starts its search from the current index record forward, towards the end of the index. Because the master data set index has unique values, SAS will not find a match as it traverses onward from the current index record. Subsequent transaction observations with the same key variable value will result in a "match not found" condition and will not be represented in the new output SAS data set.

Here is an example of the problem. Consider this portion of a master SAS data set that is to be matched, via SEQNUM, by a very small transaction SAS data set containing two observations:

Master SAS Data Set

SEQNUM	STATE	ACTUAL	PREDICT
11111	Arizona	$112,955	$110,000
22222	**Arizona**	**$101,787**	**$100,000**
33333	Arizona	$ 97,467	$200,000

Transaction SAS Data Set

SEQNUM	STATE	NEWACTUAL	NEWPREDICT
22222	Arizona	$200,453	$200,000
22222	Arizona	$450,250	$350,000

The first transaction observation finds a match on SEQNUM = 22222 in the master SAS data set. The corresponding master data set observation is output to the new SAS data set. When the second transaction attempts to make a match through the KEY option on the SET statement, the KEY variable has the same value, SEQNUM=22222, as in the previous index search. Because the key variable value did not change, SAS does not start its index search back at the beginning of the index. Instead, it starts searching for SEQNUM=22222 in subsequent index records. The first value it sees is SEQNUM=33333; therefore, SAS does not find a match for the second transaction observation. The result is that the second transaction observation is not used to create an observation in the new SAS data set.

This situation can be remedied by using the UNIQUE option on the SET statement. The UNIQUE option specifies that SAS is to go back to the beginning of the index for *every* index search. It enables every transaction with a duplicate index key value to be matched with the corresponding master SAS data set transaction and then to be output to the new SAS data set. "Example13. 2: Duplicate Index Key Variable Values in the Transaction SAS Data Set," illustrates the SAS code you can use to work with this type of situation.

Note that you must be *very* careful to consider whether this is what you really want for the new SAS data set. Consider these two side effects:

Using this technique leads to having observations with duplicate key variable values in the new SAS data set. For example, the master SAS data set with SEQNUM equal to 22222 would be output to the new SAS data set twice, using this technique. (Let's assume that the DATA step code sets ACTUAL equal to NEWACTUAL and PREDICT equal to NEWPREDICT.) The resulting new data set would contain these two observations:

New SAS Data Set

SEQNUM	STATE	ACTUAL	PREDICT
22222	Arizona	$200,453	$200,000
22222	Arizona	$450,250	$350,000

If this is *truly* the result you want, then this is the technique to use.

Another caution is that this situation can lead to duplicate observations in the new SAS data set. It happens when you use the transaction data set as a *lookup* data set and merely output matching master data set observations without updating them in the Program Data Vector. Here is what the new SAS data set would look like for SEQNUM equal to 22222:

New SAS Data Set

SEQNUM	STATE	ACTUAL	PREDICT
22222	Arizona	$101,787	$100,000
22222	Arizona	$101,787	$100,000

In this example, the SAS code in the DATA step output the matching master data set observations when a match occurred. There was no logic to update any of the variables in the master observation before it was output. Consequently, the same master data set observation was matched by two different transaction observations. Each time, it was output to the new SAS data set. The result is that you have one duplicate new observation for every duplicate transaction observation that matched a master observation through the index search. It is very unlikely that you would ever want this situation to happen!

Duplicate Index Key Variable Values in the Master SAS Data Set and Unique Key Variable Values in the Transaction SAS Data Set

By default, an index search returns the first master data set observation with the specified index key variable value. If there are master data set observations with duplicate index key variable values, only the first one will be fetched by the transaction observation and output to the new SAS data set. That is probably not what you would want to have happen. More than likely, you would want all master data set observations with the matching index key variable value to be returned, updated in memory, and then output to the data set.

Here is an example of this situation:

Master SAS Data Set

SEQNUM	STATE	ACTUAL	PREDICT
22222	**Arizona**	**$112,955**	**$110,000**
22222	Arizona	$101,787	$100,000
22222	Arizona	$ 97,467	$200,000
33333	Arizona	$ 19,995	$101,010

Transaction SAS Data Set

SEQNUM	STATE	NEWACTUAL	NEWPREDICT
22222	Arizona	$450,250	$350,000
33333	Arizona	$200,453	$200,000

In the example, the first master data set observation with SEQNUM equal to 22222 is matched by the first transaction observation, updated in the Program Data Vector, and output to the new SAS data set. This results in ACTUAL being set to $450,250 and PREDICT being set to $350,000 in the new SAS data set. SAS then reads the next transaction observation, with SEQNUM equal to 33333, and attempts a match with the master SAS data set. Consequently, the other master data set observations with SEQNUM equal to 22222 are not matched with the first transaction observation and are not output to the new SAS data set.

You can force SAS to continue to read subsequent master data set observations with duplicate key variable values by using a DO loop. The DO loop directs SAS to continue to use the index to return master data set observations with the same key variable value. The DO loop does this until SAS cannot find another match in the index. This technique is illustrated in "Example 13.3: Duplicate Index Key Variable Values in the Master SAS Data Set."

This is another case where you have to ask yourself if this is really what you want to have happen. This situation can lead to observations with duplicate variable values in the new SAS data set. For example, an index match for the data sets above would result in the following observations in the new data set with SEQNUM equal to 22222:

New SAS Data Set

SEQNUM	STATE	ACTUAL	PREDICT
22222	Arizona	$450,250	$350,000
22222	Arizona	$450,250	$350,000
22222	Arizona	$450,250	$350,000

In this example, the DATA step logic sets ACTUAL equal to NEWACTUAL and PREDICT equal to NEWPREDICT. This results in observations with duplicate values for SEQNUM, STATE, ACTUAL, and PREDICT in the new SAS data set. *Be very careful* when you have observations with duplicate key variable values in the master SAS data set but unique key variable values in the transaction data set. You can easily end up with duplicate observations in the new SAS data set.

This caution may not be needed if you are only using the transaction SAS data set as a *lookup* data set and are not going to modify values in the master data set observations as they are written to the new SAS data set. Here is an example of what the new SAS data set would look like in this case for observations in the new data set with SEQNUM equal to 22222:

New SAS Data Set

SEQNUM	STATE	ACTUAL	PREDICT
22222	Arizona	$112,955	$110,000
22222	Arizona	$101,787	$100,000
22222	Arizona	$ 97,467	$200,000

In this example, no attempt was made to set ACTUAL equal to NEWACTUAL and PREDICT equal to NEWPREDICT in the DATA step. Rather, when a match was found, the master data set observation was written (OUTPUT) to the new SAS data set. The new SAS data set does not have observations with duplicate values for ACTUAL and PREDICT. It is far more likely that you would want this result than the previous one where you would end up with new observations containing duplicate values for non-key variables.

Duplicate Index Key Variable Values in Both the Master and the Transaction SAS Data Sets

This is the most complex of all possible output situations. In this case, you want to have all master data set observations with a specific index key variable value matched by all transaction data set observations containing that same value. When each match occurs, you want to have the matching master data set observation output to the new SAS data set. Some master data set observations might be unique and have duplicate corresponding transaction data set observations. Conversely, some transaction data set observations might be unique and have duplicate corresponding master data set observations. Or, there could be multiple master and transaction data set observations with the same key variable values.

Here is an example of this type of situation:

Master SAS Data Set

Observation	SEQNUM	STATE	ACTUAL	PREDICT
2046	22222	Arizona	$112,955	$110,000
2047	22222	Arizona	$101,787	$100,000
2048	22222	Arizona	$ 97,467	$200,000

Transaction SAS Data Set

Observation	SEQNUM	STATE	NEWACTUAL	NEWPREDICT
1	22222	Arizona	$450,250	$350,000
2	22222	Arizona	$200,453	$200,000
3	33333	Arizona	$321,453	$300,000

In this example, the intent is to have an updated value of ACTUAL in the new SAS data set by adding the value of NEWACTUAL from the transaction SAS data set to the value of ACTUAL in the master data set. The value of PREDICT from the master observation is set equal to the value found in the transaction data set. The new data set observations would look like this:

New SAS Data Set

Observation	SEQNUM	STATE	ACTUAL	PREDICT
1	22222	Arizona	$ 563,205	$350,000
2	22222	Arizona	$552,037	$350,000
3	22222	Arizona	$547,726	$350,000
4	22222	Arizona	$313,408	$200,000
5	22222	Arizona	$302,240	$200,000
6	22222	Arizona	$297,929	$200,000

The preceding table shows the results of transaction observation 1 matching the following master observations and updating ACTUAL and PREDICT:

- observation 2046: ACTUAL = $112,955 + $450,250 = $563,205, PREDICT = $350,000

- observation 2047: ACTUAL = $101,787 + $450,250 = $552,037, PREDICT = $350,000

- observation 2048: ACTUAL = $ 97,467 + $450,250 = $547,726, PREDICT = $350,000

The table also reflects the results of transaction observation 2 matching the following master observations and updating them:

- observation 2046: ACTUAL = $112,955 + $200,453 = $313,408, PREDICT = $200,000

- observation 2047: ACTUAL = $101,787 + $200,453 = $302,240, PREDICT = $200,000

- observation 2048: ACTUAL = $ 97,467 + $200,453 = $297,929, PREDICT = $200,000

For the updating to work, you must control both how SAS searches the index and how it traverses the transaction SAS data set. This requires that you do the following:

1. Pre-sort the transaction data set.

2. Use BY statement processing for the transaction data set.

3. Use a DO loop to read the master data set (through the index) for all observations with a given key variable value.

4. Use a dummy key value to go back to the top of the index when the next transaction has the same value as the current one.

This technique (Moorman and Warner 1999) is demonstrated in "Example 13.4: Duplicate Index Key Variable Values in Both the Master and the Transaction SAS Data Sets."

You should always sort your transaction SAS data set into ascending order of the key variable(s) value(s). This improves performance by increasing the possibility that the index file pages and data set pages that are needed to satisfy the next index match are currently held in index and data buffers. Sorting the transaction file before using the KEY option on a SET statement increases the possibility that you can avoid costly I/Os.

Example 13.1: Unique Index Key Variable Values in Both SAS Data Sets

In this example, all observations in the INDEXLIB.PRODFILE master SAS data set have unique key variable values. The observations in the INDEXLIB.TRANFILE transaction SAS data set also have unique key variable values. The master data set has a composite index named COUNTRY_STATE that is built from the COUNTRY and STATE variables. The DATA step creates a new SAS data set containing updated master data set observations that match the values of COUNTRY and STATE in the transaction data set observations.

```
data  extract(drop=newactual newpredict);
set   indexlib.tranfile;
set   indexlib.prodfile key=country_state;

length errormessage $200.;
drop errormessage;

select (_iorc_);
  when(%sysrc(_sok)) do;      /* A match was found */
      actual = newactual;
      predict = newpredict;
      output;
  end;
  when (%sysrc(_dsenom)) do; /* No match was found */
      _error_ = 0;
  end;
  otherwise do;
      errormessage = iorcmsg();
      put "ATTENTION: unknown error condition: "
            errormessage;
  end;
end;

run;
```

The DATA statement creates the EXTRACT SAS data set and excludes, via a DROP option, the NEWACTUAL and NEWPREDICT variables that are found in the transaction data set. The KEY option on the SET statement for INDEXLIB.PRODFILE specifies that the COUNTRY_STATE composite index is to be used to search for observations in the master SAS data set. The _IORC_ automatic variable is queried to determine the success of the attempted index key variable value match. When a match is found, the values of ACTUAL and PREDICT are updated in the master data set observation held in the program data vector. The updated master data set observation is written (OUTPUT) to the EXTRACT SAS data set. If a match is not found, the _ERROR_ automatic variable is reset to ensure that no error messages are written to the SAS log.

Here is the SAS log from the execution of this example DATA step:

```
4     data extract(drop=newactual newpredict);
5     set  indexlib.tranfile;
6     set  indexlib.prodfile key=country_state;
7
8     length errormessage $200.;
9     drop errormessage;
10
11    select (_iorc_);
12       when(%sysrc(_sok)) do;      /* A match was found */
13            actual = newactual;
14            predict = newpredict;
15            output;
16       end;
17       when (%sysrc(_dsenom)) do; /* No match was found */
18            _error_ = 0;
19       end;
20       otherwise do;
21            errormessage = iorcmsg();
22            put "ATTENTION: unknown error condition: "
23                 errormessage;
24       end;
25    end;
26
27    run;


NOTE: There were 11 observations read from the data set
      INDEXLIB.TRANFILE.
NOTE: The data set WORK.EXTRACT has 4 observations and 12 variables.
NOTE: DATA statement uséd:
      real time               0.07 seconds
      user cpu time           0.01 seconds
      system cpu time         0.03 seconds
      Memory                             170k
```

In the log, you can see that 11 observations were read from INDEXLIB.TRANFILE, the transaction data set. The EXTRACT data set has 4 observations; therefore, there were only 4 matches on the index search of INDEXLIB.PRODFILE using the COUNTRY_STATE composite index. The 4 observations in the EXTRACT data set have updated values for variables ACTUAL and PREDICT. All other variables in the new data set that originated in INDEXLIB.PRODFILE have the same values that they originally had—even if there were same-named variables in INDEXLIB.TRANFILE.

You may have noticed that the SAS log does not contain any notes stating that an index was used. SAS writes index usage notes in the log when MSGLEVEL=I has been specified, and it uses an index to optimize a WHERE or BY statement. No notes are necessary in this program because the KEY option on a SET statement *always* uses the specified index. This differs from WHERE and BY statements where SAS may or may not use an index, depending on its estimation as to whether doing so would be optimal.

Use this example program to craft your own index searches when both the indexed master SAS data set and the transaction SAS data set contain unique index key variable values. But be certain that the index key variable values are unique in both data sets. If they are not, then you will not get the results that you want in your new SAS data set.

Example 13.2: Duplicate Index Key Variable Values in the Transaction SAS Data Set

In this example, the master SAS data set has unique index key variable values, but the transaction data set does not. Therefore, there are multiple transaction observations with the same index key variable values that are to be matched against the master SAS data set. The purpose of this DATA step is to create a new data set with one observation for each transaction observation that finds a match in the master data set. Within the new data set observations, the values of ACTUAL and PREDICT are updated.

The transaction data set contains the following:

- 5 observations with SEQNUM = 501
- 4 observations with SEQNUM = 506
- 1 observation with SEQNUM = 10171897
- 1 observation with SEQNUM = 4271955

Only the first two SEQNUM values, 501 and 506, are found in the master SAS data set.

Here is the SAS code:

```
data extract(drop=newactual newpredict);
set  indexlib.tranfile;
set  indexlib.prodfile key=seqnum / unique;
```

```
length errormessage $200.;
drop errormessage;
select (_iorc_);
  when(%sysrc(_sok)) do;      /* A match was found */
      actual = actual + newactual;
      predict = predict + newpredict;
  output;
  end;
  when (%sysrc(_dsenom)) do; /* No match was found */
      _error_ = 0;
  end;
  otherwise do;
      errormessage = iorcmsg();
      put "ATTENTION: unknown error condition: "
            errormessage;
  end;
end;

run;
```

The UNIQUE option on the SET statement causes SAS to start its index search at the beginning of the SEQNUM simple index whenever a new observation is read from INDEXLIB.TRANFILE. Therefore, observations in the transaction data set with duplicate SEQNUM values are able to find their matches in the master SAS data set. This would not be the case if the UNIQUE option were not used. (See "Unique Key Variable Values in the Master SAS Data Set and Duplicate Key Variable Values in the Transaction SAS Data Set," earlier in this chapter.)

Here is the log for this DATA step:

```
92   data extract(drop=newactual newpredict);
93   set  indexlib.tranfile;
94   set  indexlib.prodfile key=seqnum / unique;
95
96   length errormessage $200.;
97   drop errormessage;
98
99   select (_iorc_);
100     when(%sysrc(_sok)) do;      /* A match was found */
101         actual = actual + newactual;
102         predict = predict + newpredict;
103     output;
104     end;
```

(continued on next page)

(continued)

```
105       when (%sysrc(_dsenom)) do; /* No match was found */
106           _error_ = 0;
107       end;
108       otherwise do;
109           errormessage = iorcmsg();
110           put "ATTENTION: unknown error condition: "
111               errormessage;
112       end;
113   end;
114
115   run;


NOTE: There were 11 observations read from the data set
      INDEXLIB.TRANFILE.
NOTE: The data set WORK.EXTRACT has 9 observations and 12 variables.
NOTE: DATA statement used:
      real time            0.09 seconds
      user cpu time        0.00 seconds
      system cpu time      0.00 seconds
      Memory                          167k
```

From the log, we can see that 9 observations were written to the EXTRACT data set. That accounts for the 5 transaction observations in which SEQNUM equals 501. Each observation matched the one master data set observation with the SEQNUM value of 501 and was output to the new data set. Additionally, the 4 transaction observations with SEQNUM = 506 each matched the single master observation with that value of SEQNUM and were output. The new data set observations have values of ACTUAL set as equal to the value of NEWACTUAL in the transaction observation and added to ACTUAL in the master observation. These new observations also show values of PREDICT as equal to the value of NEWPREDICT in the transaction observation added to PREDICT in the master observation.

Example 13.3: Duplicate Index Key Variable Values in the Master SAS Data Set

This example features *duplicate* index key variable values in the master SAS data set and *unique* key variable values in the transaction data set. The transaction data set is going to be used as a *lookup* data set. This means that its only purpose is to identify master data set observations that should be output to the new data set. No variables in the master data set observations are updated by values in the transaction observations.

The master SAS data set has a non-unique composite index built from the COUNTRY and STATE variables and named COUNTRY_STATE. The transaction data set contains only one observation for each of these three Country/State values: *U.S.A./Arizona*, *U.S.A./Florida*, *U.S.A./Massachusetts*, as well as some other Country/State values. However, the master SAS data set contains the following:

- 11 observations where Country/State equals *U.S.A./Arizona*
- 40 observations where Country/State equals *U.S.A./Florida*
- 10 observations where Country/State equals *U.S.A./Massachusetts*

Having multiple observations with the same Country/State values presents a problem because an index search just returns the first master data set observation with the specified index key variable value. When there are multiple master data set observations with duplicate index key variable values, only the first observation is matched by the transaction observation and output to the new data set. To overcome this problem, you must put the master data set's SET statement inside of a DO loop.

Here is the SAS code for this DATA step:

```
data extract;
set  indexlib.tranfile;

length errormessage $200.;
drop errormessage;

do until (_iorc_=%sysrc(_dsenom));
   set  indexlib.prodfile key=country_state;

   select (_iorc_);
      when(%sysrc(_sok)) do;      /* A match was found */
            output;
      end;
```

```
        when (%sysrc(_dsenom)) do; /* No match was found */
            _error_ = 0;
        end;
        otherwise do;
                errormessage = iorcmsg();
                put "ATTENTION: unknown error condition: "
                        errormessage;
        end;
    end;
end;

run;
```

SAS first reads an observation from the INDEXLIB.TRANFILE transaction data set.
The DO UNTIL statement forces SAS to repetitively attempt to read observations in the
master SAS data set via the COUNTRY_STATE composite index for a match for the
values of COUNTRY/STATE found in the transaction observation. When a match is
found, the master observation is written to the EXTRACT data set. SAS continues to
attempt to find matching master observations via the index until a non-matching
condition is found; it is signified by *_IORC_= %sysrc(_dsenom)*. Then the DO UNTIL
loop is satisfied and SAS goes back to the top of the DATA step. The next transaction
observation is read and the index search begins again.

Here is the SAS log from this DATA step:

```
219   data extract;
220   set   indexlib.tranfile;
221
222   length errormessage $200.;
223   drop errormessage;
224
225   do until (_iorc_=%sysrc(_dsenom));
226       set   indexlib.prodfile key=country_state;
227
228       select (_iorc_);
229           when(%sysrc(_sok)) do;      /* A match was found */
230                output;
231           end;
232           when (%sysrc(_dsenom)) do; /* No match was found */
233                _error_ = 0;
234           end;
```

(continued on next page)

(continued)

```
235          otherwise do;
236              errormessage = iorcmsg();
237              put "ATTENTION: unknown error condition: "
238                  errormessage;
239          end;
240      end;
241  end;
242
243  run;


NOTE: There were 11 observations read from the data set
      INDEXLIB.TRANFILE.
NOTE: The data set WORK.EXTRACT has 61 observations and 14 variables.
NOTE: DATA statement used:
      real time            0.01  seconds
      user cpu time        0.00  seconds
      system cpu time      0.01  seconds
      Memory                            173k
```

The log shows that the EXTRACT data set has 61 observations. As mentioned previously, the transaction data set contained only 3 observations that had matches in the master data set for the COUNTRY_STATE index. Those were observations with values of Country/State equal to *U.S.A./Arizona*, *U.S.A./Florida*, and *U.S.A./Massachusetts*. Each of those observations matched consecutively with the following master data set observations:

- 11 observations where Country/State equals *U.S.A./Arizona*
- 40 observations where Country/State equals *U.S.A./Florida*
- 10 observations where Country/State equals *U.S.A./Massachusetts*

That is a total of 61 matching master data set observations. Consequently, the output SAS data set contains only those matching master data set observations.

Example 13.4: Duplicate Index Key Variable Values in Both the Master and the Transaction SAS Data Sets

The most complicated of all index matches takes place when both the master and the transaction data sets have observations with duplicate key variable values. It is difficult because every master observation with a given key variable value must be matched by every transaction observation with the same key variable value. Then these must be output. You need to employ a technique that helps SAS keep track of where it is in both the index file and the transaction data set.

The basic steps to the technique that you must use are the following:

1. Use BY statement processing (with the NOTSORTED option) for the transaction data set.

2. Use a DO loop to read the master data set (through the index) for all observations with a given key variable value.

3. Use a dummy key value to go back to the top of the index to match master observations with the next transaction observation having a duplicate key value.

In this example, there are duplicate index key variable values in both the master and transaction SAS data sets. The master SAS data set has a non-unique composite index, named COUNTRY_STATE, built from the COUNTRY and STATE variables. The master SAS data set contains the following:

- 11 observations where Country/State equals *U.S.A./Arizona*

- 40 observations where Country/State equals *U.S.A./Florida*

- 10 observations where Country/State equals *U.S.A./Massachusetts*

- 939 observations with various other values for Country/State

The transaction SAS data set contains the following:

- 3 observations where Country/State equals *U.S.A./Arizona*

- 1 observation where Country/State equals *U.S.A./Florida*

- 3 observations where Country/State equals *U.S.A./Massachusetts*

- 4 observations with various Country/State values not found in the master data set

We would expect that there would be 103 observations *output* to the new SAS data set after executing the example DATA step. The 103 observations would be for the following key variable value matches:

- Country/State equals *U.S.A./Arizona:* (3 transaction obs) * (11 master obs) = 33
- Country/State equals *U.S.A./Florida:* (1 transaction obs) * (40 master obs) = 40
- Country/State equals *U.S.A./Massachusetts*: (3 transaction obs) * (10 master obs) = 30

The example SAS code follows this basic algorithm:

1. Read a transaction observation.

2. Attempt to match the transaction observation with a master observation through the index.

3. If there is a match, update the master observation in the Program Data Vector, output that observation to the new data set, and return to step 2 to find the next master observation with the same key variable value.

4. If there is not a match, determine if this is the last transaction with this specific key variable value.

5. If it is the last transaction with that specific key variable value, return to step 1.

6. If it is not the last transaction with that specific key variable value, set the key variable value to a nonsense value (to reset the index search back to the beginning) and go to step 2. (This will fail, and then it will iterate again and attempt to match the real value.)

Here is the SAS code:

```
data extract(drop=newactual newpredict flag);
set  indexlib.tranfile;
  by notsorted country state;   ❶

flag = 0;   ❷

length errormessage $200.;
drop errormessage;

do until (_iorc_=%sysrc(_dsenom));   ❸

   if flag = 1 then country = input('0000'x,$10.);   ❹

   set  indexlib.prodfile key=country_state;
```

```
select (_iorc_);
    when(%sysrc(_sok)) do;      /* A match was found */  ❺
          actual = actual + newactual;
          predict = predict + newpredict;
          output;
    end;
    when (%sysrc(_dsenom)) do; /* No match was found */  ❻
      _error_ = 0;
      if not last.country and not last.state and not flag
          then do;  ❼
            flag = 1;
            _IORC_ = 0;
      end;
    end;
    otherwise do;
          errormessage = iorcmsg();
          put "ATTENTION: unknown error condition: "
                errormessage;
    end;
  end;

end;

run;
```

Here are the annotations for this example:

❶ The BY statement with the NOTSORTED option tells SAS that transaction observations with the same BY value are grouped together but are not necessarily sorted. This statement is necessary so that you can use the "last." automatic variable later on in this DATA step. Using the NOTSORTED option enables you to avoid sorting the transaction data set. The BY statement in the example specifies that the transaction data set sort order is COUNTRY and STATE.

❷ The FLAG variable is used to specify when you want to read the first master observation with a given key variable value after a transaction observation with a duplicate value is read.

❸ The DO UNTIL loop enables iterative reading of the master SAS data set via the index. As long as a match is found, this loop is executed. Therefore, multiple master data set observations are output for a single transaction observation within this loop. When there is no longer a match on the index key variable value (that is, it has run out of matching master observations), this loop will be exited.

❹ This IF statement accounts for the condition when a new transaction observation has the same key variable value as the previous one. The index search for the matching master transaction would begin from where the index pointer is currently located and search towards the end of the index. Consequently, it would miss all of the matching master transactions. Therefore, we must fake out the index by setting the value of one of the key variable fields to '0000'x. This forces the index to search again starting from the top.

This value, '0000'x, is used because it is *very* unlikely to occur in the variable COUNTRY. It has the added advantage that SAS can quickly determine that there is no matching entry by looking at only the very first index nodes.

❺ A match is found; update the master observation in the Program Data Vector with values from the transaction observation and output it to the new SAS data set.

❻ When no match is found, reset _ERROR_ and check to see if this is the last transaction with the specific key variable values.

❼ This IF statement checks to see if this is the last transaction observation with a given key variable value. At this point, the previous transaction observation has been matched with all master observations with the same key variable value. If this is a transaction observation with the same key variable value as the previous transaction observation, then set the FLAG variable to 1 and _IORC_ to 0. You want to stay in the DO UNTIL loop and create a bogus value for COUNTRY to force the index to begin its search again at the beginning. Then, the index falls through the DO UNTIL loop, goes back to the top of the DATA step, and reads a new transaction observation.

Here is the SAS log for this DATA step:

```
259  data extract(drop=newactual newpredict flag);
260  set  indexlib.tranfile;
261     by notsorted country state;
262
263  flag = 0;
264
265  length errormessage $200.;
266  drop errormessage;
267
268  do until (_iorc_=%sysrc(_dsenom));
269
270     if flag = 1 then country = input('0000'x,$10.);
271
```

(continued on next page)

(continued)

```
272        set   indexlib.prodfile key=country_state;
273
274      select (_iorc_);
275         when(%sysrc(_sok)) do;        /* A match was found */
276              actual = actual + newactual;
277              predict = predict + newpredict;
278              output;
279         end;
280         when (%sysrc(_dsenom)) do; /* No match was found */
281              _error_ = 0;
282              if not last.country and not last.state and not
                 flag then do;
283                  flag = 1;
284                  _IORC_ = 0;
285              end;
286         end;
287         otherwise do;
288              errormessage = iorcmsg();
289              put "ATTENTION: unknown error condition: "
290                  errormessage;
291         end;
292      end;
293
294   end;
295
296   run;


NOTE: There were 11 observations read from the data set
      INDEXLIB.TRANFILE.
NOTE: The data set WORK.EXTRACT has 103 observations and
      12 variables.
NOTE: DATA statement used:
      real time                0.03 seconds
      user cpu time            0.01 seconds
      system cpu time          0.01 seconds
      Memory                              242k
```

The log shows that there were 103 observations written to the EXTRACT SAS data set. So, each one of the master observations was matched by each one of the matching transaction observations, updated, and output to the new SAS data set.

Note that the resulting EXTRACT SAS data set is likely to have observations with duplicate values of ACTUAL and PREDICT. This is discussed in the earlier section, "Duplicate Index Key Variable Values in Both the Master and the Transaction SAS Data Sets." It may be what you want; or it may not be what you want. Whatever the case, be aware that having duplicate values for ACTUAL and PREDICT is a strong possibility.

Summary

The KEY option on a SET statement provides a way for you to create a new SAS data set by matching observations from a *transaction* SAS data set with those from an indexed *master* data set. SAS reads through the transaction data set and uses the transaction variable(s) specified in the KEY option to search the master data set' s index for a match. When a match is found, your program logic dictates whether or not the master data set observation is updated before being output to the new data set. When no match is found, you can either output the transaction observation to the new data set or skip it. You should use the _IORC_ automatic variable in your program to determine when matches are made.

There are four possibilities that you may encounter when attempting to read master data set observations via the KEY option on the SET statement. The first possibility arises when there are only unique index key variable values in the observations in both the master and transaction data sets. The second possibility occurs when there are unique index key variable values in the master data set, but duplicate key variable values in the transaction data set. The third possibility is that there are observations with duplicate index key variable values in the master SAS data set, but unique ones in the transaction data set. The fourth possibility is when there are observations with duplicate index key variable values in both the master and transaction SAS data sets. This chapter discussed the implications of each of the four possibilities and provided examples for them.

Chapter 14

Overriding Default Index Usage

Introduction

Normally, SAS does a good job of determining when using an index is more efficient than performing a sequential read of an entire SAS data set. However, there may be times when you want to exercise direct control and override the SAS default index behavior. Perhaps an index's centiles have not been updated in a while, although the data set has been updated, and you do not believe SAS can make a good decision with out-of-date centiles. (See Chapter 4, "Index Centiles," for a complete discussion of centiles.) Perhaps there are multiple indexes, and you have a specific preference that SAS use a particular index. Whatever the case, you can override this indexing decision through the use of the IDXNAME and IDXWHERE data set options. These options can be used for SAS data sets specified in a SET statement in a DATA step and in a DATA statement in a SAS procedure. And they can be used for the input SAS table specified in the FROM clause of a SELECT statement in the SQL procedure.

The IDXNAME Option

The IDXNAME option directs SAS to use a specific index to satisfy the conditions in a WHERE expression. When IDXNAME is specified, SAS does not use its internal algorithms to determine whether reading the data set sequentially is more efficient than using an index. Nor does SAS attempt to determine which index is optimal if the data set happens to have multiple indexes. Instead, SAS attempts to use the specified index to return observations to the program. It uses the specified index only when the following conditions are true:

- The specified index exists.
- One of the index variables matches a condition in the WHERE expression *and* the WHERE expression follows the specific rules for using a simple or compound index. (See Chapter 10, "Using Indexes with a WHERE Expression.")
- If the index was originally created with the NOMISS option, then the WHERE expression *must not* return any observations that contain missing values.

The IDXNAME data set option is a good tool to use with SAS data sets that have several indexes when you know that one is a better candidate for improving program performance than another. When a data set has a single index, you can use IDXNAME to override the default algorithms to force SAS to definitely use that index. In either case, the IDXNAME option gives you the ability to override SAS and take control of the use of a particular index.

The IDXWHERE Option

The IDXWHERE option overrides the decision by SAS to use or not use an index to satisfy the conditions of a WHERE expression. There are two values that you can specify:

YES   Directs SAS to use an index and to not attempt to read the data set sequentially. SAS then determines which will best optimize a WHERE expression and uses that index to return observations to the program.

NO   Directs SAS to read the data set sequentially and to not attempt to use an index. SAS reads the data set sequentially and returns observations that satisfy the conditions of a WHERE expression.

The IDXWHERE option can be helpful in cases where you want to force SAS to use an index. Similarly, it can be useful when you know that you want to turn off index use. You should be careful that your use of the IDXWHERE option to override the default behavior in SAS really does improve the performance of your SAS programs.

Example 14.1: Using the IDXNAME Option in a DATA Step

Here is an example of how the IDXNAME option can be used:

```
data Illinois;
      set indexlib.prodindx(IDXNAME=state);
      where state eq 'Illinois' and product in('BED' 'DESK');
run;
```

In the example, suppose that the INDEXLIB.PRODINDX SAS data set has two indexes:

- STATE, a simple index composed of the values of the state variable
- STATE_PRODUCT, a composite index composed of the combined values of variables STATE and PRODUCT.

Also, suppose the following:

- INDEXLIB.PRODINDX has been updated a lot recently.
- The UPDATECENTILES value for the STATE_PRODUCT index has been set to 30.
- Because SAS has not recalculated the STATE_PRODUCT index centiles, you do not want SAS to use that index.

The IDXNAME option directs SAS to specifically use the STATE index to return observations that meet the WHERE expression conditions. Because the STATE index exists and the STATE variable matches a condition in the WHERE expression, SAS *will* use the STATE index.

Here is the SAS log from running the example program:

```
32        data Illinois;
33            set indexlib.prodindx(IDXNAME=state);
34            where state eq 'Illinois' and product in('BED' 'DESK');
INFO: Index STATE selected for WHERE clause optimization.
35        run;

NOTE: There were 288000 observations read from the data set
      INDEXLIB.PRODINDX.
      WHERE (state='Illinois') and product in ('BED', 'DESK');
NOTE: The data set WORK.ILLINOIS has 288000 observations and 12
      variables.
NOTE: DATA statement used:
      real time            3.18 seconds
      user cpu time        0.93 seconds
      system cpu time      0.17 seconds
      Memory                         159k
```

In the log, you can see that SAS used the STATE index to create the ILLINOIS SAS data set from observations in the INDEXLIB.PRODINDX SAS data set. It did so even though the STATE_PRODUCT index would have been a more natural choice for SAS to use under normal circumstances. The use of the IDXNAME option forced SAS to use the STATE index.

Example 14.2: Using the IDXNAME Option in a Procedure

Here is an example of using the IDXNAME option in a SAS procedure:

```
proc univariate
data=indexlib.prodindx(where=(year <= 2005 and quarter = 1 and
                              actual > 1000)
                       idxname=year);
run;
```

In the example, suppose that the INDEXLIB.PRODINDX SAS data set has two indexes:

- YEAR, a simple index composed of the values of the state variable
- YEAR_AND_QUARTER, a composite index composed of the combined values of variables YEAR and QUARTER

Also, suppose the following:

- The YEAR index was not created with the NOMISS option.
- You have reasons to not want to use the YEAR_AND_QUARTER index.

The IDXNAME option directs SAS to specifically use the YEAR index to satisfy the WHERE expression. Because the YEAR index *does* exist, the YEAR variable matches a condition in the WHERE expression, and the NOMISS option was not used when the index was created, SAS uses the YEAR index.

Here is the SAS log from running the example program:

```
64    proc univariate
65    data=indexlib.prodindx(where=(year = 2005 and quarter = 1 and
                                    actual > 1000)
66                                  idxname=year);
INFO: Index YEAR selected for WHERE clause optimization.
67    run;
```

(continued on next page)

(continued)

```
NOTE: PROCEDURE UNIVARIATE used:
      real time              0.32 seconds
      user cpu time          0.18 seconds
      system cpu time        0.01 seconds
      Memory                                424k
```

The SAS log specifies that the YEAR index was selected for WHERE clause optimization—as was directed by the IDXNAME option. SAS had no choice but to use the YEAR index even though the YEAR_AND_QUARTER index may have been more efficient in this instance.

Example 14.3: Using the IDXWHERE Option in a DATA Step

Here is an example of how the IDXWHERE option can be used:

```
data y2000_q3_4;
      set indexlib.prodindx(IDXWHERE=yes);
      where year gt 2000 and quarter > 2;
run;
```

In this example, SAS is directed to specifically use an index if possible. SAS does not consider whether using an index is more efficient than a sequential read of the entire SAS data set to satisfy the WHERE expression. Because INDEXLIB.PRODINDX has more than one index, SAS determines which index is more efficient and uses it. In the example, there is a single simple index built from variable YEAR and a composite index, YEAR_AND_QUARTER, built from variables YEAR and QUARTER.

Here is the SAS log for this example:

```
39    data y2000_q3_4;
40           set indexlib.prodindx(IDXWHERE=yes);
41           where year gt 2000 and quarter > 2;
INFO: Data set option (IDXWHERE=YES)forced an index to be used rather
      than a sequential pass for where-clause processing.
INFO: Index YEAR selected for WHERE clause optimization.
42       run;
NOTE: There were 518400 observations read from the data set
      INDEXLIB.PRODINDX.
      WHERE (year>2000) and (quarter>2);
NOTE: The data set WORK.Y2000_Q3_4 has 518400 observations and
      12 variables.
NOTE: DATA statement used:
      real time              16.28 seconds
      user cpu time          1.18 seconds
      system cpu time        0.46 seconds
      Memory                              159k
```

The first INFO message reports that IDXWHERE=YES was specified, forcing an index to be used rather than a sequential pass of the data set. The second INFO message reports that the YEAR index was the one used to optimize the WHERE clause.

Example 14.4: Using the IDXWHERE Option in a Procedure

Here is an example of using the IDXWHERE option in a SAS procedure:

```
proc summary nway data=indexlib.prodindx(where=(1999 < year < 2004)
                                      IDXWHERE=no);
     class product;
     var actual predict;
output out=sales2000_2003 sum=;
run;
```

In this example, SAS is directed to forget about any indexes that data set INDEXLIB.PRODINDX has; it proceeds to read the entire data set sequentially. SAS does not even consider whether or not using one of the INDEXLIB.PRODINDX indexes would be more efficient. It simply reads the entire data set sequentially and returns observations that meet the WHERE expression's conditions.

Here is the SAS log for this example:

```
43     proc summary nway data=indexlib.prodindx(where=(1999 < year <
                                                2004) IDXWHERE=no);

INFO: Data set option (IDXWHERE=NO) forced a sequential pass of the
      data rather than use of an index for where-clause processing.
44        class product;
45        var actual predict;
46     output out=sales2000_2003 sum=;
47     run;

NOTE: There were 576000 observations read from the data set
      INDEXLIB.PRODINDX.
      WHERE ((year>1999 and year<2004));
NOTE: The data set WORK.SALES2000_2003 has 4 observations and 5
      variables.
NOTE: PROCEDURE SUMMARY used:
      real time            15.35 seconds
      user cpu time         0.92 seconds
      system cpu time       0.21 seconds
      Memory                                152k
```

The INFO message in the log notes that IDXWHERE=NO was specified, forcing a sequential pass of the SAS data set. Even though there is a simple index for INDEXLIB.PRODINDX built from the YEAR variable, SAS did not use it. Instead, it read the entire INDEXLIB.PRODINDX SAS data set.

Example 14.5: Using the IDXWHERE Option in the SQL Procedure

This final example illustrates the use of the IDXWHERE option in the SQL procedure:

```
proc sql;
   create table ontario as
       select * from indexlib.prodcomp(idxwhere=no)
           where country eq 'Canada' and state eq 'Ontario';
quit;
```

In this SQL procedure, the specification of IDXWHERE=NO directs SAS to not use any indexes to optimize the WHERE clause when subsetting the INDEXLIB.PRODINDX table. When PROC SQL is executed SAS must read the entire table to populate the new ONTARIO table with observations that meet the criteria of the WHERE expression.

Here is the SAS log for this example:

```
41    proc sql;
42        create table ontario as
43            select * from indexlib.prodcomp(idxwhere=no)
44                where country eq 'Canada' and state eq 'Ontario';
INFO: Data set option (IDXWHERE=NO) forced a sequential pass of the
      data rather than use of an index for where-clause processing.
NOTE: Table WORK.ONTARIO created, with 115200 rows and 12 columns.

45    quit;
NOTE: PROCEDURE SQL used:
      real time           1.35 seconds
      cpu time            0.84 seconds
```

The SAS log contains an INFO message noting that IDXWHERE=NO was specified and that a sequential pass of the data set was made, instead of SAS using an index.

Summary

From time to time circumstances may arise when you want to override SAS on whether to use or not to use indexes. You can do that via the IDXNAME and the IDXWHERE data set options. The IDXNAME option directs SAS to use the index that you specify and not consider using any other index. As long as some minimal criteria are met, SAS unconditionally uses the index that you specify in the IDXNAME option. The IDXWHERE option forces SAS to either not use any indexes at all or to use an index when SAS may have chosen not to. You can specify IDXWHERE=NO in cases where you do not want SAS to use indexes and IDXWHERE=YES when you want to force SAS to use indexes.

Both the IDXNAME and IDXWHERE options override the normally sound index-choosing logic in SAS. Therefore, you should be very careful when using these options.

Chapter 15

Preserving Indexes During Data Set Manipulations

Introduction

Having gone through the effort of creating indexes for your SAS data sets, you will want to make sure that those indexes are preserved when you use them within your SAS programs. Fortunately, many of the common ways that you would normally process indexed SAS data sets do not compromise your indexes. While Chapter 16, "Removing Indexes—Deliberately and Accidentally," discusses ways that indexes can be removed, this chapter discusses common programming actions that do not disturb the integrity of your indexes. You should familiarize yourself with both chapters so you feel comfortable that the indexes you build will be there when you need them.

Simple Actions That Do Not Compromise Indexes

There are a number of simple programmatic actions that do not compromise SAS indexes. Many of them are somewhat obvious. But they are noted here to give you a convenient list to refer to in case you are ever in doubt.

Using an Indexed SAS Data Set in a SET Statement. Using an indexed SAS data set in a SET statement does not affect the data set or its indexes in any way as long as the DATA statement does specify the same data set as the SET statement. This is true because you are using the indexed SAS data set as *input* to a DATA step, which means that it is in read-only mode. Indexes may aid in the subsetting or ordering of data input to the DATA step, but no aspect of the input data set named in the SET statement can be physically changed.

Consider this example:

```
data newsales;
set  indexlib.prodindx;

     variance = actual - predict;

run;
```

The INDEXLIB.PRODINDX SAS data set has several indexes. However, they are not exploited in the DATA step because there is no use of a WHERE or BY statement. Because the INDEXLIB.PRODINDX data set is used as *input*, no change is made to either the data set or to its indexes.

Here is another example:

```
data quebec_sales;
set  indexlib.prodindx (where=(state eq 'Quebec'));

    variance = actual - predict;

run;
```

As in the previous example, INDEXLIB.PRODINDX is used as *input* to the DATA step. This time, the STATE index is used to subset the data. Because INDEXLIB.PRODINDX is used as input, the data set and its indexes remain static throughout execution of the DATA step.

A final example illustrates this concept with the BY statement:

```
data canada;
set  indexlib.prodindx(where=(state in('British Columbia' 'Ontario'
                                  'Quebec' 'Saskatchewan')));
    by state;
run;
```

Here, the STATE index is being used to both subset and order the observations read from the INDEXLIB.PRODINDX SAS data set. Because the data set is used for *input*, observations are returned from INDEXLIB.PRODINDX with no effect on either the data set or its indexes.

Using an Indexed SAS Data Set as Input to a SAS Procedure. SAS data sets are input to SAS procedures in read-only mode. Neither the SAS data sets nor their indexes are changed in any way. For example, consider this:

```
proc summary nway data=indexlib.prodindx(where=(state='Florida'));
    class product;
    var actual predict;
output out=Florida sum=;
run;
```

The SUMMARY procedure inputs observations from INDEXLIB.PRODINDX where the value of STATE is equal to Florida. In doing so, it uses an index built from the STATE variable. Because the INDEXLIB.PRODINDX SAS data set is used as input, it is in read-only mode and not changed in any way.

If the example had not made use of an index for data set INDEXLIB.PRODINDX, there would also be no change to that data set or its indexes. Again, this is the case because the data set was accessed in read-only mode.

Renaming Index Key Variables. Renaming index key variables does not remove indexes built from those variables. This is true whether the variables are used to create simple or composite indexes. SAS makes the variable name change in the SAS data set's header page and the index file header page and maintains all indexes with which the variable is associated.

In the following example, data set INDEXLIB.PRODINDX has a simple index built from the YEAR variable, as well as several other indexes.

```
proc datasets library=indexlib;
modify prodindx;

rename year= sale_year;

run;
```

The DATASETS procedure renames the YEAR variable to SALE_YEAR. This does not affect the index built from YEAR. After the DATASETS procedure executes, the "Alphabetic List of Indexes and Attributes" of a PROC CONTENTS listing reveals the following:

#	Index	Unique Option	Nomiss Option	# of Unique Values	Variables
1	COUNTY			6	
2	PRODUCT			4	
3	SEQNUM	YES	YES	2304000	
4	**SALE_YEAR**		**YES**	**14**	
5	STATE		YES	16	

-----Alphabetic List of Indexes and Attributes-----

As you can see, SALE_YEAR, which is YEAR renamed, continues to be an index key variable in the INDEXLIB.PRODINDX SAS data set.

NOTE: In composite indexes, the index name is different from the names of the variables used to create it. When one of the composite index variable names is changed, the actual name of the composite index itself remains unchanged. This differs from simple indexes where the name of the index is the same as the name of the index variable, as in the example.

Renaming an Indexed SAS Data Set. Renaming a SAS data set with the DATASETS procedure does not affect its indexes. Both the SAS data set and its index file are renamed.

Here is an example of renaming the INDEXLIB.PRODINDX SAS data set, which has several simple indexes:

```
proc datasets library=indexlib;
  change prodindx = allsales;
run;
quit;
```

This code specifies that SAS data set PRODINDX is to be renamed ALLSALES. Here is a portion of the SAS log from executing this procedure:

```
67    proc datasets library=indexlib;
. . . . . . . . . . . . .
68    change prodindx = allsales;
69    run;
70    quit;


NOTE: Changing the name INDEXLIB.PRODINDX to INDEXLIB.ALLSALES
      (memtype=DATA).
```

The SAS data set is renamed to ALLSALES.sas7bdat, and its index file is renamed to ALLSALES.sas7bndx. Nothing within either the data set or the index file has been changed.

Adding, Deleting, or Updating Observations in an Indexed SAS Data Set. Modifying the contents of a SAS data set using the KEY option on the MODIFY statement does not remove its indexes. Index entries are updated by adding, deleting, and modifying observations. That is normal behavior. However, the indexes themselves remain intact within the data set's index file.

Here is an example of updating a SAS data set via the KEY option on the MODIFY statement:

```
data indexlib.prodindx;
set prod.tranfile;
modify  indexlib.prodindx key=seqnum /unique;
select (_iorc_);
   when (%sysrc(_sok)) do;
        if delflag = 1 then remove;
        else do;
               actual = new_actual;
               predict = new_predict;
               replace indexlib.prodindx;
        end;
   end;
   when (%sysrc(_dsenom)) do;
        _error_ = 0;
        output indexlib.prodindx;
   end;
   otherwise;
end;

run;
```

In this example, the INDEXLIB.TRANFILE SAS data set is used to either remove, replace, or add observations to the INDEXLIB.PRODINDX SAS data set. The SEQNUM simple index is used to directly access observations in INDEXLIB.PRODINDX. This is the normal way that you would use an index to update an indexed SAS data set from a transaction SAS data set.

The partial SAS log from executing this DATA step is as follows:

```
NOTE: There were 11 observations read from the data set
      PROD.TRANFILE.
NOTE: The data set INDEXLIB.PRODINDX has been updated.  There
      were 8 observations rewritten, 1 observations added and 2
      observations deleted.
NOTE: DATA statement used:
      real time              0.01 seconds
      user cpu time          0.01 seconds
      system cpu time        0.00 seconds
      Memory                                162k
```

Though observations were rewritten, added, and deleted, none of these actions affected the integrity or existence of any indexes that exist for the INDEXLIB.PRODINDX SAS data set.

Preserving Indexes While Using the APPEND Procedure

The APPEND procedure offers a convenient way to add a large quantity of observations to an existing SAS data set. As the name implies, the APPEND procedure *appends* the observations by concatenating them to the *end* of the base SAS data set. When the base SAS data set is indexed, SAS appends the observations and then adds the appropriate entries to the index file based on the index key variable values that it finds in the new observations. Consequently, the index is updated to reflect the new observations that were appended to the SAS data set.

Here is an example:

```
proc append base=indexlib.prodindx data=indexlib.tranfile;
run;
```

In this example, the INDEXLIB.TRANFILE SAS data set is being appended to the INDEXLIB.PRODINDX SAS data set, which has several simple indexes. The log for this PROC APPEND reports that the append took place and added 100 new observations to the base SAS data set:

```
128   proc append base=indexlib.prodindx data=indexlib.tranfile;
129   run;


NOTE: Appending INDEXLIB.TRANFILE to INDEXLIB.PRODINDX.
INFO: Engine's fast-append process in use.
NOTE: There were 100 observations read from the data set
      INDEXLIB.TRANFILE.
NOTE: 100 observations added.
NOTE: The data set INDEXLIB.PRODINDX has 2304100 observations
      and 12 variables.
NOTE: PROCEDURE APPEND used:
      real time            0.09 seconds
      cpu time             0.07 seconds
```

A CONTENTS procedure listing for INDEXLIB.PRODINDX would show that all of its indexes still exist. What it would not show is that index entries were updated to include the 100 new observations that were appended.

An interesting phenomenon occurs when you are appending observations to an index that has a *unique* key and there are duplicate index key values in the appending SAS data set.

Here is what happens:

1. SAS appends *all* of the observations in the transaction data set to the base data set.

2. SAS updates the index entries in the base data set.

3. If SAS finds that a new observation's index key variable value already exists in the base SAS data set, the following occurs:

   - SAS does not create an index entry for that new observation because this would violate the uniqueness of the index.

   - SAS deletes the new observation that has just been physically appended to the base SAS data set. Of course, the new observation physically remains in the SAS data set; it is just marked for deletion and is not used.

The upshot of having transaction observations with duplicate index key variable values is that the base SAS data set ends up with wasted space. It contains a number of deleted observations that bloat the size of the data set and cannot be used by any program.

In SAS Version 6, each observation was appended one at time. SAS would update the index as it appended each observation. When duplicate values were found in a unique index, the observation was rejected and not appended to the base SAS data set. Consequently, the base SAS data set was not distended with deleted observations. The penalty for this old method of appending was that it took more computer resources and more time to address each observation individually.

If you know that your transaction data sets may have a number of observations with duplicate unique index key values, you can revert to the SAS 6 append method by using the APPENDVER=V6 option. Here is an example:

```
proc append base=indexlib.prodindx data=indexlib.tranfile
          appendver=v6;
run;
```

The APPENDVER=V6 option directs SAS to append one INDEXLIB.TRANFILE observation at a time to the INDEXLIB.PRODINDX SAS data set. For this reason, observations with duplicate index key values are rejected right away and INDEXLIB.PRODINDX is not bloated with unneeded deleted observations. The only downside to this is that the greater the number of observations in INDEXLIB.TRANFILE, the greater the computer resources and time expended in appending them to the base SAS data set.

Preserving Indexes While Using the APPEND Statement in PROC DATASETS

The APPEND statement in the DATASETS procedure works the same way that PROC APPEND does. It appends all of the observations in a SAS data set to a *base* SAS data set. Like the APPEND procedure, this does not affect an index if the base SAS data set is indexed.

This example does exactly what the example in the previous section does; it appends the INDEXLIB.TRANFILE SAS data set to the INDEXLIB.PRODINDX SAS data set.

```
proc datasets;
      append base=indexlib.prodindx data=indexlib.tranfile;
run;
quit;
```

Here's an excerpt from the log for this execution of PROC DATASETS:

```
144  proc datasets;
145      append base=cdir.prodindx data=cdir.tranfile;
146  run;
147  quit;


NOTE: Appending INDEXLIB.TRANFILE to INDEXLIB.PRODINDX.
INFO: Engine's fast-append process in use.
NOTE: There were 100 observations read from the data set
      INDEXLIB.TRANFILE.
NOTE: 100 observations added.
NOTE: The data set INDEXLIB.PRODINDX has 2304100 observations and 12
      variables.
```

INDEXLIB.PRODINDX now has 100 new observations and a fully updated index file.

Note the discussion about the consequences of attempting to append observations with duplicate index key variable values for unique indexes in the preceding section, "Preserving Indexes While Using the APPEND Procedure." The same holds true for appending observations via the DATASETS procedure.

Preserving Indexes While Using the COPY Procedure

The COPY procedure lets you copy SAS data sets from one SAS data library to another. Though you may not be aware of it, the COPY procedure has an option named INDEX= that determines whether indexes are copied along with their SAS data sets. In actuality, indexes are not really *copied* to the new SAS data library. Instead, SAS copies the *index metadata* to the receiving SAS data library and then uses the metadata to re-create the indexes for the new data set.

The value of the INDEX option is either YES to copy all indexes or NO to not copy any indexes. *Fortunately, the default value for the INDEX option on the COPY statement is INDEX=YES.* Using PROC COPY to copy an indexed SAS data set, without specifying the INDEX option, normally results in the SAS data set being copied and its indexes being re-created at the target destination.

Here is an example SAS log where the INDEXLIB.PRODINDX SAS data set is copied and the default of INDEX=YES is in effect:

```
86    proc copy in=indexlib out=ctemp;
87        select prodindx;
88    run;


NOTE: Copying INDEXLIB.PRODINDX to CTEMP.PRODINDX (memtype=DATA).
NOTE: Simple index COUNTY has been defined.
NOTE: Simple index PRODUCT has been defined.
NOTE: Simple index SEQNUM has been defined.
NOTE: Simple index STATE has been defined.
NOTE: Simple index YEAR has been defined.
NOTE: There were 2304000 observations read from the data set
      INDEXLIB.PRODINDX.
NOTE: The data set CTEMP.PRODINDX has 2304000 observations and 12
      variables.
NOTE: PROCEDURE COPY used:
      real time           2:49.98
      cpu time            20.95 seconds
```

The log shows that SAS copied the data set and re-created the indexes. A CONTENTS procedure listing would show that CTEMP.PRODINDX contains all five indexes.

Preserving Indexes While Using the CPORT and CIMPORT Procedures

The CPORT procedure is used to write SAS data sets, catalogs, or entire data libraries to sequential file formats called *transport files*. The transport files can be transported to another site where they can be translated back to SAS data sets, catalogs, or data libraries via the CIMPORT procedure. SAS programmers often use PROC CPORT to move SAS data between different sites or to load SAS data on different computer operating systems.

The CPORT procedure has the INDEX option that specifies whether indexes are to be included when a transport file is created from SAS data sets that have indexes. The default value is INDEX=YES, which means that SAS will include the metadata necessary to reconstruct the indexes in the transport file along with a copy of the data set itself. (The index metadata is used by SAS to reconstruct all indexes when the data set is re-created via the CIMPORT procedure.)

Here is an example of using the CPORT procedure to copy a SAS data set that contains indexes:

```
filename tranfile 'c:\windows\temp\prodindx';

proc cport data=indexlib.prodindx file=tranfile;
run;
```

In this code, a transport file named PRODINDX is being created in the c:\windows\temp directory from SAS data set INDEXLIB.PRODINDX. Here is the log from an execution of this CPORT procedure:

```
407   filename tranfile 'c:\windows\temp\prodindx';
408
409   proc cport data=indexlib.prodindx file=tranfile;
410   run;

NOTE: Proc CPORT begins to transport data set INDEXLIB.PRODINDX
NOTE: The data set contains 12 variables and 2304000 observations.
      Logical record length is 128.
NOTE: Transporting data set index information.
NOTE: PROCEDURE CPORT used:
      real time             4:51.31
      user cpu time         13.28 seconds
      system cpu time       2.12 seconds
      Memory                            44k
```

Not only has the data been transferred to the transport file, but all index information has been transported, as evidenced by the third NOTE in the SAS log.

Transport files can be transformed back to SAS data sets via the CIMPORT procedure. The CIMPORT procedure imports a SAS data set and builds its indexes (if index information is present) from a transport file onto the host computer. This example is presented to show you that both INDEXLIB.PRODINDX and its indexes can successfully be retrieved from the transport data set created in the previous example.

```
filename tranfile 'c:\windows\temp\prodindx';

libname newlib 'c:\windows\temp\sas files';

proc cimport data=newlib.prodindx infile=tranfile;
run;
```

The CIMPORT procedure reads the PRODINDX SAS transport file and creates SAS data set NEWLIB.PRODINDX. Here is the SAS log:

```
418   filename tranfile 'c:\windows\temp\prodindx';
419
420   libname newlib 'c:\windows\temp\sas files';
NOTE: Libref NEWLIB was successfully assigned as follows:
      Engine:        V8
      Physical Name: c:\windows\temp\sas files
421
422   proc cimport data=newlib.prodindx infile=tranfile;
423   run;


NOTE: Proc CIMPORT begins to create/update data set
      NEWLIB.prodindx
NOTE: The data set index PRODUCT is defined.
NOTE: The data set index YEAR is defined.
NOTE: The data set index COUNTRY is defined.
NOTE: The data set index STATE is defined.
NOTE: The data set index SEQNUM is defined.
NOTE: Data set contains 12 variables and 2304000 observations.
      Logical record length is 128
```

(continued on next page)

(continued)

```
NOTE: PROCEDURE CIMPORT used:
      real time              4:10.81
      user cpu time          29.46 seconds
      system cpu time        4.21 seconds
      Memory                 2221k
```

As you can see, all of the indexes whose information was originally sent via CPORT to the PRODINDX SAS transport file from INDEXLIB.PRODINDX have been re-created for the new NEWLIB.PRODINDX SAS data set. When you use the CPORT procedure with the INDEX=YES default option in effect, a subsequent transporting of that data set using the CIMPORT procedure rebuilds the SAS data set as well as all of its indexes.

Preserving Indexes While Using the UPLOAD Procedure

The UPLOAD procedure enables you to upload a SAS data set and its index(es) to other computers. Those computers could be running SAS on the same operating system or running SAS on different operating systems. When an indexed SAS data set is uploaded, only the data set is actually transferred. SAS does not actually upload the existing index file to the connected computer. Instead, SAS transfers information about indexes to the remote SAS session. Once the data set has been completely uploaded, the SAS/CONNECT program, running on the remote computer, builds the indexes based on the index information that was transmitted. The result is a fully uploaded SAS data set and all its indexes on the remote computer.

Unfortunately, it is very easy to accidentally drop an index when using the UPLOAD procedure. (See the example of losing indexes with PROC UPLOAD in Chapter 16, "Removing Indexes—Deliberately and Accidentally.") You must be careful to use PROC UPLOAD only in one of the following three ways to successfully upload an indexed SAS data set and its indexes:

1. **Specify INLIB and OUTLIB options and use the SELECT statement to transfer individually indexed SAS data sets**. When you upload an entire SAS data library using the INLIB and OUTLIB options, all SAS data sets and indexes are uploaded as well as every other SAS object, such as catalogs, format libraries, etc. If you would like to upload a single indexed SAS data set, you can use the SELECT statement.

Here is an example:

```
libname pclib "C:\TEMP";

rsubmit;

   libname indexlib '/home/production';

   proc upload inlib=pclib outlib=indexlib;
        select prodindx;
   run;

endrsubmit;
```

In the example, we have a Windows SAS data library, C:\TEMP, and a UNIX SAS data library, /home/production. The UPLOAD procedure uses the INLIB and OUTLIB options to point to the two SAS data libraries. The SELECT statement specifies that only the PRODINDX SAS data set is to be uploaded. If that data set contains any indexes, they will be built on the UNIX server after PRODINDX has been uploaded.

Here is a portion of the SAS log for this program:

```
23        proc upload inlib=pclib outlib=indexlib;
24            select prodindx;
25        run;



NOTE: Upload in progress from data=PCLIB.PRODINDX to
      out=INDEXLIB.PRODINDX
NOTE: 294912000 bytes were transferred at 1590448 bytes/second.
NOTE: Sending index information.  Index creation/transfer in
      progress.
NOTE: The data set PCLIB.PRODINDX has 2304000 observations and
      12 variables.
NOTE: Single index DAYMONYR has been defined.
NOTE: Single index MONTH has been defined.
NOTE: Single index seqnum has been defined.
```

(continued on next page)

(continued)

```
NOTE: Single index YEAR has been defined.
NOTE: Single index STATE has been defined.
NOTE: Index transfer complete.
NOTE: Uploaded 2304000 observations of 12 variables.
NOTE: The data set INDEXLIB.PRODINDX has 2304000 observations
      and 12 variables.
NOTE: PROCEDURE UPLOAD used (Total process time):
      real time              3:35.43
      cpu time               27.69 seconds
```

The third NOTE specifies that PROC UPLOAD is "Sending index information" and that "Index creation/transfer [is] in progress." There are NOTEs specifying that each index has been "defined" (created), followed by a NOTE stating "Index transfer complete." This lets you know that the indexes were successfully created for the newly uploaded SAS data set.

If the SELECT statement had not been specified, then *all* SAS objects in the C:\TEMP Windows SAS data library would have been uploaded to the /home/production UNIX SAS data library. Any other SAS data sets containing indexes would have had them built on the UNIX server.

If you need to upload several SAS data sets and their indexes, you can do so with the SELECT statement. You can code multiple SAS data set names in the same SELECT statement. Or you can code each one in a separate SELECT statement. Either method results in the SAS data sets being uploaded and their indexes being rebuilt on the remote server.

2. **Specify the IN option on the UPLOAD procedure and the USER option in an OPTIONS statement to upload a data set and its indexes.** The USER option specifies the default libref that SAS must use when no other libref is specified. When you use the USER option in conjunction with PROC UPLOAD, SAS uploads a SAS data set to that SAS data library by default.

Here is an example of uploading an indexed SAS data set to a UNIX server from a Windows workstation:

```
libname pclib "C:\TEMP";

rsubmit;

    libname indexlib '/home/production';

    options user=indexlib;

    proc upload in=pclib.prodindx;
    run;

endrsubmit;
```

In this example, the OPTIONS statement specifies that INDEXLIB is the default UNIX libref. That libref is allocated on the UNIX server because it falls within the RSUBMIT/ENDRSUBMIT block. When the UPLOAD procedure executes, it uploads the PRODINDX SAS data set from the C:\TEMP Windows directory (with a libref of pclib) to the /home/production directory (with a libref of indexlib). All of the PRODINDX indexes are created once the data set has been successfully uploaded to the UNIX server.

3. **Specify the IN option and let the uploaded SAS data set load into the WORK SAS data library on the other computer.** If you identify the SAS data set that is to be uploaded via the IN option and do not specify the OUT option, that data set is uploaded to the other computer's SAS WORK data library. (The exception to this rule is when the USER option is in effect, as in the previous example.) In this case, SAS uploads the SAS data set to the WORK library and then builds all of its indexes there.

Here is an example:

```
libname pclib "C:\TEMP";

rsubmit;

  proc upload in=pclib.prodindx;
  run;

endrsubmit;
```

In this example, SAS data set PCLIB.PRODINDX is uploaded from a PC directory to a UNIX directory. SAS uploads it to the UNIX directory that is being used as the WORK SAS data library. Then, all the PRODINDX indexes are created on the UNIX server.

The big caution with this particular type of upload is that the data set and its indexes end up residing in a temporary SAS WORK data library. After your SAS/CONNECT session has ended, the data set, its index file, and all other SAS constructs in the SAS WORK data library are lost when the library is deleted. If you want a SAS data set and its indexes to remain after the SAS/CONNECT session has ended, then you should use one of the previously discussed methods of using PROC UPLOAD.

These three methods of uploading a SAS data set will preserve its indexes. The first two are probably used most often because they lead to permanent SAS data sets and indexes on the remote server after the SAS/CONNECT session has terminated. However, the third method may be handy when you have some processing to do and do not want to leave a large SAS data set and its indexes on the remote server after it has been completed.

Preserving Indexes While Using the DOWNLOAD Procedure

The DOWNLOAD procedure permits you to download a SAS data set and its index(es) from another computer. That computer could be running SAS on the same operating system or running SAS on a different operating system. When an indexed SAS data set is downloaded, only the data set is actually transferred. SAS does not actually download the existing index file to the connected computer. Instead, it sends index information along with the downloaded SAS data set. When the data set has been completely downloaded, SAS builds the indexes. The result is a completely downloaded SAS data set with all of its indexes.

It is easy to accidentally drop an index when using the DOWNLOAD procedure. (See the example of losing indexes with PROC DOWNLOAD in Chapter 16, "Removing Indexes—Deliberately and Accidentally.") However, if you use any one of the following three download methods, you can successfully download an indexed SAS data set and its indexes:

1. **Specify INLIB and OUTLIB options and use the SELECT statement to transfer individual indexed SAS data sets.** When you download an entire SAS data library using the INLIB and OUTLIB options, all SAS objects, including SAS data sets, are downloaded. Any indexes existing in the INLIB SAS data library are rebuilt in the OUTLIB SAS data library on the other server. You can download a single indexed SAS data set by specifying it in a SELECT statement. If you do so, only that particular SAS data set is downloaded and its indexes are rebuilt. Here is an example:

```
libname pclib "C:\TEMP\SAS Downloads";

rsubmit;

    libname indexlib '/home/production';

proc download inlib=indexlib outlib=pclib;
     select prodindx;
run;

endrsubmit;
```

In this example, we want to download SAS data set PRODINDX from a UNIX SAS data library, /home/production, to a Windows SAS data library, C:\TEMP. PROC DOWNLOAD uses the INLIB and OUTLIB options to point to the two SAS data libraries. The SELECT statement specifies that only the PRODINDX SAS data set is to be downloaded. Because that data set contains indexes, they are built on the Windows server *after* PRODINDX has been downloaded from the UNIX server.

Here is a portion of the SAS log for this program:

```
33       proc download inlib=indexlib outlib=pclib;
34          select prodindx;
35       run;



NOTE: Download in progress from data=INDEXLIB.PRODINDX to
      out=PCLIB.PRODINDX
NOTE: 294912000 bytes were transferred at 1470971
      bytes/second.
NOTE: Receiving index information.  Index creation/transfer
      in progress.
```

(continued on next page)

(continued)

```
NOTE: Single index STATE has been defined.
NOTE: Single index YEAR has been defined.
NOTE: Single index seqnum has been defined.
NOTE: Single index MONTH has been defined.
NOTE: Single index DAYMONYR has been defined.
NOTE: Index transfer complete.
NOTE: The data set PCLIB.PRODINDX has 2304000 observations
      and 12 variables.
NOTE: Downloaded 2304000 observations of 12 variables.
NOTE: The data set INDEXLIB.PRODINDX has 2304000
      observations and 12 variables.
NOTE: PROCEDURE DOWNLOAD used (Total process time):
      real time              23:12.07
cpu time               4.03 seconds
```

The third NOTE specifies that PROC DOWNLOAD is "Receiving index information" and that "Index creation/transfer [is] in progress." Then there are NOTEs specifying that each index has been "defined" (created), followed by a NOTE stating "Index transfer complete." This message tells you that the indexes were successfully created for the newly downloaded SAS data set.

If the SELECT statement had not been specified, then all SAS objects in the C:\TEMP Windows SAS data library would have been downloaded to the /home/production UNIX SAS data library. Other indexed SAS data sets would have had their indexes built on the Windows server.

You can use the SELECT statement to download several SAS data sets and their indexes from the same SAS data library. Simply code multiple SAS data set names in the same SELECT statement. Or you can code each SAS data set name in a separate SELECT statement. Both methods override the default behavior of the INLIB/OUTLIB options and result in only the specified SAS data sets and their indexes being downloaded.

2. **Specify the IN option on the DOWNLOAD procedure and the USER option in an OPTIONS statement to download a data set and have its indexes built.** The USER option specifies the default libref that SAS is to use when no other libref is specified. When you use the USER option in combination with PROC DOWNLOAD, SAS downloads a SAS data set to the USER SAS data library by default.

Here is an example:

```
libname pclib "C:\TEMP";

options user=pclib;

rsubmit;

   libname indexlib '/home/production';

   proc download in=indexlib.prodindx;
   run;

endrsubmit;
```

In the example, the OPTIONS statement specifies that PCLIB is the default libref on the Windows server. When the DOWNLOAD procedure executes, it downloads the PRODINDX SAS data set from the UNIX /home/production directory to the Windows C:\TEMP Windows directory. It uses that Windows directory because the USER option specified that it is the default directory on the Windows server. The indexes for SAS data set PRODINDX are created by SAS/CONNECT once the data set has been successfully downloaded to the Windows server.

3. **Specify the IN option and let the downloaded SAS data set load into the WORK SAS data library on the client computer**. If you identify the SAS data set that is to be downloaded via the IN option and do not specify the OUT option, that data set is downloaded to your client computer's SAS WORK data library. (The exception to this is when you have specified the USER option, as in the previous example.) SAS downloads the SAS data set to the WORK library and then builds all of its indexes there.

Here is an example:

```
rsubmit;

   libname indexlib '/home/production';

   proc download in=unixlib.prodindx;
   run;

endrsubmit;
```

In the example, UNIX SAS data set PCLIB.PRODINDX is downloaded to an unspecified directory on a Windows workstation. SAS downloads it to the Windows directory that is being used as the SAS WORK data library. Once PRODINDX is completely downloaded, all of its indexes are created in the SAS WORK data library on the Windows server.

Because the downloaded SAS data set and its indexes reside in the SAS WORK data library, they will be deleted when you end your SAS session. You should be cautious when doing this type of download for a SAS data set and its indexes.

These three methods all result in successfully downloaded SAS data sets and their indexes. The first two methods are more utilitarian because they produce permanent indexed SAS data sets and provide the most control over where those data sets reside.

Summary

Though it is possible to accidentally remove indexes, most of the ways that you would normally process indexed SAS data sets do not delete them. Events such as using indexed SAS data sets as input to DATA or PROC steps, renaming index key variables, renaming indexed SAS data sets, and updating indexed SAS data sets via the KEY option on the MODIFY statement have no adverse effect on the indexes.

When you manipulate SAS data sets with SAS procedures, you need to be careful that you specify options that allow indexes to be preserved. This chapter discussed several of the more commonly used SAS procedures and the options that allow indexes to be preserved. By familiarizing yourself with these options, you can avoid the accidental deletion of your indexes and continue to use them to promote good performance in your SAS applications.

Chapter 16

Removing Indexes—Deliberately and Accidentally

Introduction

It should be somewhat comforting to know that you can remove SAS indexes whenever you feel that they are no longer needed. On the other hand, it may be discomforting to know that indexes can be accidentally removed by some of the simple data set manipulations that you often use in SAS programming. This chapter first discusses the two tools that you can use to deliberately delete SAS indexes: PROC DATASETS and PROC SQL. Then it explains how a number of common SAS data set manipulations can result in the accidental loss of all of the indexes associated with a SAS data set.

Explicitly Removing Indexes

You can use the DATASETS procedure to *delete* an index or the SQL procedure to *drop* an index. Both procedures do the same thing, though the terminology is slightly different. They both *remove* the designated index from the SAS data set. If a SAS data set has multiple indexes and some are removed, SAS does not release the unused space from the SAS index file as long as at least one index remains. SAS holds onto the space in case it is needed for the expansion of an existing index or for a new index. You would not see a lower value for the "Number of Index File Pages" in a CONTENTS procedure listing produced after a few indexes were deleted. Once all indexes associated with a SAS data set are removed, SAS automatically deletes the SAS index file.

Deleting Indexes with PROC DATASETS

This is the general format for deleting an index with PROC DATASETS:

```
PROC DATASETS LIBRARY=libref;
    MODIFY data-set-name;
    INDEX DELETE index1 <index2> <index...n>;
RUN;
QUIT;
```

In the form, above, the INDEX DELETE statement specifies the name of the index that is to be deleted. If you want to delete multiple indexes, you can either include them on a single INDEX DELETE statement or code them on separate INDEX DELETE statements.

Here is an example of deleting two indexes at the same time:

```
proc datasets library=indexlib;
  modify prodindx;
      index delete county product;
  run;
quit;
```

In this example, the COUNTY and PRODUCT indexes are deleted from the
INDEXLIB.PRODINDX SAS data set.

Here is the resulting SAS log:

```
16    proc datasets library=indexlib;
                                  -----Directory-----
Libref:         INDEXLIB
Engine:         9.0101M3
Physical Name: C:\Data Files
File Name:      C:\Data Files


        #  Name         Memtype    File Size  Last Modified

        1  PRODCOMP    DATA       297255936   05FEB2005:18:20:28
           PRODCOMP    INDEX       57377792   05FEB2005:18:20:28
        2  PRODINDX    DATA       296332288   06MAR2005:10:14:17
           PRODINDX    INDEX      170344960   06MAR2005:10:14:17
        3  PRODSALE    DATA       298021888   15JAN2005:18:03:25
        4  TRANCAN     DATA        22475776   28MAR2004:13:41:42
17       modify prodindx;
18          index delete county product;
NOTE: Index COUNTY deleted.
NOTE: Index PRODUCT deleted.
19          run;
20    quit;
```

The two NOTEs in the SAS log show that both the COUNTY and the PRODUCT
indexes were successfully deleted. The size of the PRODINDX INDEX file, 170344960
bytes, remains the same after the two indexes were deleted. This means that
INDEXLIB.PRODINDX has one or more remaining indexes. The index file continues to
exist until either the PRODINDX SAS data set is deleted or all of its indexes are deleted.

Dropping Indexes with PROC SQL

This is the general format for dropping an index with the SQL procedure:

```
PROC SQL;
    DROP INDEX index-name FROM table-name;
QUIT;
```

As the form illustrates, the DROP INDEX statement is used to remove an index. You must identify the name of the index that is to be dropped and the SAS table that it is associated with. Only one index may be removed in a DROP INDEX statement; if you have multiple indexes to drop, you must use multiple DROP INDEX statements.

In this example two indexes are dropped via PROC SQL:

```
proc sql;
   drop index state from indexlib.prodindx;
   drop index year from indexlib.prodindx;
quit;
```

In the example, the first DROP INDEX statement drops the STATE index from the INDEXLIB.PRODINDX SAS table. The second one drops the YEAR index.

Here is the resulting SAS log:

```
27   proc sql;
28   drop index state from indexlib.prodindx;
NOTE: Index state has been dropped.
29   drop index year from indexlib.prodindx;
NOTE: Index year has been dropped.
30   quit;
NOTE: PROCEDURE SQL used:
      real time            3.17 seconds
      cpu time             0.23 seconds
```

The two NOTEs in the SAS log report that the STATE and the YEAR index have been dropped. Notice that this output is much simpler than the output from deleting indexes with PROC DATASETS.

How Integrity Constraints Affect Index Deletion

Integrity constraints are a set of data validation rules specified by users to restrict the data values that can be stored in a variable in a SAS data set. They are created by the SQL procedure, by the DATASETS procedure, or in the SAS Component Language (SCL).

When users create *unique*, *primary key*, and *foreign key* integrity constraints, SAS stores the data values in an index file.

If an index for a particular integrity constraint variable does not exist, SAS builds one. If an index for a particular variable that is being defined as having an integrity constraint already exists, SAS uses the existing index for two purposes: as an index that facilitates accessing data and to enforce the integrity constraint. When this happens, SAS marks the index as having two owners. The first one is the user who created the index and the second one is the integrity constraint itself. SAS does not delete the index until both owners request that it be deleted.

When you attempt to remove an index that is also an integrity constraint by using the DATASETS or SQL procedure, SAS marks only that the ownership for the user who created the index has been removed from the index. The index continues to exist and will be used to enforce integrity constraints within the data set. To permanently remove the index, you must remove the integrity constraint via the SQL procedure, the DATASETS procedure, or in SCL code. If you attempt to remove an index via PROC DATASETS or PROC SQL and see that it still exists, it is most likely caused by an existing integrity constraint that you were not aware of.

Accidentally Removing Indexes

It can be very aggravating to accidentally remove a SAS index, especially if it happens deep within a program and you were counting on using the index to optimize the program's computer resource usage. The unfortunate fact is that accidentally deleting an index is easy to do. It is easy because some very common types of SAS data set manipulations actually remove all indexes associated with a SAS data set.

The most common ways that indexes are accidentally removed are as follows:

1. **When an indexed SAS data set is "written" over by being in both the DATA and SET statements, its indexes are deleted.** This is probably the easiest mistake to make and the easiest mistake to avoid. You can use the DATASETS procedure to make simple changes to variable characteristics such as labels, formats, informats, etc. It can also be avoided by using the KEY option on a MODIFY statement when you need to add, update, or delete observations within an indexed SAS data set. (See Chapter 12, "Using Indexes with the KEY Option on a Modify Statement," for a more thorough discussion.)

In this example, SAS data set INDEXLIB.PRODINDX, containing multiple indexes, is specified in both the DATA and SET statements so that the new variable VARIANCE can be created:

```
52
53    data indexlib.prodindx;
54    set  indexlib.prodindx;
55
56    variance = actual - predict;
57
58    run;

NOTE:  There were 2304000 observations read from the data set
       INDEXLIB.PRODINDX.
NOTE:  The data set INDEXLIB.PRODINDX has 2304000
       observations and 11 variables.
NOTE:  DATA statement used:
       real time            59.99 seconds
       cpu time             11.45 seconds
```

As you can see, though INDEXLIB.PRODINDX has been re-created from the old data set with the same name to contain the new variable, there are no messages in the log to indicate that all of the indexes were removed. But all indexes have indeed been removed. Consequently, a subsequent use of a subsetting WHERE or an ordering BY statement results in a sequential read of the entire INDEXLIB.PRODINDX SAS data set.

Here is another example where all indexes are lost because the indexed SAS data set was specified in both the DATA and SET statements. In this example log, a misguided attempt is made to update a *master* SAS data set with a *transaction* data set using the KEY option on a SET statement.

```
365   data indexlib.prodindx;
366   set tranfile;
367   set indexlib.prodind key=seqnum ;
368   select (_iorc_);
369      when (%sysrc(_sok)) do;
370          actual = new_actual;
371          predict = new_predict;
372          output;
373      end;
```

(continued on next page)

(continued)

```
374         when (%sysrc(_dsenom)) do;
375             _error_ = 0;
376         end;
377         otherwise;
378   end;
379
380   run;


NOTE: There were 11 observations read from the data set
      WORK.TRANFILE.
NOTE: The data set INDEXLIB.PRODINDX has 10 observations and 14
      variables.
NOTE: DATA statement used:
      real time              0.01 seconds
      user cpu time          0.00 seconds
      system cpu time        0.00 seconds
      Memory                             170k
```

Because the intent of the program was to update observations in
INDEXLIB.PRODINDX when SEQNUM matches were found in TRANFILE, this
program should really have used the KEY option on the MODIFY statement, instead
of on a SET statement. Because of this error, not only did INDEXLIB.PRODINDX
have all of its indexes stripped away, but it dropped from 2,304,000 observations to
just 10 observations. This is clearly not what the program's author would have
wanted; it is simply the result of a common index-deleting error.

2. **When a new data set is created from an indexed SAS data set in a DATA step,
   the new SAS data set *is not* indexed.** SAS copies only the observations in the data
   set specified in the SET statement to the data set specified in the DATA statement.
   Existing indexes *are not* copied to the new data set. If you want an index for the new
   data set, you may specify the INDEX data set option on the DATA statement. Or
   you may build the index by using the DATASETS or SQL procedure after the new
   data set has been created.

   In this SAS log, data set CTEMP.PRODINDX is created from the indexed SAS data
   set INDEXLIB.PRODINDX in a DATA step. Even though
   INDEXLIB.PRODINDX contained five simple indexes, the new data set does not
   contain any indexes.

```
104   data ctemp.prodindx;
105   set  indexlib.prodindx;
106   run;


NOTE: There were 2304000 observations read from the data set
      INDEXLIB.PRODINDX.
NOTE: The data set CTEMP.PRODINDX has 2304000 observations
      and 12 variables.
NOTE: DATA statement used:
      real time            59.29 seconds
      cpu time             1.65 seconds
```

The SAS log makes no mention of indexes because SAS did not copy, use, or create any indexes during execution of the DATA step. Now that CTEMP.PRODINDX exists, indexes may be created with either PROC DATASETS or PROC SQL.

3. **When an indexed SAS data set is sorted into itself with the FORCE option enabled, its indexes are deleted.** The FORCE option specifies that SAS is to sort and replace an indexed (or subsetted) data set when the OUT option is not specified. Unfortunately, all user-created indexes are removed when the FORCE option is used. (Indexes created by integrity constraints are not removed when the FORCE option is used.) Fortunately, the default SAS sort option is NOFORCE; you would have to use the FORCE option to have your indexes deleted.

If you attempt to sort a SAS data set containing indexes without the FORCE option, SAS produces an error message and does not sort the data set. Here is an example SAS log from an attempt to sort (without the FORCE option) the INDEXLIB.PRODINDX SAS data set, which contains several indexes:

```
33
34    proc sort data=indexlib.prodindx;
35        by country;
36    run;


ERROR: Indexed data set cannot be sorted in place unless the
       FORCE option is used.
NOTE:  The SAS System stopped processing this step because
       of errors.
NOTE:  PROCEDURE SORT used:
       real time            0.00 seconds
       cpu time             0.00 seconds
```

The example shows clearly that SAS refuses to sort the indexed data set.

Here is the SAS log with the FORCE option used:

```
38    proc sort data=indexlib.prodindx force;
39        by country;
40    run;


NOTE: SAS sort was used.
NOTE: There were 2304000 observations read from the data set
      INDEXLIB.PRODINDX.
NOTE: The data set INDEXLIB.PRODINDX has 2304000
      observations and 10 variables.
NOTE: PROCEDURE SORT used:
      real time              57.53 seconds
      cpu time                9.71 seconds
```

SAS does not put any messages in the log to report the removal of the indexes. However, if you were to execute PROC CONTENTS, you would find that INDEXLIB.PRODINDX does not contain a single index after the sort.

4. **When you use the SORT procedure to input an indexed SAS data set and then sort and output to a new SAS data set, the new SAS data set *is not* indexed.** SAS does not re-create the indexes in the new SAS data set. This is true even if you use the FORCE option on the SORT statement.

   The following SAS code inputs SAS data set INDEXLIB.PRODINDX, sorts the observations by COUNTRY, and outputs to a new SAS data set named CTEMP.PRODINDX.

   ```
   proc sort in=indexlib.prodindx out=ctemp.prodindx force;
        by country;
   run;
   ```

   Even though the FORCE option is used in PROC SORT, none of the five indexes that reside in INDEXLIB.PRODINDX are re-created in CTEMP.PRODINDX. Consequently, new indexes have to be created by using the DATASETS or SQL procedure.

   Note that the five indexes could have been created for the new CTEMP.PRODINDX by specifying the INDEX data set option on the OUT statement in the SORT procedure. See Chapter 7, "Creating Indexes with the INDEX Data Set Option," for more details.

5. **When an indexed data set is copied via the COPY procedure with the INDEX=NO coded for the INDEX parameter, its indexes are not created for the new copy of the data set.** Fortunately, the default value for the INDEX option on the COPY statement is INDEX=YES. Because coding INDEX=NO is such an overt action, it is unlikely that you would accidentally delete indexes this way.

Here is an example SAS log where the INDEXLIB.PRODINDX SAS data set is copied and the default of INDEX=YES is in effect:

```
86    proc copy in=indexlib out=ctemp;
87        select prodindx;
88    run;


NOTE: Copying INDEXLIB.PRODINDX to CTEMP.PRODINDX
      (memtype=DATA).
NOTE: Simple index COUNTY has been defined.
NOTE: Simple index PRODUCT has been defined.
NOTE: Simple index SEQNUM has been defined.
NOTE: Simple index STATE has been defined.
NOTE: Simple index YEAR has been defined.
NOTE: There were 2304000 observations read from the data set
      INDEXLIB.PRODINDX.
NOTE: The data set CTEMP.PRODINDX has 2304000 observations
      and 12 variables.
NOTE: PROCEDURE COPY used:
      real time              2:49.98
      cpu time               20.95 seconds
```

The log shows that SAS copied the data set and rebuilt the indexes for CTEMP.PRODINDX. A CONTENTS procedure listing would show that CTEMP.PRODINDX does indeed contain five indexes.

Contrast the example above with this one where INDEX=NO is specified:

```
95    proc copy in=indexlib out=ctemp index=no;
96        select prodindx;
97    run;


NOTE: Copying INDEXLIB.PRODINDX to CTEMP.PRODINDX
      (memtype=DATA).
NOTE: Index copy suppressed at user's request.
```

(continued on next page)

(continued)

```
NOTE: There were 2304000 observations read from the data set
      INDEXLIB.PRODINDX.
NOTE: The data set CTEMP.PRODINDX has 2304000 observations
      and 12 variables.
NOTE: PROCEDURE COPY used:
      real time              55.06 seconds
      cpu time                1.49 seconds
```

The NOTE in the log clearly states that the index copy was suppressed. Running PROC CONTENTS validates the fact that the CTEMP.PRODINDX SAS data set does not have any indexes associated with it.

6. **When you use the SAS XPORT engine to create a transport file, indexes are not copied to the transport file**. Many programmers use the SAS XPORT engine to create transport files to either transport SAS files to other operating systems or to create backup copies of SAS files. However, SAS transport files do not support indexes. If your indexed SAS data sets need to be transported to another operating system, use the CPORT procedure instead of the XPORT engine to create your SAS transport file. See the "Preserving Indexes While Using the CPORT Procedure" section in Chapter 15, "Preserving Indexes During Data Set Manipulations," for more details on PROC CPORT.

Here is an example of SAS code that creates a transport file from a SAS data set that has five indexes:

```
libname templib "C:\windows\temp";

libname xportlib xport "C:\windows\temp\prodfile.xpt";

proc copy in=templib out=xportlib;
    select prodindx;
run;
```

In the example, indexed SAS data set PRODINDX, in the TEMPLIB SAS data library, is input to the SAS XPORT engine to create the PRODFILE.XPT SAS transport file. This is accomplished via the XPORT keyword in the second LIBNAME statement and the COPY procedure.

Here is the resulting SAS log:

```
8     libname templib "C:\windows\temp";
NOTE: Libref TEMPLIB was successfully assigned as follows:
      Engine:        V8
      Physical Name: C:\windows\temp
9
10    libname xportlib xport "C:\windows\temp\prodfile.xpt";
NOTE: Libref XPORTLIB was successfully assigned as follows:
      Engine:        XPORT
      Physical Name: C:\windows\temp\prodfile.xpt
11
12    proc copy in=templib out=xportlib;
13        select prodindx;
14    run;


NOTE: Copying TEMPLIB.PRODINDX to XPORTLIB.PRODINDX
      (memtype=DATA).
WARNING: Indexes for TEMPLIB.PRODINDX.DATA cannot be copied.
WARNING: Engine XPORT does not support index create
         operations.
NOTE: There were 2304000 observations read from the data set
      TEMPLIB.PRODINDX.
NOTE: The data set XPORTLIB.PRODINDX has 2304000
      observations and 12 variables.
NOTE: PROCEDURE COPY used:
      real time          1:13.43
      cpu time           5.03 seconds
```

As you can see from the two WARNING messages in the log, the SAS XPORT engine does not support indexes. Therefore, no index metadata is created in the SAS transport file. When the PRODFILE.XPT transport file is reconverted to a SAS data set on another computer, it will not contain any indexes.

7. **When you use PROC UPLOAD to upload a SAS data set to another computing platform and use both the DATA and OUT options, indexes are not created for the uploaded data set.** It is common practice to use both the DATA and the OUT options when uploading a single SAS data set with PROC UPLOAD through SAS/CONNECT. However, this practice has unintended negative consequences when the SAS data set specified by the DATA option is indexed. No indexes will be created for the SAS data set specified by the OUT option when it is uploaded to the other computer platform.

Here is an example:

```
libname pclib "C:\TEMP";

rsubmit;

    libname unixlib '/home/production';

    proc upload data=pclib.prodindx out=unixlib.prodindx;
    run;

endrsubmit;
```

The intent of the example is to upload the PCLIB.PRODINDX SAS data set from a Windows workstation to the /home/production directory on a UNIX server. The SAS code is syntactically correct and uploads the SAS data set. However, because both the DATA and the OUT options are not specified, no indexes are created for UNIXLIB.PRODINDX by PROC UPLOAD.

The PROC UPLOAD portion of the SAS log for this program looks like this:

```
5          proc upload data=pclib.prodindx
           out=unixlib.prodindx;
6          run;


NOTE: Upload in progress from data=PCLIB.PRODINDX to
      out=UNIXLIB.PRODINDX
NOTE: 294912000 bytes were transferred at 419027
      bytes/second.
NOTE: The data set PCLIB.PRODINDX has 2304000 observations
      and 12 variables.
NOTE: Uploaded 2304000 observations of 12 variables.
NOTE: The data set UNIXLIB.PRODINDX has 2304000 observations
      and 12 variables.
NOTE: PROCEDURE UPLOAD used (Total process time):
      real time              11:45.13
cpu time              6.06 seconds
```

Notice that the log does not mention SAS indexes, even though INDEXLIB.PRODINDX contains three of them. The UNIXLIB.PRODINDX SAS data set is index-free after the upload.

If you try specifying the INDEX=YES option to override the problem of the DATA/OUT option combination dropping indexes, it does not work. It produces the following warning message in your SAS log:

```
WARNING: INDEX=YES option is invalid when the OUT option is
         specified; INDEX=YES will be ignored.
```

The section, "Preserving Indexes While Using the UPLOAD Procedure," in Chapter 15, "Preserving Indexes During Data Set Manipulations," provides several methods of avoiding the loss of indexes when uploading SAS data sets with PROC UPLOAD.

8. **When you use PROC DOWNLOAD to download a SAS data set from another computing platform and use both the DATA and OUT options, the downloaded SAS data set is not indexed.** As with the UPLOAD procedure, it is common practice to use both the DATA and the OUT options when downloading specific SAS data sets using PROC DOWNLOAD with SAS/CONNECT. When both options are used, indexes *are not* created for the SAS data set specified by the OUT option when it is downloaded.

Here is an example:

```
libname pclib "C:\TEMP\SAS Downloads";

rsubmit;

   libname unixlib '/home/indexdir';

   proc download data=unixlib.prodindx out=pclib.prodindx;
   run;

endrsubmit;

   run;
```

In the example, the PCLIB.PRODINDX SAS data set is downloaded from a UNIX server to the C:\TEMP\SAS Downloads directory on a Windows workstation. Because both the DATA and the OUT options were specified, no indexes are created for PCLIB.PRODINDX by the DOWNLOAD procedure.

This is how the PROC DOWNLOAD portion of the SAS log looks:

```
24         proc download data=unixlib.prodindx
           out=pclib.prodindx;
25         run;


NOTE: Download in progress from data=UNIXLIB.PRODINDX to
      out=PCLIB.PRODINDX
NOTE: 294912000 bytes were transferred at 1588050
      bytes/second.
NOTE: The data set PCLIB.PRODINDX has 2304000 observations
      and 12 variables.
NOTE: Downloaded 2304000 observations of 12 variables.
NOTE: The data set UNIXLIB.PRODINDX has 2304000 observations
      and 12 variables.
NOTE: PROCEDURE DOWNLOAD used (Total process time):
      real time          3:14.86
      cpu time           3.92 seconds
```

The SAS log does not contain index messages even though UNIXLIB.PRODINDX
has three simple indexes. Consequently, the INDEXLIB.PRODINDX SAS data set
does not contain a single index after the download has completed.

Do not attempt to circumvent this problem by also specifying the INDEX=YES
option. It does not work and produces the following warning message in your SAS
log:

```
WARNING: INDEX=YES option is invalid when the OUT option is
         specified; INDEX=YES will be ignored.
```

The section, "Preserving Indexes While Using the DOWNLOAD Procedure," in
Chapter 15, "Preserving Indexes During Data Set Manipulations," provides several
methods of avoiding the loss of indexes when downloading SAS data sets via PROC
DOWNLOAD.

9. **When you copy a SAS data set and its index file from a different operating
   system and access it using Cross-Environment Data Access (CEDA), SAS
   cannot use the indexes.** Starting with SAS Version 7, users can copy SAS data sets
   from other operating systems and process them using SAS on a different system.
   SAS uses its CEDA engine to understand the internal composition of the SAS data
   set that has a foreign data representation. However, CEDA poses some strict
   limitations on how the data set can be processed. One of the limitations is that SAS
   does not recognize that the data set is indexed.

For example, consider data set INDEXLIB.PRODINDX, which resides on a Linux server. A partial listing of the CONTENTS procedure, as run on Linux, shows the following:

```
                          The CONTENTS Procedure

Data Set Name        INDEXLIB.PRODINDX              Observations          2304000
Member Type          DATA                          Variables             12
Engine               V9                            Indexes               5
Created              Thursday, May 05, 2005 03:45:55 PM  Observation Length    128
Last Modified        Thursday, May 05, 2005 03:45:55 PM  Deleted Observations  0
Protection                                         Compressed            NO
Data Set Type                                      Sorted                NO
Label
Data Representation  LINUX_32, INTEL_ABI
```

Note that INDEXLIB.PRODINDX has five indexes.

Now, we transfer PRODINDX.sas7bdat and PRODINDX.sas7bndx, the SAS data set and its index, to a Windows server using a binary FTP. Then, using Windows SAS, we execute a PROC CONTENTS against the Linux SAS data set now residing on the Windows server. We first observe the following in the SAS log:

```
3      proc contents data=linxdata.prodindx;
4      run;


INFO: Data file LINXDATA.PRODINDX.DATA is in a format native
      to another host or the file encoding does not match
      the session encoding. Cross Environment Data Access
      will be used, which may require additional CPU
      resources and reduce performance.
```

Here is the partial CONTENTS listing for LINXDATA.PRODINDX:

```
                        The CONTENTS Procedure

Data Set Name    LINXDATA.PRODINDX              Observations          2304000
Member Type      DATA                           Variables             12
Engine           V9                             Indexes               0
Created          Thursday, May 05, 2005 03:45:55 PM  Observation Length    128
Last Modified    Thursday, May 05, 2005 03:45:55 PM  Deleted Observations  0
Protection                                      Compressed            NO
Data Set Type                                   Sorted                NO
Label
Data Representation    LINUX_32, INTEL_ABI
Encoding              latin1  Western (ISO)
```

Notice that there are zero indexes for LINXDAT.PRODINDX in the CONTENTS listing. Even though both the SAS data set (PRODINDX.sas7bdat) and its index (PRODINDX.sas7bndx) are sitting side by side in the same Windows directory, SAS does not recognize the indexes. When you are processing SAS data sets from foreign operating systems via CEDA, no indexes, if there are any, are available for your use.

By carefully avoiding the actions that remove SAS indexes, you ensure that your SAS applications will successfully exploit them. Be sure to check your SAS log from time to time to ensure that your WHERE and BY statements *are indeed* using the indexes that you want them to use. If these statements cease to use a particular index, check a CONTENTS procedure listing to determine if the index still exists. Make sure that other applications that use your SAS data sets have not inadvertently compromised the indexes.

Summary

Indexes can be removed both deliberately and accidentally in SAS. You can deliberately *delete* individual indexes using the INDEX DELETE statement in the DATASETS procedure. The SQL procedure enables you to *drop* indexes using the DROP INDEX statement. Though the syntax and terminology is different, both procedures essentially enable you to remove indexes for a specific SAS data set. When all of a SAS data set's indexes are removed, SAS deletes the index file from your system.

Some very common data set manipulations can accidentally remove all indexes associated with a SAS data set. These include various uses of the DATA step, the SORT procedure, the COPY procedure, the UPLOAD and DOWNLOAD procedures, and restrictions imposed by CEDA. You should familiarize yourself with the types of data set manipulations that remove indexes. Then, you can avoid putting them in your SAS programs and ensure that the indexes you rely on are there to serve you when you need them.

Chapter **17**

Recovering and Repairing Indexes

Introduction

Like other types of computer files, SAS index files can sometimes go missing or become physically damaged. For example, a system administrator might accidentally delete an index file while cleaning up a production directory. Or an index file might run out of disk space during an update operation and be only partially complete. Fortunately, SAS has a couple of features that usually enable you to recover a missing or damaged index. This chapter discusses how you can use SAS to recover an index file that is missing and to repair an index file that is damaged.

Though this chapter discusses missing and damaged index files separately, SAS internal code makes no such distinction between the two. It views a missing index file or a damaged index file as just one of several reasons to consider that the SAS data set itself is damaged. When you encounter an index problem it is likely to be because an index is missing or because one is damaged. This chapter divides index problems into two categories: missing index files and damaged index files.

The DLDMGACTION Option and Missing or Damaged Indexes

The DLDMGACTION system option specifies which action SAS is to take when a damaged data set (or catalog) is opened. As noted, a missing or damaged index file is just one of several reasons that SAS could consider a SAS data set to be damaged. The data set itself could be compromised in some way that makes it unreadable. Whatever the problem with a SAS data set, the current setting of the DLDMGACTION option dictates whether or not SAS attempts to rebuild or repair it.

The possible settings for DLDMGACTION are as follows:

FAIL   SAS immediately stops the DATA or PROC step and writes an error message to the log. *This is the default setting for batch mode.*

REPAIR   SAS automatically rebuilds indexes and writes a warning message to the log. *This is the default setting for interactive mode.*

ABORT   SAS terminates the DATA or PROC step, writes an error message to the SAS log, and aborts the SAS session.

PROMPT   SAS displays a window that enables the user to select either FAIL, REPAIR, or ABORT to process the damaged index.

A good all-around value for DLDMGACTION is REPAIR. This value facilitates the successful completion of your interactive and batch SAS programs if an index file ever becomes compromised. With this value, SAS rebuilds a missing index and repairs a damaged index when one of these problems is encountered.

You can specify the DLDMGACTION system option in a system configuration file, a user configuration file, the SAS invocation, an OPTIONS statement, and in the SAS System Options window in a SAS windowing environment. Here is an example of specifying the DLDMGACTION option in an OPTIONS statement:

```
options dldmgaction = repair;
```

If DLDMGACTION is not set to REPAIR and SAS encounters an index problem, your program fails. Here is an example:

```
21    options dldmgaction=fail;
22
23    proc contents data=indexlib.prodindx;
ERROR: The open failed because library member
       INDEXLIB.PRODINDX.DATA is damaged.
24    run;


NOTE: Statements not processed because of errors noted above.
NOTE: PROCEDURE CONTENTS used:
      real time              0.18 seconds
      cpu time               0.00 seconds


NOTE: The SAS System stopped processing this step because of
      errors.
```

In this example, the index for SAS data set INDEXLIB.PRODINDX is missing. The OPTIONS statement set DLDMGACTION to FAIL. When the CONTENTS procedure attempted to open the INDEXLIB.PRODINDX SAS data set, the open failed. The ERROR message in the SAS log states that the open failed because the data set is damaged. However, the log does not state exactly how the data set is damaged.

Recovering Missing Index Files

By default, SAS creates an index file in the same directory as the SAS data file. It gives the index file the same name as the SAS data file except that it has a suffix of .sas7bndx.[1] Consequently, SAS expects the index file to reside in the same directory as the data file and to have the same name but not the same suffix. When the file resides elsewhere, SAS considers the index file to be missing and makes an attempt to recover it, but only if DLDMGACTION is set to REPAIR.

An index file could go missing for a number of reasons:

- It may have been deleted.
- It may have been moved to another directory.
- It may have been renamed.
- The SAS data file may have been renamed while the index file was not.

These actions must have been done using an operating system command, the execution of some other type of program, or a GUI action. *Note that SAS cannot rebuild an index that has either been deleted deliberately or accidentally.* For details see Chapter 16, "Removing Indexes—Deliberately and Accidentally."

Because SAS stores index information in the header page of a SAS data set, it can rebuild an index file that is missing. When a SAS data set is opened after an index file goes missing, SAS recognizes the problem. If DLDMGACTION is set to REPAIR, SAS rebuilds the index file. SAS reconstructs all of the simple and/or composite indexes that resided within the original index file. Because this is an innate feature of SAS, you do not have to perform any specific action to recover a missing index file.

---

[1] The exception to this is SAS indexes on the z/OS platform that are not created in the Hierarchical File System (HFS). Under z/OS, a SAS data library is a single OS data set with an organization of Physical Sequential (PS) and a record format of Fixed Standard (FS). Items such as SAS data sets, indexes, and catalogs all exist within the OS data set considered to be a SAS library. They do not exist as independent SAS files. However, SAS knows where within the OS data set each SAS file is stored. See the *SAS Companion for z/OS* for more information.

Here is an example of SAS rebuilding a missing index file. The following CONTENTS procedure listing of a SAS data library contains three SAS data sets, two of which have indexes.

```
                        The CONTENTS Procedure


                             Directory


                   Libref          INDEXLIB
                   Engine          V9
                   Physical Name   c:\Data Files
                   File Name       c:\Data Files



                         Member
         #   Name        Type      File Size   Last Modified

         1   PRODCOMP    DATA      296125440   26Feb05:15:14:55
             PRODCOMP    INDEX      58803712   26Feb05:15:14:55
         2   PRODINDX    DATA      296125440   14Aug05:11:36:06
             PRODINDX    INDEX     188311552   14Aug05:11:36:01
         3   PRODSALE    DATA      298021888   26Feb05:14:43:16
```

In this example, consider that the PRODINDX index file is inadvertently deleted in Windows Explorer and that the physical file (c:\Data Files\prodindx.sas7bndx) no longer exists. Executing the CONTENTS procedure for the INDEXLIB *SAS data library* rebuilds the PRODINDX index file with all of its indexes:

```
4
5          proc contents data=indexlib._all_ details directory;
6          run;

NOTE: Indexes recreated:
  4 Simple indexes
NOTE: PROCEDURE CONTENTS used (Total process time):
        real time          17.79 seconds
        cpu time           16.00 seconds
```

You can see from the NOTE in the SAS log and the line that follows it that SAS re-created four simple indexes along with the index file itself.

This would also have occurred if you had run PROC CONTENTS against the PRODINDX *SAS data set*, as opposed to running it against the INDEXLIB *SAS data library* as in the previous example:

```
7
8          proc contents data=indexlib.prodindx details directory;
NOTE: Indexes recreated:
 4 Simple indexes
9          run;

NOTE: PROCEDURE CONTENTS used (Total process time):
      real time             23.27 seconds
      cpu time              16.07 seconds
```

Again, you can see that the SAS log indicates that indexes were re-created.

SAS also re-creates an index file and rebuilds all of the missing indexes when the data set is opened in a DATA step or in a PROC step. In this example, the PRODCOMP index file (c:\Data Files\prodindx.sas7bndx) was accidentally deleted. The following DATA step first re-creates the index file and the indexes, and then it executes.

```
4
5    data florida;
6    set  indexlib.prodcomp(where=(state='Florida'));
NOTE: Indexes recreated:
 3 Composite indexes
INFO: Index STATE_PRODUCT selected for WHERE clause
      optimization.
7
8    run;

NOTE: There were 115200 observations read from the data set
      INDEXLIB.PRODCOMP.
      WHERE state='Florida';
NOTE: The data set WORK.FLORIDA has 115200 observations and 12
      variables.
NOTE: DATA statement used (Total process time):
      real time             10:41.08
      user cpu time         22.36 seconds
      system cpu time       31.06 seconds
      Memory                         68708k
```

Notice that the SAS log first has messages indicating that the indexes were re-created. Then it has messages that report on the outcome of executing the DATA step.

The common thread in all of the examples is that SAS opened the data set, realized that the index file was missing, and rebuilt the indexes and the index file. Once SAS opens a data set that has a missing index file, it rebuilds that file without any intervention on your part.

On operating systems such as UNIX and Linux, there is a subtle problem that could adversely affect the rebuild of SAS indexes for SAS data sets that are shared by multiple users. On such systems one user usually owns a SAS data set and has full read-write permissions, while others generally have read-only permissions. If an index is deleted and a user who has read-only permission attempts to open the data set, that person's program fails. Here is an example:

```
1          libname unixlib "/home/raithel_m/indexes/data";
NOTE: Libref UNIXLIB was successfully assigned as follows:
      Engine:        V9
      Physical Name: /home/raithel_m/indexes/data
2
3      proc contents data=unixlib.prdsale;
ERROR: User does not have appropriate authorization level for
       file UNIXLIB.PRDSALE.DATA.
ERROR: Library member UNIXLIB.PRDSALE.DATA could not be
       repaired.
4      run;

NOTE: Statements not processed because of errors noted above.
NOTE: PROCEDURE CONTENTS used (Total process time):
      real time           0.01 seconds
      cpu time            0.02 seconds

NOTE: The SAS System stopped processing this step because of
      errors.
```

In the example, the LIBNAME statement executed successfully because the user had permission to access the /home/raithel_m/indexes/data UNIX directory. However, the CONTENTS procedure failed. The first ERROR message states that the user did not have the appropriate authorization level for the SAS data set. That would be confusing to a user who is accustomed to processing data sets in this directory if it were not for the second ERROR message. The second ERROR message states that the SAS data set could not be repaired. This was the case because the user did not have *write* permission for files in the /home/raithel_m/indexes/data UNIX directory.

If this situation occurs in your UNIX or Linux environment, you could choose to give your users *write* permission to the directory in question. Or you could do nothing and have users with this type of problem contact you. That would enable you to track the frequency of missing indexes in your directory and to personally rebuild the indexes.

Repairing Damaged Index Files

Though it does not occur very often, it is possible for a SAS index file to become damaged. Some of the more common ways for damage to occur are as follows:

- During an index update the disk where the index file resides becomes full before the update can be completed.
- An I/O error occurs while the index file is being updated.
- An operating system failure occurs while the index is being updated.
- The storage device on which the index file exists becomes damaged.

Whatever the reason for the problem, SAS cannot use a damaged index. The next time that SAS opens the index, it detects that it is damaged and may attempt to repair it. It attempts to rebuild the index only if the DLDMGACTION option is set to REPAIR.

Here is an example of SAS determining that an index is damaged and repairing the index because the DLDMGACTION option is set to REPAIR:

```
8
9    libname indexlib "C:\Data Files";
NOTE: Libref INDEXLIB was successfully assigned as follows:
      Engine:        V9
      Physical Name: C:\Data Files
10
WARNING: File 'INDEXLIB.PRODCOMP.INDEX' is shorter than
         expected.
WARNING: File 'INDEXLIB.PRODCOMP.INDEX' is shorter than
         expected.
11   proc contents data=indexlib.prodcomp;
NOTE: Indexes recreated:
 3 Composite indexes
12   run;
```

(continued on next page)

(continued)

```
NOTE: PROCEDURE CONTENTS used (Total process time):
      real time            8:44.43
      user cpu time        23.33 seconds
      system cpu time      20.00 seconds
      Memory                          68643k
```

In this example, the PRODCOMP SAS data set had a damaged index file (C:\Data Files\prodcomp.sas7bndx). SAS detected the damaged index file and repaired the file by re-creating it. You can see the WARNING message as well as the NOTE about the indexes being re-created in the SAS log.

If you ever have a damaged index and your SAS program stops because the DLDMGACTION option was set to either FAIL or ABORT, all is not lost. You can repair your damaged index. To do so, execute the REPAIR statement in the DATASETS procedure. The REPAIR statement is used to repair damaged SAS data sets, SAS indexes, and SAS catalogs. When you specify the PROC DATASETS REPAIR statement for a SAS data set, SAS examines and repairs the data set, if necessary, as well as its index file.

Here is an example of using the REPAIR statement in the DATASETS procedure:

```
proc datasets library=indexlib nolist;
     repair prodindx;
   run;
quit;
```

In this example, the PRODINDX SAS data set in the INDEXLIB SAS data library has all of its indexes repaired. Here is the log from executing this SAS code:

```
9     proc datasets library=indexlib nolist;
10          repair prodindx;
11        run;

NOTE: Repairing INDEXLIB.PRODINDX (memtype=DATA).
12   quit;

NOTE: PROCEDURE DATASETS used:
      real time            0.01 seconds
      cpu time             0.01 seconds
```

The NOTE in the SAS log affirms that SAS is repairing the INDEXLIB.PRODINDX SAS data set and its associated indexes. The quick turnaround time (0.01 seconds) is a result of there not being a problem with the data set or its indexes.

Occasionally, you may have an index file that is so corrupted that SAS cannot repair it. Consider this DATA step that ended in an error because of a damaged index file:

```
4
ERROR:  Read Access Violation In Task [ DATASTEP )
Exception occurred at (6779BD59)
Task Traceback
Address    Frame      (DBGHELP API Version 4.0 rev 5)
6779BD59   05AFF17C   0001:0000AD59 sase7xrt.dll
677984C9   05AFF2D0   0001:000074C9 sase7xrt.dll
67796575   05AFF428   0001:00005575 sase7xrt.dll
67218C67   05AFF6CC   0001:00007C67 sase7opn.dll
671B1A32   05AFFC14   0001:00010A32 sasyoio.dll
671AF2EF   05AFFD54   0001:0000E2EF sasyoio.dll
672F7F88   05AFFDEC   0001:00006F88 sasdsa.dll
672B9F72   05AFFE74   0001:00008F72 sasdsc.dll
67871CA3   05AFFF04   0001:00030CA3 sasxshel.dll
67871331   05AFFF14   0001:00030331 sasxshel.dll
672B1891   05AFFF48   0001:00000891 sasdsc.dll
673111E9   05AFFF88   0001:000001E9 sasds.dll
67E228F2   05AFFFA0   0001:000118F2 sashost.dll
67E26A00   05AFFFB4   0001:00015A00 sashost.dll
77E7D28E   05AFFFEC   kernel32:RegisterWaitForInputIdle+0x43


NOTE: DATA statement used (Total process time):
      real time           0.86 seconds
      user cpu time       0.30 seconds
      system cpu time     0.10 seconds
      Memory                          119k


NOTE: The SAS System stopped processing this step because of errors.
5    data florida;
6    set  indexlib.prodcomp(where=(state='Florida'));
7
8    run;
9
```

There is nothing in the error messages above that would alert you to the fact that the index file is corrupted. However, in this case the author knew that the index file was corrupted. Attempting to fix the corrupted file results in another half page of error messages:

```
10      proc datasets library=indexlib nolist;
11              repair prodcomp;
12          run;


NOTE: Repairing INDEXLIB.PRODCOMP (memtype=DATA).
ERROR:  Read Access Violation In Task [ DATASETS )
Exception occurred at (6779BD59)
Task Traceback
Address     Frame       (DBGHELP API Version 4.0 rev 5)
6779BD59    05AFE3A4    0001:0000AD59 sase7xrt.dll
677984C9    05AFE4F8    0001:000074C9 sase7xrt.dll
67796575    05AFE650    0001:00005575 sase7xrt.dll
67218C67    05AFE8F4    0001:00007C67 sase7opn.dll
5FDC1136    05AFEED8    0001:00000136 sase7ms.dll
5FAB1C82    05AFF02C    0001:00000C82 sasyio2.dll
671B214E    05AFF56C    0001:0001114E sasyoio.dll
5FAB1CAE    05AFF6C0    0001:00000CAE sasyio2.dll
670C3290    05AFFE3C    0001:00002290 sasqutil.dll
670C1AD7    05AFFE58    0001:00000AD7 sasqutil.dll
6787258C    05AFFEB4    0001:0003158C sasxshel.dll
670FC02B    05AFFEF0    0001:0003B02B sasqutil.dll
670C1449    05AFFF88    0001:00000449 sasqutil.dll
67E228F2    05AFFFA0    0001:000118F2 sashost.dll
67E26A00    05AFFFB4    0001:00015A00 sashost.dll
77E7D28E    05AFFFEC    kernel32:RegisterWaitForInputIdle+0x43


NOTE: The SAS System stopped processing this step because of errors.
NOTE: PROCEDURE DATASETS used (Total process time):
        real time            0.95 seconds
        user cpu time        0.29 seconds
        system cpu time      0.04 seconds
        Memory                            49k

quit;
```

Because the index file cannot be repaired, the best course of action is to do the following:

1. Delete the index file outside of SAS. You may use a system command, another program, or a GUI to delete the file.

2. Run PROC CONTENTS against the SAS data library that the data set with the missing index resides in. That will force SAS to open the data set and rebuild its index file and indexes.

Following these steps gives you a new index file with rebuilt index(es).

Information about Index Repairs

If you happen to miss information about index recoveries and repairs in your SAS logs, you may be able to find some clues in the CONTENTS procedure listings. The "Engine / Host Dependent Information" section of your PROC CONTENTS output provides information on *data set repairs*. *Data set repairs* is a broad-brush category that may mean a repair to the SAS data set, an index rebuild, or an index repair.

Here is a portion of a CONTENTS procedure listing for a SAS data set that has had its indexes rebuilt:

```
                           The CONTENTS Procedure

Data Set Name    INDEXLIB.PRODINDX            Observations
2304000
Member Type      DATA                         Variables              12
Engine           V9                           Indexes                9
Created          Sat, Feb 26, 2005 01:53:40 PM   Integrity Constraints  1
Last Modified    Saturday, October 01, 2005 11:08:07 AM  Observation Length   128
Protection                                    Deleted Observations   0
Data Set Type                                 Compressed             NO
Label                                         Sorted                 NO
Data Representation    WINDOWS_32
Encoding               wlatin1  Western (Windows)
```

(continued on next page)

(continued)

```
                    Engine/Host Dependent Information

        Data Set Page Size            32768
        Number of Data Set Pages      9037
        First Data Page               1
        Max Obs per Page              255
        Obs in First Data Page        237
        Index File Page Size          4096
        Number of Index File Pages    54815
        Number of Data Set Repairs    1
        Last Repair                   12:54 Sunday, August 14, 2005
        File Name                     C:\Data Files\prodindx.sas7bdat
        Release Created               9.0101M3
        Host Created                  XP_PRO
```

In the example, "Number of Data Set Repairs" and "Last Repair" provide information about the rebuild of the indexes. "Number of Data Set Repairs" is set to 1, meaning that there was a single data set repair event. In this case, we happen to know that this event was rebuilding the index file, which had accidentally been deleted. "Last Repair" specifies the time and date on which the last repair was made. The example shows that it took place at 12:54 on Sunday, August 14, 2005. The repair was not to the SAS data set; rather the repair re-created the indexes associated with the SAS data set.

Because metrics for "Number of Data Set Repairs" and "Last Repair" may actually be reporting repairs to a SAS data set and not reporting an index rebuild or an index repair, you should regard these metrics with some skepticism. SAS considers the *SAS data set* to be damaged if its index is missing or damaged. SAS makes no attempt to separate index damage from data set damage in this metric.

The metrics may signal that there was a problem with an index file or a problem with your SAS data set. When the CONTENTS procedure shows that there have been data set repairs, you should look at your SAS logs to see if there are any index rebuild or index repair messages. If so, you need to know why your index file was compromised.

Summary

This chapter discussed how you can handle a missing or damaged index. Fortunately, SAS has a built-in facility for handling problems with indexes. It rebuilds a missing index file and all of its indexes or repairs a damaged index when the indexed data set is next opened. The current setting of the DLDMGACTION option dictates whether or not SAS attempts a repair. The best overall setting for the DLDMGACTION option is REPAIR, which forces SAS to rebuild missing indexes and fix damaged indexes that it encounters in both interactive and batch SAS programs. When an index is damaged to the point that SAS cannot repair it, you can delete the index and then open its data set via the CONTENTS procedure. Then SAS can automatically rebuild the index. Whether an index is lost or damaged, recovering it is a straightforward process.

Appendix **A**

CONTENTS Procedure Listing of INDEXLIB.PRODSALE

```
                              The SAS System
                           The CONTENTS Procedure

Data Set Name        INDEXLIB.PRODSALE              Observations          2304000
Member Type          DATA                           Variables             12
  Engine             V9                             Indexes               0
Created              Sat, Feb 26, 2005 01:40:01 PM  Observation Length    128
Last Modified        Sat, Feb 26, 2005 01:40:01 PM  Deleted Observations  0
Protection                                          Compressed            NO
Data Set Type                                       Sorted                YES
Label
Data Representation  WINDOWS_32
Encoding             wlatin1  Western (Windows)
```

(continued on next page)

(continued)

```
                    Engine/Host Dependent Information

          Data Set Page Size            12288
          Number of Data Set Pages      24253
          First Data Page              1
          Max Obs per Page             95
          Obs in First Data Page       77
          Number of Data Set Repairs   0
          File Name                    c:\data files\prodsale.sas7bdat
          Release Created              9.0101M3
          Host Created                 XP_PRO


                 Alphabetic List of Variables and Attributes

      #   Variable    Type    Len    Format        Informat    Label

      4   ACTUAL      Num     8      DOLLAR12.2                Actual Sales
      1   COUNTRY     Char    10     $CHAR10.                  Country
      3   COUNTY      Char    20     $CHAR20.                  County
     10   DAYMONYR    Num     8      DATE7.        MONYY.      Day/Month/Year
     11   MONTH       Num     8                                Month
      5   PREDICT     Num     8      DOLLAR12.2                Predicted Sales
      6   PRODTYPE    Char    10     $CHAR10.                  Product Type
      7   PRODUCT     Char    10     $CHAR10.                  Product
      9   QUARTER     Num     8      8.                        Quarter
     12   SEQNUM      Num     8                                Sequence Number
      2   STATE       Char    22     $CHAR22.                  State/Province
      8   YEAR        Num     8      4.                        Year


                           Sort Information

                    Sortedby        SEQNUM
                    Validated       YES
                    Character Set    ANSI
```

Appendix B

CONTENTS Procedure Listing of INDEXLIB.PRODINDX

```
                              The SAS System

                          The CONTENTS Procedure

Data Set Name      INDEXLIB.PRODINDX              Observations           2304000
Member Type        DATA                           Variables              12
Engine             V9                             Indexes                5
Created            Sat, Feb 26, 2005 01:53:40 PM  Observation Length     128
Last Modified      Sat, Feb 26, 2005 02:01:27 PM  Deleted Observations   0
Protection                                        Compressed             NO
Data Set Type                                     Sorted                 NO
Label
Data Representation   WINDOWS_32
Encoding             wlatin1  Western (Windows)
```

(continued on next page)

(continued)

```
                    Engine/Host Dependent Information

              Data Set Page Size          32768
              Number of Data Set Pages     9037
              First Data Page              1
              Max Obs per Page             255
              Obs in First Data Page       237
              Index File Page Size         32256
              Number of Index File Pages   3459
              Number of Data Set Repairs   0
              File Name                    C:\Data Files\prodindx.sas7bdat
              Release Created              9.0101M3
              Host Created                 XP_PRO



            Alphabetic List of Variables and Attributes

    #    Variable    Type    Len    Format        Informat    Label

    4    ACTUAL      Num      8     DOLLAR12.2                 Actual Sales
    1    COUNTRY     Char    10     $CHAR10.                   Country
    3    COUNTY      Char    20     $CHAR20.                   County
   10    DAYMONYR    Num      8     DATE7.        MONYY.       Day/Month/Year
   11    MONTH       Num      8                                Month
    5    PREDICT     Num      8     DOLLAR12.2                 Predicted Sales
    6    PRODTYPE    Char    10     $CHAR10.                   Product Type
    7    PRODUCT     Char    10     $CHAR10.                   Product
    9    QUARTER     Num      8     8.                         Quarter
   12    SEQNUM      Num      8                                Sequence Number
    2    STATE       Char    22     $CHAR22.                   State/Province
    8    YEAR        Num      8     4.                         Year
```

(continued on next page)

(continued)

```
                    Alphabetic List of Indexes and Attributes

                                          Current    # of
            Unique   NoMiss    Update     Update     Unique
  #  Index  Option   Option    Centiles   Percent    Values    Variables

  1  COUNTY                       5          0          6




                                                              Adams
                                                              Cook
                                                              Fayette
                                                              McLean
                                                              Winnebago
  2  PRODUCT                      5          0          4
                                                              BED
                                                              BED
                                                              BED
                                                              BED
                                                              BED
                                                              BED
                                                              CHAIR
                                                              CHAIR
```

(continued on next page)

(continued)

							CHAIR
							CHAIR
							CHAIR
							DESK
							DESK
							DESK
							DESK
							DESK
							SOFA
							SOFA
							SOFA
							SOFA
							SOFA
3	SEQNUM	YES	YES	5	0	2304000	
							1
							115200
							230400
							345600
							460800
							576000
							691200
							806400
							921600
							1036800
							1152000
							1267200
							1382400
							1497600
							1612800
							1728000
							1843200
							1958400
							2073600
							2188800
							2304000
4	STATE		YES	5	0	16	
							Baja California Norte
							Baja California Norte

(continued on next page)

(continued)

						British Columbia
						California
						Campeche
						Colorado
						Florida
						Illinois
						Illinois
						Illinois
						Illinois
						Illinois
						Michoacan
						New York
						North Carolina
						Nuevo Leon
						Ontario
						Quebec
						Saskatchewan
						Texas
						Washington
5	YEAR	YES	5	0	14	
						1995
						1996
						1996
						1997
						1997
						1998
						1998
						1998
						1999
						1999
						2000
						2001
						2001
						2002
						2003
						2004
						2005
						2006
						2007
						2008

Appendix C

CONTENTS Procedure Listing of INDEXLIB.PRODCOMP

```
                              The SAS System

                           The CONTENTS Procedure

Data Set Name         INDEXLIB.PRODCOMP              Observations           2304000
Member Type           DATA                           Variables              12
Engine                V9                             Indexes                3
Created               Sat, Feb 26, 2005 02:06:30 PM  Observation Length     128
Last Modified         Sat, Feb 26, 2005 02:12:27 PM  Deleted Observations   0
Protection                                           Compressed             NO
Data Set Type                                        Sorted                 NO
Label
Data Representation   WINDOWS_32
Encoding              wlatin1  Western (Windows)
```

(continued on next page)

(continued)

```
                    Engine/Host Dependent Information

        Data Set Page Size            32768
        Number of Data Set Pages      9037
        First Data Page               1
        Max Obs per Page              255
        Obs in First Data Page        237
        Index File Page Size          32256
        Number of Index File Pages    1823
        Number of Data Set Repairs    0
        File Name                     C:\Data Files\prodcomp.sas7bdat
        Release Created               9.0101M3
        Host Created                  XP_PRO

              Alphabetic List of Variables and Attributes
```

#	Variable	Type	Len	Format	Informat	Label
4	ACTUAL	Num	8	DOLLAR12.2		Actual Sales
1	COUNTRY	Char	10	$CHAR10.		Country
3	COUNTY	Char	20	$CHAR20.		County
10	DAYMONYR	Num	8	DATE7.	MONYY.	Day/Month/Year
11	MONTH	Num	8			Month
5	PREDICT	Num	8	DOLLAR12.2		Predicted Sales
6	PRODTYPE	Char	10	$CHAR10.		Product Type
7	PRODUCT	Char	10	$CHAR10.		Product
9	QUARTER	Num	8	8.		Quarter
12	SEQNUM	Num	8			Sequence Number
2	STATE	Char	22	$CHAR22.		State/Province
8	YEAR	Num	8	4.		Year

(continued on next page)

(continued)

```
                      Alphabetic List of Indexes and Attributes

                            Current   # of
                NoMiss    Update  Update Unique
# Index         Option  Centiles Percent Values Variables

1 COUNTRY_STATE  YES          5       0     16 COUNTRY STATE
                                              Canada      ,British Columbia
                                              Canada      ,British Columbia
                                              Canada      ,Ontario
                                              Canada      ,Quebec
                                              Canada      ,Saskatchewan
                                              Mexico      ,Baja California Norte
                                              Mexico      ,Campeche
                                              Mexico      ,Michoacan
                                              Mexico      ,Nuevo Leon
                                              U.S.A.      ,California
                                              U.S.A.      ,Colorado
                                              U.S.A.      ,Florida
                                              U.S.A.      ,Illinois
                                              U.S.A.      ,Illinois
                                              U.S.A.      ,Illinois
                                              U.S.A.      ,Illinois
                                              U.S.A.      ,Illinois
                                              U.S.A.      ,New York
                                              U.S.A.      ,North Carolina
                                              U.S.A.      ,Texas
                                              U.S.A.      ,Washington
2 STATE_PRODUCT               5       0     64 STATE PRODUCT
                                              Baja California Norte ,BED
                                              Baja California Norte ,SOFA
                                              British Columbia      ,SOFA
                                              California            ,SOFA
                                              Campeche              ,SOFA
                                              Colorado              ,SOFA
                                              Florida               ,SOFA
                                              Illinois              ,BED
```

(continued on next page)

(continued)

					Illinois	,CHAIR
					Illinois	,DESK
					Illinois	,SOFA
					Illinois	,SOFA
					Michoacan	,SOFA
					New York	,SOFA
					North Carolina	,SOFA
					Nuevo Leon	,SOFA
					Ontario	,SOFA
					Quebec	,SOFA
					Saskatchewan	,SOFA
					Texas	,SOFA
					Washington	,SOFA
3	YEAR_AND_QUARTER	5	0	56	YEAR QUARTER	
					1995,1	
					1995,4	
					1996,2	
					1996,4	
					1997,2	
					1997,4	
					1998,2	
					1998,3	
					1998,4	
					1999,2	
					1999,4	
					2000,4	
					2001,2	
					2001,4	
					2002,4	
					2003,4	
					2004,4	
					2005,4	
					2006,4	
					2007,4	
					2008,4	

Appendix **D**

Estimating the Number of Pages for a SAS 9 Index

This program is found on the SAS Web site, support.sas.com. It enables you to estimate the number of pages for an index. To be sure that you have the latest copy, access the Web site and search for this string: "Estimate the Number of Pages for a SAS V9 Index." Information on how to use this program is provided in the "Estimating the Size of an Index" section in Chapter 1, "Introduction to Indexes."

```
/*----------------------------------------------------------------*/
/* Title: Estimate the number of pages required for an V9 index   */
/*                                                                */
/*                                                                */
/* NOTES:                                                         */
/* 1. This program is for V9 SAS index files.                     */
/* 2. The algorithm expects all values to be integers. Thus the need */
/*    to use the round function.                                  */
/* 3. This program is based upon the algorithm published in a paper */
/*    written by Clifford, et al, for SUGI 14 - Using new SAS     */
/*    Database Features and Options.                              */
/* 4. This program estimates the size of one index. If your       */
/*    application has multiple indexes, you must run the program  */
/*    once (specifying the characteristics of each index) for each */
/*    index.                                                      */
/* 5. To estimate the size of your particular index, change the   */
/*    values below in the "User-supplied values" section and run  */
/*    the program.                                                */
/*----------------------------------------------------------------*/

data _null_;
length host $5;


/*----------------------------------------------------------------*/
/* User-supplied values                                           */
/*----------------------------------------------------------------*/
psize = 6000;   /* page size of index file                        */
vsize = 32;     /* total number of bytes in the value to be indexed. */
                /* For a composite index, this is the sum of the  */
                /* constituent variable sizes.                    */
uval  =  3000;  /* number of unique values                        */
nrec  = 20000;  /* total number of records (ie, observations)     */
                /* NOTE: if uval and nrec are equal, this is assumed */
                /* to be a unique index.                          */
host  = "MVS";  /* HOST   PLATFORM                          SIZE   */
                /* ====   ================================ ====== */
                /* MVS - OS/390                             32 bit */
                /* WIN - Windows NT/2000/XP                 32 bit */
                /* LNX - RedHat Linux on Intel              32 bit */
                /* ALP - OpenVMS Alpha                      64 bit */
                /* ALX - Compaq Digital UNIX                64 bit */
                /* H64 - HP 64                              64 bit */
                /* S64 - Solaris 64                         64 bit */
                /* R64 - AIX 64                             64 bit */
                /* H6I - HP/UX for Itanium Platform Family  64 bit */
                /* W64 - Windows for IPF                    64 bit */
/*----------------------------------------------------------------*/
```

```
/*------------------------------------------------------------------*/
/* Program-generated values                                         */
/*------------------------------------------------------------------*/
/*    lpages   - number of leaf (bottom) index pages                */
/*    upages   - number of upper level (non-leaf) index pages       */
/*    maxent   - maximum number of entries on an upper-level page   */
/*    totpgs   - total number of index pages                        */
/*    bytes    - total number of pages converted to bytes           */
/*    offset   - size of offset                                     */
/*    levels   - number of levels in the index tree                 */
/*    entry    - the space needed to store a single indexed value and */
/*               all of its RIDs (Record IDs). For a unique index   */
/*               there is one RID per indexed value. For a non-unique */
/*               index there will be unval/nrec RIDs.               */
/*    noperpg  - number of entries per leaf page                    */
/*    cont     - continuation leaf pages (for non-unique index)     */
/*------------------------------------------------------------------*/


/*------------------------------------------------------------------*/
/* Host-specific values                                             */
/*------------------------------------------------------------------*/
/* shrtsize - sizeof(short)                                         */
/* header   - sizeof(struct IDXPAGES)                               */
/*              struct IDXPAGES                                      */
/*                {                                                 */
/*                uint32_t pageid;                                  */
/*                long  spare1;                                     */
/*                long  nextpage;                                   */
/*                long  idxid;                                      */
/*                short flags;                                      */
/*                short ctr;                                        */
/*                short nbrentry;                                   */
/*                short free;                                       */
/*                char  level;                                      */
/*                char  spare2[3];                                  */
/*                };                                                */
/* longsize - sizeof(long)                                          */
/* rsize    - sizeof(struct BASE_RID). This is the size of the      */
/*              pointer (RID) to the record in the data set stored in */
/*              the index.                                          */
/*------------------------------------------------------------------*/


if (host eq "ALP"   or
    host eq "ALX"   or
    host eq "H64"   or
    host eq "S64"   or
    host eq "R64"   or
```

```
      host eq "H6I"   or
      host eq "W64") then do;
  /* 64-bit hosts */
  shrtsize =  2;
  header   = 44;
  longsize =  8;
  rsize    = 16;
end;
else do;
  /* 32-bit hosts */
  shrtsize =  2;
  header   = 28;
  longsize =  4;
  rsize    =  8;
end;

if (uval eq nrec) then do;
  /* Unique index. No offset for a unique index.           */
  offset = 0;
end;
else do;
  /* Non-unique index. Assume each value occurs nrec/uval times.  */
  /* So there will be nrec/uval RIDs and one value.               */
  offset = shrtsize;
  rsize  = round( ((nrec / uval) * rsize), 1 );
end;

entry   = vsize + (offset * 2) + rsize;
noperpg = round( ((psize - header) / entry ) , 1 );

if (noperpg lt 1) then do;
    /*-------------------------------------------------------------*/
    /* An entire entry will not fit on a page. This is possible only */
    /* for non-unique indexes. Remember that 'entry' is the size of  */
    /* the indexed value plus all of its RIDs. Here we calculate cont,*/
    /* the number of continuation pages needed for the extra RIDs.   */
    /*-------------------------------------------------------------*/
    noperpg = 1;
    cont = round( (entry / (psize - header)), 1 );
end;
else cont = 0;

lpages = round( uval / noperpg, 1 );   /* number of leaf pages */
if ((lpages * noperpg) ne uval) then lpages = lpages + 1;

lolev  = lpages;
lpages = lpages + cont;
```

```
maxent = round ( ((psize - header) / (offset + vsize + longsize)), 1 );

/*------------------------------------------------------------*/
/* Simulate index creation and count the number of leaf and  */
/* non-leaf pages.                                           */
/*------------------------------------------------------------*/
upages = 0;
levels = 1;
do while (lolev > 1);
   curlev = round( ((lolev + maxent - 1) / maxent) , 1);
   upages = upages + curlev;
   lolev  = curlev;
   levels = levels + 1;
end;

totpgs = lpages + upages;
bytes  = totpgs * psize;

/*------------------------------------------------------------*/
/* All values have been calculated. Create the report.       */
/*------------------------------------------------------------*/

put "============================================================";
put "   ";
put "Index characteristics:";
put "    Host Platform             = " host;
put "    Page Size (bytes)         = " psize;
put "    Index Value Size (bytes)  = " vsize;
put "    Unique Values             = " uval;
put "    Total Number of Values    = " nrec;
put "    Number of Index Levels    = " levels;
put " ";
put "Estimated storage requirements for a V9 index:";
put "    Number of Upper Level Pages = " upages 8.;
put "    Number of Leaf Pages        = " lpages 8.;
put "    Total Number of Index Pages = " totpgs 8." or " bytes comma14."
bytes";
put " ";
put "Note: the above estimate does not include storage for the index";
put "      directory (usually one page) or the host header page.";
put "   ";
put "Estimation of index size complete.";
put "   ";
put "============================================================";

run;
```

References

Clifford, W. (2005), "Frequently Asked Questions about SAS Indexes," *Proceedings of the Thirtieth Annual SAS Users Group International Conference.* Cary, NC: SAS Institute Inc.

Moorman, D. J. and D. Warner (1999), "Updating Data Using the MODIFY Statement and the KEY= Option," *Observations: The Technical Journal for Software Users,* Third Quarter, http://support.sas.com/documentation/periodicals/obs/obswww19. Cary, NC: SAS Institute Inc.

Olson, D. (2000), "Power Indexing: A Guide to Using Indexes Effectively in Nashville Releases," *Proceedings of the Twenty-fifth Annual SAS Users Group International Conference.* Cary, NC: SAS Institute Inc.

Raithel, M. A. (2005), "The Basics of Using SAS Indexes," *Proceedings of the Thirtieth Annual SAS Users Group International Conference.* Cary, NC: SAS Institute Inc.

Raithel, M. A. (2004), "Creating and Exploiting SAS Indexes," *Proceedings of the Twenty-ninth Annual SAS Users Group International Conference.* Cary, NC: SAS Institute Inc.

Raithel, M. A. (2003), *Tuning SAS Applications in the OS/390 and z/OS Environments, Second Edition.* Cary, NC: SAS Institute Inc.

SAS Institute Inc. (2005), *Companion for z/OS*, SAS OnlineDoc, Version 9.1.3. Cary, NC: SAS Institute Inc.

SAS Institute Inc. (2005), SAS OnlineDoc, Version 9.1.3. Cary, NC: SAS Institute Inc.

SAS Institute Inc. (2005), "Understanding SAS Indexes," *SAS Language Reference: Concepts*, SAS OnlineDoc 9.1.3 CD-ROM, Cary, NC: SAS Institute Inc.

Index

Books Available from SAS® Press

Advanced Log-Linear Models Using SAS®
by **Daniel Zelterman**

Analysis of Clinical Trials Using SAS®: A Practical Guide
by **Alex Dmitrienko, Geert Molenberghs, Walter Offen,** *and* **Christy Chuang-Stein**

Annotate: Simply the Basics
by **Art Carpenter**

Applied Multivariate Statistics with SAS® Software, Second Edition
by **Ravindra Khattree** *and* **Dayanand N. Naik**

Applied Statistics and the SAS® Programming Language, Fourth Edition
by **Ronald P. Cody** *and* **Jeffrey K. Smith**

An Array of Challenges — Test Your SAS® Skills
by **Robert Virgile**

Carpenter's Complete Guide to the SAS® Macro Language, Second Edition
by **Art Carpenter**

The Cartoon Guide to Statistics
by **Larry Gonick** *and* **Woollcott Smith**

Categorical Data Analysis Using the SAS® System, Second Edition
by **Maura E. Stokes, Charles S. Davis,** *and* **Gary G. Koch**

Cody's Data Cleaning Techniques Using SAS® Software
by **Ron Cody**

Common Statistical Methods for Clinical Research with SAS® Examples, Second Edition
by **Glenn A. Walker**

The Complete Guide to SAS® Indexes
by **Michael A. Raithel**

Debugging SAS® Programs: A Handbook of Tools and Techniques
by **Michele M. Burlew**

Efficiency: Improving the Performance of Your SAS® Applications
by **Robert Virgile**

The Essential PROC SQL Handbook for SAS® Users
by **Katherine Prairie**

Genetic Analysis of Complex Traits Using SAS®
by **Arnold M. Saxton**

A Handbook of Statistical Analyses Using SAS®, Second Edition
by **B.S. Everitt** *and* **G. Der**

Health Care Data and SAS®
by **Marge Scerbo, Craig Dickstein,** *and* **Alan Wilson**

The How-To Book for SAS/GRAPH® Software
by **Thomas Miron**

support.sas.com/pubs

Instant ODS: Style Templates for the Output Delivery System
by **Bernadette Johnson**

In the Know... SAS® Tips and Techniques From Around the Globe
by **Phil Mason**

Integrating Results through Meta-Analytic Review Using SAS® Software
by **Morgan C. Wang**
and **Brad J. Bushman**

Learning SAS® in the Computer Lab, Second Edition
by **Rebecca J. Elliott**

The Little SAS® Book: A Primer
by **Lora D. Delwiche**
and **Susan J. Slaughter**

The Little SAS® Book: A Primer, Second Edition
by **Lora D. Delwiche**
and **Susan J. Slaughter**
(updated to include Version 7 features)

The Little SAS® Book: A Primer, Third Edition
by **Lora D. Delwiche**
and **Susan J. Slaughter**
(updated to include SAS 9.1 features)

Logistic Regression Using the SAS® System: Theory and Application
by **Paul D. Allison**

Longitudinal Data and SAS®: A Programmer's Guide
by **Ron Cody**

Maps Made Easy Using SAS®
by **Mike Zdeb**

Models for Discrete Date
by **Daniel Zelterman**

Multiple Comparisons and Multiple Tests Using SAS® Text and Workbook Set
(books in this set also sold separately)
by **Peter H. Westfall, Randall D. Tobias, Dror Rom, Russell D. Wolfinger,**
and **Yosef Hochberg**

Multiple-Plot Displays: Simplified with Macros
by **Perry Watts**

Multivariate Data Reduction and Discrimination with SAS® Software
by **Ravindra Khattree**
and **Dayanand N. Naik**

Output Delivery System: The Basics
by **Lauren E. Haworth**

Painless Windows: A Handbook for SAS® Users, Third Edition
by **Jodie Gilmore**
(updated to include Version 8 and SAS 9.1 features)

The Power of PROC FORMAT
by **Jonas V. Bilenas**

PROC TABULATE by Example
by **Lauren E. Haworth**

Professional SAS® Programming Shortcuts
by **Rick Aster**

Quick Results with SAS/GRAPH® Software
by **Arthur L. Carpenter**
and **Charles E. Shipp**

Quick Results with the Output Delivery System
by **Sunil Gupta**

Quick Start to Data Analysis with SAS®
by **Frank C. Dilorio**
and **Kenneth A. Hardy**

Reading External Data Files Using SAS®: Examples Handbook
by **Michele M. Burlew**

Regression and ANOVA: An Integrated Approach Using SAS® Software
by **Keith E. Muller**
and **Bethel A. Fetterman**

SAS® Applications Programming: A Gentle Introduction
by **Frank C. Dilorio**

support.sas.com/pubs

Using the SAS® Windowing Environment:
A Quick Tutorial
by **Larry Hatcher**

Visualizing Categorical Data
by **Michael Friendly**

Web Development with SAS® by Example
by **Frederick Pratter**

Your Guide to Survey Research Using the
SAS® System
by **Archer Gravely**

JMP® Books

JMP® for Basic Univariate and Multivariate Statistics:
A Step-by-Step Guide
by **Ann Lehman, Norm O'Rourke, Larry Hatcher,**
and **Edward J. Stepanski**

JMP® Start Statistics, Third Edition
by **John Sall, Ann Lehman,**
and **Lee Creighton**

Regression Using JMP®
by **Rudolf J. Freund, Ramon C. Littell,**
and **Lee Creighton**

support.sas.com/pubs